Teach®
Yourself

Understand
Philosophy

Mel Thompson

For UK order enquiries: please contact Bookpoint Ltd,
130 Milton Park, Abingdon, Oxon OX14 4SB.
Telephone: +44 (0) 1235 827720. Fax: +44 (0) 1235 400454.
Lines are open 09.00–17.00, Monday to Saturday, with a 24-hour
message answering service. Details about our titles and how to
order are available at www.teachyourself.com

For USA order enquiries: please contact McGraw-Hill
Customer Services, PO Box 545, Blacklick, OH 43004-0545, USA.
Telephone: 1-800-722-4726. Fax: 1-614-755-5645.

For Canada order enquiries: please contact McGraw-Hill
Ryerson Ltd, 300 Water St, Whitby, Ontario L1N 9B6, Canada.
Telephone: 905 430 5000. Fax: 905 430 5020.

Long renowned as the authoritative source for self-guided
learning – with more than 50 million copies sold worldwide –
the **Teach Yourself** series includes over 500 titles in the fields of
languages, crafts, hobbies, business, computing and education.

British Library Cataloguing in Publication Data: a catalogue record
for this title is available from the British Library.

Library of Congress Catalog Card Number: on file.

First published in UK 1995 by Hodder Education, part of
Hachette UK, 338 Euston Road, London NW1 3BH.

First published in US 1995 by The McGraw-Hill Companies, Inc.

This edition published 2010.

The **Teach Yourself** name is a registered trade mark of
Hodder Headline.

Typeset by MPS Limited, A Macmillan Company.

Printed in Great Britain for Hodder Education, an Hachette UK
Company, 338 Euston Road, London NW1 3BH, by CPI Cox &
Wyman, Reading, Berkshire RG1 8EX.

The publisher has used its best endeavours to ensure that the URLs for
external websites referred to in this book are correct and active at the
time of going to press. However, the publisher and the author have no
responsibility for the websites and can make no guarantee that a site
will remain live or that the content will remain relevant, decent
or appropriate.

Hachette UK's policy is to use papers that are natural, renewable
and recyclable products and made from wood grown in sustainable
forests. The logging and manufacturing processes are expected to
conform to the environmental regulations of the country of origin.

Impression number   10 9 8 7 6 5 4 3 2 1
Year   2014 2013 2012 2011 2010

Contents

Acknowledgements

The author and publishers would like to thank the following for their permission to use copyright material in this book:

The Observer, *The Sunday Telegraph* and *The Daily Telegraph* for extracts from their respective newspapers; Chatto and Windus for the extract from Iris Murdoch's *Metaphysics as a Guide to Morals*; Penguin Books Ltd for the extract from Descartes' *Discourse on Method* and *Chambers Concise Dictionary*, 2nd edition, 2009, ISBN: 9780550103345 for it's definition of Philosophy.

Meet the author

Welcome to *Understand Philosophy*!

We're all philosophers. When there's a tough choice to be made, when faced with the facts of birth, love or death, or simply when thinking about what we want to do with our lives or what we hold dear, we all tend to ask fundamental questions and to use our reason to try to make sense of our situation. Work is no escape from it; whether it's examining the logic of a business decision, sifting the relevance of scientific data, or trying to express oneself as clearly as possible in an email, we are exercising our philosophical muscles. To me, philosophy is doing what comes naturally, but doing it in a rigorous and systematic way, not opting out when the mental going gets tough. It's a wonderful discipline for clearing the mind; a skill like no other. It's also a point of entry into the history of ideas, perusing the wisdom of the past to aid our decisions for the future.

Four decades ago, waiting to go up to university but knowing nothing of philosophy, I picked up my newly-bought copy of Bertrand Russell's *History of Western Philosophy*, sat on a river bank near my home, and started flicking through its chapters. I found that my own thoughts and questions had been aired by others before me with far greater clarity and rigor; it was an eye-opener from which I have never recovered.

Mel Thompson, 2010

Only got a minute?

According to the *Concise Chambers Dictionary*, philosophy is:

1 the search for truth and knowledge concerning the universe, human existence, perception and behaviour, pursued by means of reflection, reasoning and argument. 2 any particular system or set of beliefs established as a result of this.

3 a set of principles that serves as a basis for making judgements and decisions.

Philosophy is an activity – the attempt to understand the general principles and ideas that lie behind various aspects of life and the language we use to convey them. Political philosophy, for example, asks questions about justice and equality, about how a state should be organized.

Philosophy as a subject also involves examining 'the history of ideas' – what thinkers have said on fundamental questions over the centuries. You can examine the philosophy of a particular period – the philosophy of ancient Greece, for example, is particularly important for understanding Western thought and culture. You might look at the philosophy of the European Enlightenment, or of the twentieth century, each giving an insight into ideas that developed out of and shaped a particular period of history. But the most straightforward way of approaching philosophy is through its subject matter – the philosophy of mind, of language, of religion, of science, of politics, the theory of knowledge and so on. The latter approach is the most accessible and will therefore be the one adopted for this book.

Philosophy aims first and foremost for clarification – of thoughts, of concepts, of language. To philosophize is to think clearly and accurately. Philosophy is both an academic subject and an essential life skill.

5 Only got five minutes?

Thinking in time ...

Whatever we do, we do in time. That sounds obvious and banal, but it has implications. Consider a simple action the – decision to make a cup of tea. Do I take milk in my tea, or have it black with a slice of lemon? That might suggest to you whether I am from England or continental Europe. Do I use a cup or mug? Do I take the tea back to my desk or stroll outside to take a break from work? Each of these preferences reflects my past experience – have I previously enjoyed tea with milk, or taking a break – and influences my immediate future, since as a free agent I can have input into what happens. That does not imply that I can determine the future – after all, something dramatic might intervene to stop me making my cup of tea – but my present choices reflect my intention for that future.

Everything we do is thus a process whereby our past experiences, stored in memory, shape our intentions and choices. The crucially important present moment is no more than a fleeting transition from past to future. And that applies to absolutely everything. Without the experience of time, a symphony would be reduced to a single chord. You read a book one word at a time; it only becomes reading 'a book' if you remember the words you have already read, and anticipate following the thoughts of the author and turning the page. Without a sense of what has happened in the past, it is difficult to understand or make choices in the present, and therefore impossible to shape up our ideas for the future. Someone whose memory was totally erased would be at a loss to know what to do.

So what does this have to do with philosophy?

Philosophy is both an activity and a body of knowledge. As an activity, it takes place in the present and anticipates the future.

It is the process of thinking about and reflecting on what we know, how we know it, what we approve or disapprove, what we wish to happen. In other words, it embraces the contribution of human reason, insight and intuition, injected into each fleeting moment, to shape what will happen next. It is the crucial difference between being an inanimate object (responding in a predictable way to external forces) and a living and thinking being (able to seek out its own future); it is the point at which we make a difference. Of course everyone thinks, but not everyone considers himself or herself as a philosopher – that description is reserved for those (including you, since you are reading this book) who pay conscious attention to the process of thinking and decision-making. Philosophy is not just thinking, but thinking about thinking.

But giving attention to our thinking is greatly aided by philosophy as a body of knowledge. Although circumstances are always changing, the fundamental questions that we ask remain much the same from one generation to the next, even if the answers given to them develop over time. If we give attention to philosophy as a body of knowledge, we can thus call upon the whole history of discussions about justice – each set against the particular concerns of each thinker and the times in which they were writing – to inform our present understanding.

Whenever you take an interest in a particular set of philosophical questions – about mind, or science, or religion, or ethics, or politics – you find that your reflections have implications for many other spheres of life. For convenience, we need to divide up philosophy into its different branches, but in practice they all interpenetrate. Each of them has a history, and our views on them can be informed, our perception sharpened, and our ability to take a view and argue our case assisted by paying attention to what great thinkers in the past have had to say.

10 Only got ten minutes?

In a lecture in 1854, Louis Pasteur is reported to have said 'In the fields of observation, chance favours only the prepared mind'. Why do I mention this in an introduction to philosophy? Well, it is my view that, in life as in observation, the varied situations and crises that chance throws up present both hazards and opportunities. The person that is alert and sensitive to what life is about, and who has already considered the fundamental principles of what we can know or what we should do, will hopefully be better able to grasp and use each situation to the full. It has always been appreciated that information is needed in order to make good business decisions. At one time, an advertisement for The *Financial Times* said simply 'No FT; no comment.' To me, the same thing applies to life in general: 'No philosophy; no comment.'

In general, the aims of this book are:

- ▶ to map out the main areas of philosophy, and to introduce some of the thinkers who have contributed to them
- ▶ to give an outline of some of the arguments that have been put forward
- ▶ to provide an overview of the fundamental concepts and ways in which philosophy has developed, so that ideas and arguments can be 'placed' in their historical context.

Reading other people's thoughts is no substitute for thinking. If this book attempts to offer 'pegs' upon which to hang a reasoned argument, it is merely a way of assisting the person who is new to philosophy to present his or her case without having to re-invent the philosophical wheel!

What we shall be examining

What can we know for certain? What constitutes sound evidence?
Are there any absolute truths? These questions are dealt with
under **epistemology**: the theory of knowledge. It is particularly
useful to start with epistemology, because examining evidence for
any claim is a useful intellectual discipline. We shall see that some
philosophers (**empiricists**) start with the evidence of the senses,
while others (**rationalists**) give primacy to human reason. Making
sense of life requires skill and clarity in our thinking and reflecting
on what we already know. However, in a confusing world,
philosophy does not always offer certainties, for it often raises
more questions than it answers.

We often tend to assume that science offers a straightforward and
incontrovertible way of getting information about the world –
and indeed, by and large that is true. But even science throws up
difficult questions. Karl Popper, a major twentieth-century figure
in the **Philosophy of Science**, criticized both Marx and Freud on
the basis that they would not allow new evidence to falsify their
theories, whereas Popper insisted that science must always remain
open to have its theories overturned if new evidence contradicts
them. But it is far from clear just how willing (and appropriate)
it is for science to drop useful theories at the first appearance of
conflicting data.

Then there is the question of **language**. Early in the twentieth-
century the Logical Positivists thought that the only valid form of
language was that which described the physical world, and that
the meaning of a statement was seen in its method of verification.
Although inspired by science, it was a very narrow approach.
Originally inspired by Wittgenstein's early work, its influence
waned as Wittgenstein himself changed his view, insisting that
language should be understood in terms of how it is used. We are
easily fooled by words. The old joke, based on an advertisement
for a painkilling tablet, goes: 'Nothing works faster than …, so,

next time you have a headache, take nothing!' Silly, I know, but you may be surprised just how often we are fooled into thinking that a word automatically must refer to an entity. Controversially, 'God' has suffered from that tendency, people have been enslaved in the name of 'freedom' and treated unfairly in the name of 'justice'. The scope and significance of language is hugely important.

The Philosophy of Mind not only examines the relationship between mind and body, but explores the whole range of new ideas thrown up by cognitive science. Can the mind be fully mapped by neuroscience? Can computers replicate what goes on in the human brain? Are we animated bodies, or is there something about a human being that is beyond the physical? And, if so, might we be able – at least in theory – to survive death?

The Philosophy of Religion explores what religious beliefs mean and how we should understand words like 'God'. The traditional arguments for the existence of God form the central core of this area of philosophy – not necessarily because they are convincing as arguments, but because they help to illustrate what religious belief is about.

But human beings not only seek to understand their world, they also live in it, make choices in it, and organize themselves into societies. Philosophy therefore addresses two other practical areas of life – **Ethics** and **Political philosophy**. These are of immediate importance and relevance, since everyone is involved with making moral and political decisions at some level, and an appreciation of the values and arguments that underpin ethical principles is important for transforming personal intuition about right and wrong into rational argument.

During the twentieth century, in the English-speaking world, philosophy became much concerned with issues of evidence and language. It was often assumed that philosophers were there to unpack difficult logical problems, or to clarify terms, but were most unlikely to have anything much to say about how people should live. On the continent of Europe, however, very different approaches to philosophy were being developed; these were far more directly concerned with people's experience of their own lives. Building on the work of thinkers such as Kant in the eighteenth century, or Hegel in the nineteenth, the European tradition produced **phenomenology, existentialism** and **postmodernism** – ways of that reflect thinking the complexity of human experience which have implications for art and literature as well as philosophy.

Definite answers and progress?

When studying the natural sciences, you can generally trace a progression of ideas and a gradual expansion of knowledge. By contrast, in reading philosophy, you will find that, although you can trace out the progression of ideas (who influenced whom, and so on), you will also find that progress can sometimes appear to be circular rather than linear, that the questions explored by the ancient Greeks are still very much debated today. But philosophy is always suggesting new ways of looking at questions, new ways of expressing ideas, and new views about the purpose and function of philosophy itself. But new ideas may not necessarily be an improvement on old ones.

Is not possible to live in Western Europe, or the United States, without having your language and ideas influenced by generations of thinkers. To be aware of that heritage, gives you a greater appreciation of your own culture. There is always going to be progress, because we benefit from this developing history of ideas.

For those who crave definitive answers, philosophy is likely to prove a source of constant frustration. For those who constantly ask questions, and are prepared to examine and modify their own views, it is a source of fascination and a means of sharpening the critical faculties.

Introduction

In order to enjoy philosophy, it is important to remember that it is both an activity and a body of knowledge.

As an activity, it is a matter of asking questions, challenging assumptions, re-examining traditionally held views, unpacking the meaning of words, weighing up the value of evidence and examining the logic of arguments. It cultivates an enquiring and critical mind, even if it sometimes infuriates those who want an easy intellectual life. Philosophy is also a means of clarifying your own thinking. The clearer your thought, the better able you will be to express yourself, and the more accurate your way of examining arguments and making decisions.

As a body of knowledge, it is the cumulative wisdom of great thinkers. It offers you a chance to explore fundamental questions and to see what thinkers in different periods of history have had to say about them. This in itself is valuable, because it frees you from being limited by the unquestioned assumptions of those around you. To think through issues from first principles is a natural result of having looked at the way in which philosophers have gone about their work. So this second aspect of philosophy reinforces the first.

Philosophy is a tool with which to expose nonsense, and express ideas in a way that is as unambiguous as possible. For example, philosophy makes a distinction between 'analytic' and 'synthetic' statements. An analytic statement is known to be true once the definitions of its terms are understood. $2 + 2 = 4$ is just such a statement. You don't have to go out gathering sets of two items and counting them in order to verify it. You cannot return triumphant and proclaim that you have found a single case which disproves the rule – that you have two sets of two which actually add up to five! Proof, for analytic statements, does not require research or experimental testing. On the other hand, if I say that a certain person is at home, that cannot be true in the same way – it is a synthetic statement, based on evidence. To find out whether or not it is true, you have to phone or visit. The statement can easily be proved wrong, and it certainly cannot be true for all time.

But if someone says 'God exists', is that an analytic or a synthetic statement? Can you define 'God' in such a way that his existence is inevitable? If so, can any evidence be relevant for or against that claim? You might argue that:

▶ *God is everything that exists.*
▶ *Everything that exists, exists.*
▶ *Therefore God exists.*

This argument is sound, but it implies that 'God' and 'everything that exists' are interchangeable terms. This is **pantheism** (the idea that God and the world are identical) and it is quite logical, but is it what most people mean by the word 'God'? And what are its implications for the way we see 'everything that exists'? We observe that everything in the world is liable to change. There will come a time when nothing that exists now will remain. Does this mean that a pantheistic god is also constantly changing? Does it make sense for a word to stay the same, when the thing to which it refers changes? Is a school the same if its buildings are replaced, its staff move on to other posts, and its pupils leave year by year to be replaced by others? Am I the same, even though most of the cells in my body are changing, and my thoughts are constantly on the move? What is the 'I' that remains throughout my life?

In these questions we have touched on some of the central problems of philosophy:

▶ **metaphysics** – *the study of reality, of what actually exists*
▶ **epistemology** – *questions about what things we can know, and how we can know them*
▶ **philosophy of religion** – *the issues that lie behind religious ideas and language*
▶ **philosophy of mind** – *the study of the nature of the self.*

This illustrates another feature of philosophy, and a good reason to study it: you can start from any one question and find yourself drawn outwards to consider many others. Start with 'the self', and you find that matters of metaphysics or religion are drawn into your thinking. By using the skills of philosophy, you have the means of integrating your ideas, of relating them, and of testing them out within a wide range of issues.

Different styles of argument

Philosophy can be presented in different ways. Plato, for example, favoured the dialogue form. So his political philosophy in *The Republic* has a range of characters, each of who presents and argues for a particular viewpoint. Other philosophers gradually unpack the implications of their particular theory in a more linear fashion.

Some, of course, take an analytic approach, breaking down accepted ideas into their simplest indubitable elements, and then trying to start from scratch and give an account of what can be known for certain. There is also pure logic, which uses artificial languages in order to clarify and set out the logic of our ordinary language.

Much of the time, philosophy is concerned with language. Indeed, some philosophers see their whole task as linguistic. In this, it is important to distinguish between 'first order' and 'second order' language. Some examples:

First order:	'A caused B.'
Second order:	'What does it mean to say that A caused B?'
First order:	'Is it right to do this?'
Second order:	'What does it mean to say that something is "right"?'
First order:	'God does not exist.'
Second order:	'What is religious language, and how may religious assertions be verified?'

Second order language clarifies first order language. In doing so it also clarifies the thought that lies behind that language. Philosophy is mainly concerned with second order language, so it may not be able to tell you if something is right or wrong, but it will clarify the grounds upon which you can make that decision for yourself.

There was a phase in philosophy – starting early in the twentieth century – when some thinkers claimed that the sole task of philosophy was to clarify the meaning of words. They assumed that, once the linguistic problems were sorted out, all else would follow. Today that view is giving way to a broader perspective. Philosophy is indeed about language, and it is essential to understand the language you use, but it is also important to rise above language, to explore the basic ideas and concepts it expresses, and then to move on to examine features about the world that would not have come to light without that process of serious thinking and analysis.

Of course, philosophers do not always agree about how to do philosophy, or what is of value. The late A. J. Ayer, an Oxford philosopher best known for his work on 'logical positivism' (see p. 72), interviewed about his work in 1980, commented in his usual direct way on the work of various other philosophers, saying of the German existential philosopher Heidegger's idea about 'the Nothing' that it seemed to him to be 'sheer rubbish' and that people might sometimes be impressed because they like to be mystified. In Chapter 8 we shall be looking briefly at the work of Heidegger. You may feel inclined, after reading that, to agree with Ayer, or you might feel that Heidegger is describing something of greater importance than Ayer's more analytic approach. The essential thing to realize at this stage is that philosophers do not all agree on the topics about which to philosophize, the way to set about doing so, or the conclusions reached. Philosophy is not monolithic. There is no body of established and unquestioned work; it is an ongoing activity – and one which often raises more questions than it answers.

Eastern approaches

Philosophy is not limited to any one culture or continent. The philosophy introduced in this book, and taught in departments of philosophy in most universities in Europe and the United States, is Western philosophy – but that is only one part of a much larger tradition.

Eastern philosophy is generally taken to include the major religious and philosophical systems of India (the various traditions collectively known as Hinduism, along with Buddhist and Jain philosophy) and the Far East, including Confucian and Taoist thought and the later developments of Buddhism.

It is commonly said that the big difference between Eastern and Western philosophy is that the former is religious, and is concerned with salvation as much as with knowledge, whereas the latter is secular, seen by many as almost an alternative to religion. That is not entirely true. In the West, the Christian, Jewish and Muslim religions have had a profound influence on philosophical thought, and the philosophy of religion continues to be an important aspect of philosophy. In the East, although philosophy is seen as a matter of practical and spiritual importance, the process of reasoning can be examined in itself, quite apart from any religious connotations. It may also distort Eastern thought to try to draw a distinction between religion and philosophy: Buddhism, for example, sees the path to overcoming suffering in terms of understanding the fundamental truths of life. It is not a matter of religious doctrines on the one hand and secular thought on the other – that is a Western distinction that is not really relevant.

Since there is little enough scope within this book to introduce the main areas of Western thought, no attempt has been made to explore Eastern philosophy. A book on *Eastern Philosophy*, originally part of this series, is available from the same author – see 'Further Reading'.

Philosophy today – like the froth on the crest of a wave – is carried forward by the whole movement of thought that stretches back at least 2,500 years, and far longer if you include Eastern thought. What this book seeks to do (while acknowledging its limitations of coverage and depth) is to point to the reality of the wave, and the general direction of the water within it. A society without philosophy would be cut off from its own roots; it would have to start from scratch time and time again to sort out its values and its self-understanding. With philosophy, that process of sorting out is shown in its historical and logical perspectives. With philosophy, you start at an advantage, for you look at each problem with the benefit of knowing something of the accumulated wisdom of some of the best thinkers in Western culture.

Worth the hemlock?

One of the most remarkable moments in the history of Western philosophy was the death of Socrates in 399 BCE. The event is recorded by Plato, whose respect for his teacher was such that he set out most of his philosophy in the form of dialogues in which Socrates plays the central role. Charged with impiety, Socrates was condemned to death on the grounds that his questioning and teaching was corrupting the young (with whom he appears to have been popular for challenging conventional beliefs and ideas). Plato presents Socrates as declining to propose an acceptable alternative punishment, and being prepared to accept death (by drinking a cup of hemlock). For Plato, reason and the freedom of the individual to live in accordance with it, took priority over the social and political order. Socrates would not compromise his freedom to pursue the truth, even if it appeared subversive and a danger to the state. Indeed, as Plato was later to expound in *The Republic*, justice and the institutions of state should be based on reason, and rulers should be philosophers, willing and able to apply reason with disinterested objectivity.

For Socrates, the task of the philosopher was not peripheral to life, but central. To stop questioning and challenging accepted concepts was unthinkable; Socrates chose to accept death rather than leave Athens. He is presented as calm, rational and a man of absolute integrity.

Philosophy can be a frustrating discipline. Sometimes it appears dry and remote from life. Sometimes it takes the role of linguistic handmaid, clarifying the terms used by other disciplines without appearing to offer anything of substance to the sum of human knowledge. Sometimes philosophers insist on setting down their thoughts in a style that obscures rather than clarifies. From time to time, one may be tempted to ask, 'Is it worth it? Why not settle for established thoughts and values, however superficial? Why make life difficult by this constant questioning?' or, in the case of Socrates, 'Is it worth the hemlock?'

That I leave the reader to judge.

1

The theory of knowledge

In this chapter you will learn:

- *how Western philosophers have tackled the issue of knowledge and certainty*
- *how some of the best-known philosophers have described reality*
- *how to assess the role of your senses in understanding the world.*

There are two basic questions which have been asked throughout the history of philosophy and which affect the way in which many different topics are considered:

What can we know?

This question is about the basic features of existence; not the sort of information that science gives about particular things, but the questions that lie beneath all such enquiry: questions about the fundamental nature of space, time or causality; about whether concepts like 'justice' or 'love' have any external, objective reality; about the structure of the world as we experience it. In the collected works of Aristotle, such questions were dealt with after his material on physics and were therefore called **metaphysics**.

But as soon as we start considering metaphysics, yet another question arises:

How can we know it?

Is there anything of which we can be absolutely certain? Do we depend entirely on our senses, or can we discover basic truths simply by thinking? How can we justify or prove the truth of what we claim? All such questions are considered under **epistemology** – the theory of knowledge.

But when we deal with metaphysics or epistemology, we have to communicate our thoughts in some way. The medium for this is language. We ask 'What can we say?' and 'How can we say it?' The study of the nature of language, and the way in which statements can be shown to be true or false, is another constant preoccupation of philosophy.

In this chapter we shall be examining some basic issues in metaphysics and epistemology, before going on to look at scientific knowledge and the nature of language. Once you have a sound knowledge of these areas of philosophy, it will become much easier to examine the way they are applied to various topics to be considered later – God, the mind, ethics, politics and so on. You will find that the same fundamental problems occur in all areas of study.

Empiricism and rationalism

Within epistemology (the theory of knowledge) there is a fundamental issue about whether our knowledge originates in, and is therefore dependent upon, the data we receive through our senses, or whether (since we know that all such sense data is fallible) the only true certainties are those that come from our own minds – from the way in which we think and organize our experience, from the principles of reason and logic.

Two key terms:

- **Empiricism** – *all knowledge starts with the senses.*
- **Rationalism** – *all knowledge starts with the mind.*

An example of an empiricist position is that of Hume, while a rationalist one is illustrated by Descartes. Their arguments about how we can justify our claims to knowledge will be outlined later in this chapter.

However, the issue of experience and the way the mind categorizes it is far from straightforward. A very basic problem here concerns **reductionism,** and the existence of, or reality of, complex entities or general concepts.

Consider these questions:

- *How does a painting relate to the individual pigments or threads of canvas of which is it made?*
- *How does music relate to vibrations in the air?*
- *How does a person relate to the individual cells in his or her body?*
- *How does a nation relate to the citizens of which it is made up?*

A 'reductionist' approach to metaphysics takes the 'nothing but' view, for example that music is 'nothing but' vibrations in the air.

Reductionism and practical decisions ...

When, on Christmas Day, the British and German soldiers facing one another in the First World War came out of their trenches, played football together and shared cigarettes, they ceased to be merely representatives of nations and acted as individuals. Later, they returned to their trenches and continued to kill one another.

(Contd)

Which is more real – a nation or the individuals who make it up? Which should guide action? Should we act as individuals, framing political decisions on the basis of what individuals want, or should we give primacy to the 'nation' or the 'class', even if individuals have to suffer as a result? That is a matter for ethics, but we can go further and ask, 'Do nations actually exist? Is there any such thing as society, or are there just people and families?' These are fundamental, abstract questions, but they have important practical and moral consequences.

If you believe that the ultimate reality is matter – the solid external world that we experience through our senses – then you are probably going to call yourself a **materialist**. On the other hand, if you hold that the basic reality is mental – that the world of your experience is in fact the sum of all the sensations and perceptions that have registered in your mind – you may call yourself an **idealist**.

Insight

Although idealism sounds improbable, consider this: How can you tell whether, at this moment, you are dreaming or experiencing the external, physical world? If you just consider the experience you have, it's not quite as simple as common sense would suggest.

Knowledge and justification: are you certain?

Whenever I experience something, that experience involves two things:

1 *The sensations of sight, sound, taste, touch or smell, all of which seem to me to be coming from outside myself, and therefore to be giving me information about the world.*
2 *My own senses. If I am partially deaf, I may be mistaken in what I hear. If I am colour-blind I will not be able to*

*distinguish certain patterns, or appreciate the subtleties of a
multicoloured fabric. If I am asleep, all sorts of things may go
on around me of which I am quite unaware.*

Imagine that I am taken to a police station and questioned about
something that is alleged to have happened in the recent past. I give
my account of what I have heard or seen. If it sounds credible, or
agrees with the evidence of others, I am likely to be believed. On
the other hand, the police may ask, 'Are you sure about that? Is it
possible that you were mistaken?' The implication is that, even if I
am trying to be accurate and honest, the senses may be mistaken, and
there may be two quite different ways of interpreting an experience.

When philosophers ask, 'What can be known for certain?' or
'Are the senses a reliable source of knowledge?' they are trying to
sort out this element of uncertainty, so as to achieve statements
that are known to be true.

Basically, as we saw above, there are two ways of approaching this
problem, corresponding to the two elements in every experience.

▶ *Empiricists are those who start with the sensations of an
  experience, and say that all of our knowledge of the world is
  based on sensation.*
▶ *Rationalists are those who claim that the basis of knowledge
  is the set of ideas we have – the mental element that sorts out
  and interprets experience. Rationalists consider the mind to be
  primary, and the actual data of experience to be secondary.*

But before we look at these approaches in more detail, let us be
clear about one category of things that we can know for certain.
If I say that $2 + 2 = 4$, there is no doubt about the truth of that
statement. Mathematics and logic work from agreed definitions.
Once those are accepted, certain results follow. They do not
depend upon particular situations or experiences.

In general terms I can say that: If $A = B + C$, and if B and C are
contained in, or implied by, the definition of A, then that statement

will always be true. Understand the words and you understand its truth. Statements that are true by definition, although they are important, need not therefore detain us.

DESCARTES (1596–1650)

René Descartes placed one question centre-stage: 'Of what can I be certain?' He used the method of systematic doubt, by which he would only accept what he could see clearly and distinctly to be true. He knew that his senses could be deceived, therefore he would not trust them, nor could he always trust his own logic. He realized that he might even be dreaming what he took to be a waking reality. His approach is one that will be examined below, in the section on Scepticism. Yet the one thing Descartes could not doubt was his own existence. If he doubted, he was there to doubt; therefore he must exist. The famous phrase which expresses this is 'cogito ergo sum' ('I think, therefore I am'). His argument is set out in his *Discourse on Method* (Section 4), 1637:

> **But then, immediately, as I strove to think of everything as false, I realized that, in the very act of thinking everything false, I was aware of myself as something real; and observing that the truth: I think, therefore I am, was so firm and so assured that the most extravagant arguments of the sceptics were incapable of shaking it, I concluded that I might have no scruple in taking it as the first principle of philosophy for which I was looking.**

Penguin Classics (trans. A. Wollaston), 1960

Descartes could doubt even his own body but, while doubting, he could not deny himself as a thinking being. All else was open to the challenge that he could be mistaken.

In many ways, Descartes' argument represents the starting point of modern philosophy (modern, that is, as compared to that of the ancient Greeks and of the medieval world), not because later thinkers have been in agreement with him but because, challenged by scepticism, they have followed his quest to find the basis of certainty and knowledge. In other words, Descartes set the theory of knowledge at the heart of the philosophical agenda.

RUSSELL (1872–1970)

Bertrand Russell's early philosophy was as hugely influential as his later writings were popular. He contributed to mathematics and logic, and introduced analytic philosophy, an approach that dominated the Anglo–American philosophical scene for half a century.

Moving on from Descartes' systematic doubt, a useful next step is to look at Russell's analysis of experience in his book *The Problems of Philosophy* (1912). He examines the table at which he sits to write. He observes that its appearance changes in different light and from different positions, and comes to the conclusion that our sense perceptions (the actual experiences of colour, shape and texture) are not the same thing as the table itself (otherwise we would have to say that the table becomes black once the light is turned out, or that it gets smaller when we walk away from it), but that we have to *infer* the table from those perceptions.

He therefore distinguishes sense data from the 'physical object' that gives rise to them.

He refers to Bishop Berkeley (see p. 19), who argued that there is nothing given in our perception of something that proves it exists even when nobody is perceiving it. In order to maintain continuity when things are not being observed, Berkeley used the idea that they were being observed by God. In other words, what we call matter (the external physical world) is only known to exist in dependence upon minds that perceive it.

Having commented on Descartes' systematic doubt, Russell points out that common sense suggests that there are ongoing objects, and that they do continue to exist when not being observed.

He gives the example of a cloth thrown over a table. Once that is done, the table cannot be observed, but it is implied by the shape of the cloth, apparently suspended in mid air. He also considers the situation where a number of people look at the same table. Unless there were to be some underlying reality, there seems to be little reason why everyone should see exactly the same thing.

He takes the idea of a cat which becomes equally hungry whether it is being observed or not. If it did not exist except when being observed, this would not make sense. Indeed, he points out that the cat's hunger is something that one cannot observe directly, and therefore (in terms of sense data) it does not exist.

All this leads him to accept the idea, given in an instinctive belief which he has no reason to reject, that there is indeed an external world which gives rise to our sense experience.

The external world: appearance and reality

As we have already seen, metaphysics examines what lies behind, or is implied by, our experience of the world. It explores general ideas such as 'goodness' or 'honesty' or 'beauty' and tries to say what role they play in our understanding of reality. Without metaphysics, the world is just a jumble of experiences without overall coherence.

Of course, it is quite possible to claim that our experience of the world is in fact a jumble of sensations without overall value, sense or direction. That is a rejection of all metaphysics. It is equally possible to seek for, and have an intuition that there should be, some overall reality and unity in the world, an understanding of which would be able to give guidance in the interpretation and valuation of individual experiences. This sense of overall coherence may be expressed in terms of belief in God, or it may not. But in either case, what is being done is metaphysics.

Of course, the debate about knowledge of external reality predates Descartes, even if he is a convenient starting point because of his radical doubt. The ancient Greeks were concerned to explore both the nature of experience and the words we use to describe it.

PRE-SOCRATIC PHILOSOPHERS

The philosophers Plato (427–347 BCE) and Aristotle (384–322 BCE) are the most important of the Greek thinkers for the subsequent history of Western philosophy, and they set much of the agenda for those who followed. Plato took his inspiration from Socrates (470–399 BCE), whose ideas are known primarily through his appearance in Plato's dialogues. But before Socrates there were a number of philosophers who were concerned with metaphysics from what would later become a 'scientific' standpoint. They sought the principles that lay behind all natural phenomena.

The pre-socratics include Thales and Anaximander from the sixth century BCE, along with the philosopher and mathematician Pythagoras, and Parmenides from the following century. Although there is no scope here to discuss them individually, they are covered in most histories of Western philosophy, and are well worth studying. Of particular interest are the views of the 'atomists', Leucippus and Demoncritus, who (anticipating Newtonian and later physics) thought of all material objects as made up of atoms, operating according to fixed laws, and who recognized that many secondary qualities (colour, etc.) were dependent upon the perceiver, rather than qualities inherent in what was perceived.

There was also a fascination with the problems of permanence and change. Heraclitus (early sixth century BCE) claimed that one could not step into the same river twice, on the grounds that the water that made it up was constantly changing. Can the river be considered a permanent entity if fresh water is always flowing down it?

Insight

This was a radical question to ask in the sixth century BCE, and one that is interestingly parallel to the metaphysics being developed by the Buddha in Northern India at about the same time.

With the benefit of 2,500 years of philosophical hindsight, the earliest thinkers may seem to have primitive ideas of cosmology and physics. What is remarkable, however, is that they should have set out to give an overall explanation of the world in the first place: to make it a 'cosmos', a unified, rationally understood world. There had been, and continued to be, myths and images by which the world could be explored and given meaning, but these pre-socratic philosophers set out to examine the nature of the world in a more systematic way, and to use their reason to formulate general principles about its fundamental structure and composition. While their contemporaries were thinking in terms of fate or the influence of the gods to explain things, they pressed ahead with what was later to develop into philosophy and science.

PLATO (427–347 BCE)

It has been said that the whole of Western philosophy is a set of footnotes to Plato, and there is a great deal of truth in that, since Plato covered a wide range of issues, and raised questions that have been debated ever since.

In *The Republic*, Plato uses an analogy to illustrate his view of human experience and his theory of knowledge. A row of prisoners sit near the back of a cave, chained so that they cannot turn to face its mouth. Behind them is a fire, in front of which are paraded various objects. The fire casts shadows of these objects on to the wall at the back of the cave, and this is all the prisoners can see. Plato thinks that this corresponds to the normal way in which things are experienced: shadows, not reality itself. But he then presents a situation in which a prisoner is freed so that he can turn round and see the fire and the objects that cast the shadows. His first impression is that the objects are not as 'real' as those images he has been accustomed to seeing. But then he is forcibly dragged up to the mouth of the cave and into the sunlight and he gradually adjusts to the light of the sun. The experience of daylight and perceiving the sun is painful, and requires considerable adjustment. Only then does it become clear to the prisoner that his former perceptions were only shadows, not reality. This, for Plato, corresponds to the journey from seeing particular things, to seeing the eternal realities of which the particulars are mere shadow-like copies.

In Plato's dialogues, Socrates debates the meaning of words as a means of getting to understand the reality to which they point. So, for example, he argues that 'Justice' is not just a word that is used to bracket certain events and situations together. Justice actually exists, as a reality over and above any of the individual things that are said to be just. Indeed, the individual things can be said to be 'just' only because we already have knowledge of 'justice' itself and can see that they share in its reality.

These general realities he calls 'Forms'. If we did not have knowledge of such Forms we would have no ability to put anything into a category. The Form of something is its essential feature, the thing that makes it what it is.

An example

If I do not know the essence of dogginess, I will not be able to tell if the animal before me is a dog or a camel. Is it possible that I am looking at a tall dog with a hump, a long neck and bad breath? Equally, could that dachshund on a lead be a humpless, short-necked, particularly squat camel?

Description requires general terms, and general terms require an understanding of essences. Only with a prior appreciation of dogginess or camelity – if that is the correct term – can I hope to distinguish between then.

The ultimate Form for Plato (and the goal of the philosophical quest) is the Form of the Good. An understanding of 'the good' enables all else to be valued; it is the equivalent of the sun that the escaped prisoner sees as he leaves the cave. So, in both the doctrine of the Forms and the analogy of the cave, Plato is describing the same process that concerns modern philosophers: the way in which we can relate our present experiences to reality itself. What Plato is saying is that our ordinary experience is no more than shadows, and that reality itself lies beyond them. We can have knowledge of the Forms, because they are known by reason, whereas the most we can have of the individual things in the world of sensation is 'true belief', since it is always provisional and changing.

But how do we come by knowledge of the Forms? In his dialogues, the protagonist (generally Socrates) challenges someone to explain the meaning of a particular concept and, by introducing examples by which to test out the explanation, refines the concept. This implies that true knowledge can be developed by the use of reason alone. But how is that possible, if all experience is of particulars? He believed that we must have had direct knowledge of the Forms in the eternal realm, before our birth into this world, but that such knowledge is then cluttered by the changing experiences of the everyday world (as we sit in our cave, watching shadows). For Plato, we do not gather knowledge, we remember it.

ARISTOTLE (384–322 BCE)

In the great legacy of Greek thought, Aristotle offers an interesting contrast to Plato. Whereas Plato explored the world of the 'Forms', known only to the intellect – a perfect world, free from the limitations of the particular things we experience – Aristotle's philosophy is based on what is known through experience. He categorized the sciences (physics, psychology and economics all come from Aristotle) and gave us many of the terms and concepts that have dominated science and philosophy (including energy, substance, essence and category).

In rejecting Plato's Forms, Aristotle nevertheless acknowledged that people needed to consider 'sorts' of things, rather than each particular thing individually (try describing something without using general terms to indicate the kind of thing it is), but he believed that the Forms (to use Plato's term) were immanent in the particulars. In other words, I may look at a variety of things that are red, and say that what they have in common is redness. The quality 'redness' is actually part of my experience of those things. But what would it mean to have absolute redness; a redness that was not a red something or other? In Aristotle's philosophy, we do not go outside the world of experience in order to know the meaning of universal concepts; we simply apply them within experience. This aimed to overcome a basic problem with Plato's Forms, illustrated by the example given below:

An example

I believe that this particular in front of me is a man.

Why? Because I have knowledge of the Form of man.

But, given that all particulars are different, how do I know that this one belongs to the category 'man'? (It could be a robot, an ape, a pre-hominoid.)

Answer: There must be a concept of 'man' over above the Form and the particular, to which I refer when I claim that the one is a particular example of the other.

But how do I know that **that** is in the right category? Only by having yet another concept of 'man' to which I can refer – and so on *ad infinitum*! (Which means that I can never know for sure that this is a man!)

This problem was recognized by Plato himself. It is generally known as the 'third-man argument'. By denying that the Form is separate from the particulars, but simply a way of describing the particular sort of thing that these particulars are, Aristotle reckoned that he had avoided this problem.

For Plato, knowledge had been limited to the world of forms, whereas the world known to the senses could yield, at best, only true belief. Eternal truths were detached from particular things. By contrast, having forms immanent within particulars, Aristotle claims that we can have true knowledge of the world of the senses.

There are many other important elements in Aristotle's metaphysics. One of them, his idea of causality, is of particular interest because it has implications both for metaphysics and also for the philosophy of religion.

Aristotle argued that everything had four causes:

1 **Material** – *the matter from which the thing is made.*
2 **Formal** – *the kind of thing that something is (i.e. the issue described in the box above).*
3 **Efficient** – *the agent that brings something about (the sense in which modern science would speak of a cause).*
4 **Final** – *the goal or purpose for which a thing is the way it is, and to which it is moving. This introduces the concept of the telos, or 'end'. If the world is rational, everything has its part to play, its purpose.*

This had a considerable impact on the later philosophy of religion (as we shall see in Chapter 5) and also on the 'natural law' approach to ethics (see Chapter 6). It is also important because it acknowledges that the reality of a particular thing is not just a matter of its present substance and form, but is related to agents in the past that have produced it and goals in the future to which it moves – both of which are part of its reality.

Insight

When science asks 'Why?' it looks for an 'efficient' cause or causes. When a religious or moral thinker asks 'Why?' he or she is asking about the 'final' cause or purpose.

In some way, every metaphysical question has to take account of the fact that there are individual things which need to be known and related to one another, but also (and implied every time we use language) that there are universals, general concepts, a sense of the whole. Which of these should take priority?

This dilemma is illustrated by two major metaphysical systems, those of Spinoza and Leibniz. Both are examples of rationalism (that one can come to a knowledge of reality by means of pure reason, as opposed to empiricism, which based knowledge on the data of experience), and both follow the tradition established by Descartes of trying to move from first principles to construct an overall view of the world.

SPINOZA (1632–77)

Baruch Spinoza was born to Jewish parents in Amsterdam, and was brought up in the Orthodox Jewish community, but expelled from it at the age of 24 for his heterodox views. Thereafter he earned his living grinding lenses, which allowed him freedom to develop his ideas and to write. He was later offered a professorship, but declined it in order to maintain his freedom to explore philosophy in his own way.

For Spinoza (and for Leibniz) the reality of the world, as known to reason, is very different from the appearance of the world as it is known to us through experience. Spinoza, a radical Jewish thinker, argued that God was the only absolute substance. His argument may be summarized as:

▶ *If God is infinite, he must co-exist with everything.*
▶ *God must therefore be the only thing whose explanation lies within itself (all limited things can be caused by something external – but God can't, because there is nothing external to God).*
▶ *God is therefore the whole of the natural order.*
▶ *Although individual things may appear to be separate, they are, in reality, parts of a larger whole, which is God.*
▶ *The one true thing is the world as a whole.*

Insight

Spinoza considered that everything therefore only had its reality as part of a greater whole, and that the mental and the material were two different aspects of the same fundamental reality. In his quest for the real, his conclusions were therefore exactly the opposite of those of Descartes.

LEIBNIZ (1646–1716)

Born in Leipzig, the son of a professor of moral philosophy, Gottfried Wilhelm Leibniz was a brilliant philosopher, mathematician (he developed calculus independently of Newton) and logician.

Leibniz takes a view about particulars and wholes which is exactly the opposite of Spinoza. For Leibniz (following Descartes) the world is divided between mental things and physical or material things, and the essential difference between them is that physical things exist in space, but mental things do not. Now Leibniz saw that any material thing can be divided into its constituent parts, and these can be sub-divided again and again. Ultimately, the world must therefore consist of an infinite number of things, which cannot be divided any more. But if they are indivisible, they cannot occupy space (if they did, they could be divided), so they cannot be physical. Therefore (since things are either physical or mental) they must be mental in nature. He called them monads.

His argument might be expressed thus:

- ▶ *Every complex material thing can be divided into its constituent parts.*
- ▶ *These parts can be sub-divided again and again.*
- ▶ *Anything which has extension in space can be divided.*
- ▶ *Ultimately you arrive at an infinite number of monads, which occupy no space at all. They cannot be physical (otherwise they would be in space, and capable of being further divided), so they must be mental.*

Note

In modern usage, 'mental' is taken to refer to the process of human thought, and as such it is difficult to see how Leibniz's monads can be so described. Given that, following Descartes, everything was designated either material or mental, Leibniz did not have much of a choice. Perhaps, in modern terms, it might be better to describe his monads as having a quality of pure energy or pure activity. This would bring his concept much closer to that of modern physics, where ultimately all matter is comprised of energy.

How do these monads come together to form complex entities? Leibniz took the view that the monads – since they were not physical – could not influence one another directly. Rather, the world was arranged with a pre-established harmony, so that all the separate monads, each following its own course, actually managed to combine to give rise to the world we know, with its complex bodies.

In other words

▶ Which is more real – the whole or the parts of which the whole is comprised?
▶ Are there such things as justice and beauty (or any universal idea) or are there just individual things that we choose to describe as just or beautiful?
▶ How do you get beyond the things that appear to the senses? Is there a reality that lies beneath them and, if so, can we ever get to understand it?

These are some of the basic questions for metaphysics, raised by the philosophers we have considered so far in this chapter.

STARTING WITH EXPERIENCE

In the quest for knowledge, there are two contrasting approaches: one (rationalism) starts with the mind; the other (empiricism) starts with experience. The essential thing to grasp as we look at empiricism is that sense data (which make up the content of our experience) are not simply 'things' out there in the world. They depend upon our own faculties – the way in which we experience as well as what we experience.

The rationalism/empiricism debate can be seen by contrasting Descartes' views (as briefly outlined above) with those of John Locke, George Berkeley and David Hume, who are key figures in the development of empiricism.

LOCKE (1632–1704)

John Locke is known both for his empiricism, analysing sense experience and the way in which we learn, and also for his political philosophy. In his *Essay Concerning Human Understanding* (1689), he was on the same quest as Descartes: the desire to know what the mind can comprehend and what it cannot. But his conclusions were radically different. He claimed that there are no such things as innate ideas, and that all that we know comes to us from experience, and from reflecting upon experience.

Locke held that there are primary qualities (solidity, extension, motion, number) and secondary qualities (colour, sound, taste, etc.). The former inhere in bodies (i.e. they are independent of our perceiving them); the latter depend upon the act of perception (i.e. being able to see, hear, etc.).

He also held that we can genuinely know of the existence of bodies through our senses. The sense data we receive cannot be subjective, because we do not control them. (This is similar to the position outlined by Russell as he looks at his table – because others see it as well as he, he concludes that the table itself cannot depend upon his own sensation, even if the actual data he receives does so.)

Locke was certainly influenced by Descartes. He had to accept that substance itself was unknowable, for he could know nothing directly, only through his senses. In this he anticipated to some extent the more general conclusions of Kant (see p. 23), who later made the radical distinction between things as they are in themselves (noumena) and things as we perceive them (phenomena).

BERKELEY (1685-1753)

Bishop George Berkeley was a fascinating character. He wrote his philosophy while in his twenties, later became a Bishop, and took an interest in higher education in the American Colonies (where he lived for some time), leaving his library of books to Yale University.

Berkeley argued for 'idealism', which is the theory that everything that exists is mental. This sounds an unlikely view to hold about the world, but it follows from the way in which we perceive things. An idealist might argue as follows:

▶ *All we actually know of the world are sensations (colour, sound, taste, touch, the relative positions of things that we perceive). We cannot know the world by any other means. For us, these sensations are what we mean by 'the world'.*
▶ *All these sensations are 'ideas': they are mental phenomena. (The colour red does not exist independent of the mind perceiving something of that colour.)*
▶ *Things are therefore collections of these ideas; they exist by being perceived.*

The obvious problem for Berkeley was showing how something can exist while not being perceived.

A silly example

I am aware of a tree in front of me. I see the trunk, branches and leaves with their different colours. I may reach forward and touch the bark. The tree, for me, is the collection of all these sensations. In order

(Contd)

to test out idealism, I shut my eyes, put my hands by my side, and attempt to cut off all sensations of the tree. Convinced that the tree no longer exists, I step forward. The tree immediately reappears in the form of an acute pain in the nose and forehead!

But what does it mean to say that the tree exists in the moment between shutting my eyes and hitting the trunk?

It is possible to say that an object continues to exist if it is being perceived by someone else; but what if nobody perceives it? Berkeley's answer to this is that the tree continues to exist only because it is being perceived by God.

In thinking about Berkeley's theory, it is worth reflecting on where sensations are located. Because they take place as a result of brain and sensory activity, Berkeley says that they are mental – in effect, that they are taking place 'in' the mind. But just because a sensation varies with different conditions, as colours change with different lighting, does that imply that the whole of what we mean by colour is subjective?

Berkeley also held that there are no abstract general ideas. If you think of a triangle, you are thinking of a particular triangle. It shares its qualities with other triangles, but there is no concept of triangle that does not spring from some particular triangle. What we think of as a 'universal' is just a set of qualities abstracted from particulars.

Insight

Few things are new in philosophy. The discussion given above can be traced back to the different views of Plato and Aristotle. If you believe that universals are 'real' then you are likely to be called a 'realist' and will tend to agree with Plato, but if you think that universals are only the 'names' we give to groups of individuals, you are a 'nominalist' and will tend to agree with Aristotle.

HUME (1711–76)

David Hume was a popular and radical philosopher and man of letters who lived in Edinburgh and contributed to the eighteenth-century Scottish Enlightenment. In his day, he was better known – and more widely read – as a historian than as a philosopher, having produced a six-volume history of England. In taking an empiricist approach – that all knowledge is derived from sense experience – Hume made the important distinction (which we have already discussed) between what we have called 'analytic' and 'synthetic' statements. In other words, between:

▶ *those statements that show the relationship between ideas.*
  These are known to be true a priori (before experience)
  because their denial involved contradiction, e.g. the
  propositions of maths and logic. They offer certainty, but
  not information about the world.

and

▶ *those that describe matters of fact. These can only be known*
  a posteriori (after experience). They are not certain, but
  depend on empirical evidence.

This leads to what is known as Hume's Fork. In this, you may ask of a statement:

▶ *Does it contain matters of fact? If so, relate them*
  to experience.
▶ *Does it give the relationships between ideas?*
▶ *If neither, then it is meaningless.*

Insight

The problem with this is that it suggests that moral, religious or value statements are meaningless, since they do not simply depend on facts nor on pure logic. We shall examine this later, because it was a view taken up by the Logical Positivists in the twentieth century, but notice how this strictly empiricist approach limits the function of language to one of picturing the world as it is, rather than shaping it as we wish it to be.

Hume's argument concerning evidence runs like this:

> ▶ *I see something happen several times.*
> ▶ *I therefore expect it to happen again.*
> ▶ *I get into the mental habit of expecting it to happen.*
> ▶ *I may be tempted to project this mental habit out on to the external world in the form of a 'law' of physics.*

So, for example, 'A causes B' could be taken to mean 'B has always been seen to follow A'.

It might be tempting to say 'Therefore B will always follow A', but this would imply that nature is uniform, and you can never have enough evidence for such an absolute statement.

To the statement 'Every event must have a cause' Hume would say:

> ▶ *it can't be justified by logic, since its denial does not involve self-contradiction*
> ▶ *it can't be proved from experience, because we cannot witness every event.*

What, then, are we to do? Hume says that we can accept the idea of causality because it is a habit of the imagination, based on past observation. This may seem obvious, but an important distinction has been made between claiming that something *must be* the case, and saying that, in practice, we have always *found it to be* the case.

In section 10 of *An Enquiry Concerning Human Understanding* (1758), where Hume is considering miracles, he sets out his position about evidence:

A wise man ... proportions his belief to the evidence. In such conclusions as are founded on an infallible experience, he expects the event with the last degree of assurance, and regards his past experience as a full proof of the future existence of that event. In other cases, he proceeds with more caution: He weighs the

> *opposite experiments: He considers which side is supported by the greater number of experiments: to that side he inclines, with doubt and hesitation; and when at last he fixes his judgement, the evidence exceeds not what we properly call probability.*

Hume's approach is also valuable in assessing the question of whether or not the external world exists, and whether we could prove it to exist. He says that it cannot be proved, but gives two features of experience which lead to the idea being accepted – constancy and coherence. I see that objects remain in the same place over a period of time, and I assume that they remain there even when not observed. Also, I may see someone at different times in different places, and I infer from this that they are moving about. In other words, the assumption that the world is predictable enables me to fill in the gaps of my own experience. Once again, however, the key thing to remember is that this is not something that can be proved.

KANT (1724–1804)

Immanuel Kant is one of the most influential figures in the development of Western philosophy. His entire life was spent in Königsberg in East Prussia, where he was a professor at the university. This in itself was remarkable since, prior to the twentieth century, most philosophers were not professional academics.

In many ways, Kant's philosophy can be seen as an attempt to take seriously the claims of the Empiricists (e.g. Hume) that everything depends upon experience and is open to doubt, but to do so in the context of Newtonian physics and the rise of science. Science seeks to formulate laws which predict with certainty, and causality is an essential feature of Newtonian science. We just *know* that everything will be found to have a cause, even before we experience it. So how can you reconcile an empiricist view of knowledge with common sense and the findings of science?

Kant sought to achieve this through what he called his 'Copernican Revolution'. Just as Copernicus totally changed our perception of the world by showing that the Earth revolved round the Sun and not vice versa, so Kant argued that the world of our experience is shaped by our own means of perceiving and understanding it, making the important distinction between what we perceive with our senses (which he called **phenomena**) and the world of things as they are in themselves (which he called **noumena**).

Kant argued that certain features of experience, including space, time and causality, were not in themselves features of the external world, but were imposed by the mind on experience. This was a revolutionary way of looking at the theory of knowledge and at metaphysics. Take the example of time. When I see a sequence of things, I say that time is passing and that one thing follows another. But where is that time? Is it something that exists 'out there' to be seen? Is time there to be discovered? Kant argued that time was one of the ways in which the mind organizes its experiences; it is part of our mental apparatus.

▶ *'But what happened before the "Big Bang"?' is an example of the mind trying to impose the category of time on something to which scientists try to tell us it cannot be applied. However much I accept the idea of space and time coming from that 'singularity', my mind rebels and demands yet more space and time before and beyond it. I am given a description of the universe, and ask 'But what lies outside it?' If I am told that nothing lies outside it, I become confused, for my mind automatically tries to imagine an expanse of nothingness stretching outward from what is known.*

The same is true for causality. We assume that everything has a cause. Even when we have no evidence of a cause, we believe that one will be found eventually – because that is the way the world works. Kant would say that it is the way the mind works. We impose the idea of causality on our experience.

This was his way of reconciling these two important elements in the consciousness of the eighteenth century, and it has many implications for later thought.

'**Realism**' is a term that is frequently used in discussions of appearance and reality. It stands for the view that science is able to give us a true representation of the world 'out there', including entities that are unobservable. There are different forms of realism: 'naïve realism' is generally used for the view that what we perceive is what is actually there; 'representative realism' takes one step back from this, but says that we can form correct representations of what exists. This is particularly important for the philosophy of science, which we shall examine in the next chapter.

Intuitive knowledge

Intuitive knowledge creates particular problems for those who base their knowledge of the world on sense experience. For example, I may feel, listening to a piece of music or looking at a painting, that it 'says something' about life – something that is far beyond any analysis of the particular notes being played or the particles of pigment on canvas. I may feel caught up in an experience of a level of reality of which I am intuitively convinced, but which I subsequently fail to articulate precisely.

A little alcoholic drink can have the same effect – an opening up of intuitive faculties, and a conviction that suddenly the whole world makes sense, that there is something of universal importance that one wants to say. But somehow, once sober again, it is difficult to put into words.

A. J. Ayer, interviewed in *The Observer* in 1980, was asked whether, when listening to music, there might be something other than what is scientifically verifiable; whether, for example, there could be a sense of ecstasy, and of something that was not fully explained. He replied:

> **'I don't particularly want to reduce aesthetic experiences to anything expressible in purely physical terms, but I don't think it's more mysterious than any other statement you might make about yourself. Clearly there is a problem about communicating feelings of any kind, since one has to take the other person's word for it. I can't, as it were, get inside your head and measure your ecstasy, but the statement that you feel ecstatic doesn't seem to me to create any particular problem. I know roughly what kind of feeling you're describing, what causes it, how it leads you to behave, when you are susceptible to it, how it fits in with the general pattern of your behaviour. Is the fact that you feel ecstatic more mysterious than that you feel bored, or any other sort of feeling?'**
>
> *The Observer*, 24 February 1980, p. 35

Notice what is really happening in Ayer's answer. The questioner implied that there could be an intuition, in moments of ecstasy, which seemed to give awareness of something beyond scientific analysis. What Ayer does is to reduce it to the actual feeling – ecstasy – along with other feelings, like boredom. Having done that, the whole of the experience is one of understanding the internal workings of another person and his or her feelings. But what was being asked about was not ecstasy as 'feeling' but ecstasy as 'knowledge' – and it is just this that Ayer does not accept.

Note

Many things are intuited before they are understood – whether it be Einstein's intuition of relativity, or a mathematician who described a particular mathematical argument as 'elegant'. There may be a sense that something is right, even if, without further examination, it cannot be shown to be so.

Insight

It seems to me that a suitable analogy for the process of reducing intuitive knowledge to empirical evidence is that of taking a car engine to pieces in order to discover the joy of motoring. It's fine as an academic exercise, but you can't drive the car while it's in a dismantled state, and it certainly does not get you any closer to the experience of the road! Intuition is the driving force of creative thinking; analysis and assessment come later.

Scepticism

The term 'sceptic' is generally used of a person who claims that we cannot know anything for certain, and that one view is likely to be as valid as any other. People tend to be sceptical about particular things – the validity of scientific claims, for example, or politics or morals.

It may be helpful, however, to make a distinction between scepticism as a conclusion and sceptical questioning as a process. Philosophers need to question and challenge all claims to knowledge, so – as a process – being sceptical about a claim is both valid and important for philosophy. However, there are some sceptical conclusions – for example, that the world as we know it may not exist at all, but may all be a dream – that are an interesting challenge, because common sense tells you that they are wrong, but the arguments for them may be difficult to refute.

Descartes was particularly concerned about scepticism, and wanted to counter it by finding something that he could not doubt. In order to achieve this, he set about using the very process that proved so threatening: sceptical doubt. This is how he sets about his task in Section 4 of his *Discourse on Method* (1637):

> *I had noticed long ago ... that in matters of morality and custom, it is often necessary to follow opinions one knows to be highly*

doubtful, just as if there were no doubts attaching to them at all.
Now, however, that I intended to make the search for truth my
only business, I thought it necessary to do exactly the opposite,
and to regard as absolutely false anything which gave rise in my
mind to the slightest doubt, with the object of finding out, once
this had been done, whether anything remained which I could
take as indubitable.

(translation: A. Wollaston, Penguin Classics, 1960)

Therefore, recognizing that his senses sometimes deceived him, he
decided to assume that they always did so. Equally, he recognized
that people could be mistaken in their reasoning, so logic and
mathematics could not be accepted as indubitable. He even went
on to assume that the world as he encountered it was perhaps no
more than a dream:

Finally, in view of the fact that those very same ideas, which
come to us when we are awake, can also come when we are
asleep without one of them then being true, I resolved to pretend
that everything that had ever entered my mind was as false as
the figments of my dreams.

Having done this, he reaches the conclusion that the only thing he
cannot doubt is that he exists as a thinking being, for the very act
of doubting requires him to think. Hence his famous starting point
for knowledge 'I think, therefore I am'.

Having reached that point, he then tries to build up an account
of what he can actually know – and it is this process, along
with his one point of certainty, that the true sceptic will not
accept. Scepticism is significant within the philosophy of religion
(where the ability to know religious truths by way of reason
alone may be challenged by those who emphasize the role of
faith) and the philosophy of science (where realism is challenged
by a variety of equally valid ways of describing the same
phenomenon), as well as within discussions of the theory of
knowledge.

The proof of the pudding ...

When examining matters of epistemology, you may be tempted to take a common-sense view: that a theory would seem to be right because it is the generally accepted and practical way of looking at things. We may be justified in accepting a theory if it is useful and solves problems. There is a tradition of philosophy that follows this line of reasoning: **pragmatism**. It was developed in America and is associated in particular with C. S. Peirce (1839–1914), William James (1842–1910) and John Dewey (1859–1952). In the simplest of terms, pragmatism says:

▶ *We act; we are not just spectators. The 'facts' about the world are shaped by our concerns, and what we hope to do.*
▶ *Beliefs should accord with known facts. But what should you do if the evidence is balanced between two theories?*
▶ *The answer – according to the pragmatists – is to accept the theory which gives the richer consequences; in other words, the one which will be of the greater practical use.*

Dewey emphasized the fact that we are not detached observers, but that we need to survive in the world, and that *thinking is a problem-solving activity* related to that need. Science is a dynamic process of gaining knowledge, enabling us to get some mastery over our environment. Knowledge is therefore of practical importance in our lives, not simply something about which we might speculate.

A basic test to be applied to all statements is that of *coherence*. At any one time, we have a number of ways of seeing the world and working within it. A new theory, if it is to be accepted, needs to be compatible with existing accepted theories. Of course, this cannot be an absolute criterion of truth, or truth would be decided by committee and science would make no progress. Nevertheless, it is an important factor to be taken into account. This issue of testing out new views will be considered again when we examine the philosophy of science.

Some conclusions

Knowing is a creative activity, and always involves an element of
interpretation. We know nothing with absolute certainty, except
those things that are true by definition. On the other hand – as we
saw Russell doing as he contemplated his desk – we can gradually
build up a degree of reasonable certainty.

Early in this chapter we looked at Descartes and his systematic
doubt – his determination to set aside all previously held opinions
and accept only what he could see clearly and distinctly to be true.
In practice, however, we need to get beyond a position of total
scepticism. Descartes himself saw no reason to believe that the
created order should deceive us – and therefore he could accept as
true what he perceived clearly to be so. Russell (in *The Problem of
Philosophy*) came to accept the reality of the external object (his
table) on the grounds that it was seen by a number of different
people at the same time, and that its shared experience was a valid
basis for asserting the objectivity of the table.

Perhaps, after all, there is scope for common sense in philosophy!

In terms of epistemology, we saw that the American pragmatist
tradition looked to accept those ideas and theories that were most
productive, most useful, recognizing that human beings do not
simply contemplate the world but are – at least on a temporary
basis – part of it, and engaged in the business of living.

A similar test might be applied to metaphysics in general. Consider
the practical and emotional implications of Plato's theory of the

Forms. It is possible for a Platonic approach to lead to a view that the present world, as encountered by the senses, is inferior, partial and lacking in inherent value. The philosopher is constantly looking beyond what is present, out to another, ideal world. Justice, love, beauty, truth – if these are encountered at all in the present world they are but pale reflections of their abstract, ideal counterparts.

The religious implications of this (and indeed, the influence of Plato on the development of the Christian religion) is considerable. Reality, from this perspective, is located outside the present known world, not within it. By contrast, a materialist may insist that everything is of value in itself and needs no external or ultimate justification.

Insight

Even if we are not conscious of them, the issues considered under epistemology and metaphysics are still relevant to our ordinary concerns about the world; they shape how we see things and how we value them.

A personal postscript

A fundamental problem within Western philosophy has been caused by the view that 'self' and 'world' are separate things, with the one trying to find out if the other is actually there – a view propounded by Descartes. In my opinion, this is mistaken. In reality, what we call 'self' is a temporary and changing part of what we call 'world'. There are not two separate realities, only one, and we are part of it.

Equally, experience is not an object (sense data do not exist); it is the term we use for the relationship that all sentient beings have with the rest of the world. It is both physical and mental; it is sharing not gathering; it is plastic not fixed. If we fail to experience

(Contd)

the world around us we are likely to die, for we are part of it and depend upon the rest of it for our very existence.

In terms of metaphysics and epistemology, philosophies can be rated according to how well they account for the fundamental unity and interconnected nature of everything. On this basis, Plato, Descartes and Kant do rather badly; their worlds are fundamentally dualist. Reality, for them, is always beyond what we experience. Aristotle, Spinoza and the Pragmatists do better. For them, there is one world, and we need to engage with it and make sense of it.

10 THINGS TO REMEMBER

1 *Rationalism claims that knowledge starts with the mind; empiricism that it starts with information given by the senses.*

2 *Descartes could doubt everything except that he was thinking.*

3 *Locke distinguished between primary and secondary qualities.*

4 *For Berkeley, to be is to be perceived.*

5 *Hume argued that belief should be proportional to evidence.*

6 *Kant argued that our minds shape how we experience the world.*

7 *It is always difficult to articulate what intuition reveals.*

8 *Scepticism has a positive role in challenging claims to knowledge.*

9 *Pragmatism sees thought as a problem-solving activity.*

10 *All knowledge involves an element of interpretation.*

2

The philosophy of science

In this chapter you will learn:
- *the historical development of science in relation to philosophy*
- *the way in which scientific theories are derived from observations and experiments*
- *the issues about how science makes progress.*

The philosophy of science examines the methods used by science, the ways in which hypotheses and laws are formulated from evidence, and the grounds on which scientific claims about the world may be justified.

Philosophy and science are not in principle opposed to one another, but are in many ways parallel operations, for both seek to understand the nature of the world and its structures. Whereas the individual sciences do so by gathering data from within their particular spheres and formulating general theories for understanding them, philosophy tends to concern itself with the process of formulating those theories, and establishing how they relate together to form an overall view. We saw in Chapter 1 that metaphysics is the task of understanding the basic structures of reality that lie behind all the findings of individual sciences.

A major part of all philosophy is the process of analyzing the language people use and the criteria of truth that they accept.

Therefore, while the individual sciences use 'first order language' (speaking directly about physical, chemical or biological observations), philosophy uses 'second order language' (examining what it means to speak about those things) and examines whether the claims that are made are logically justified by the evidence on which they appear to be based.

Insight

Today, scientists specialize because it is quite impossible for anyone to have detailed knowledge of the current state of research in all the various branches of science. It is even more difficult for a philosopher to get a view of the workings of science 'as a whole'. Hence the main task of philosophy is to examine the logic of particular scientific claims, and to probe the limits of what can be said.

Scientists, mathematicians and philosophers work in separate disciplines, even if they are interested in and may benefit from the work of the others, but it was not always so. Physics was originally known as 'natural philosophy', and some of the greatest names in philosophy were also involved with mathematics and science. Aristotle examined and codified the various sciences within his overall scheme of philosophy. Descartes, Leibniz, Pascal and Russell were all mathematicians as well as philosophers. Indeed, Russell and Whitehead argued in *Principia Mathematica* (1910–13) that mathematics was a development of deductive logic – see p. 85. Bacon, Locke and others were influenced by the rise of modern scientific method, and were concerned to give it a sound philosophical basis. Kant wrote *A General Natural History and Theory of the Heavens* in 1755 in which he explored the possible origin of the solar system.

Some philosophical movements (e.g. Logical positivism, in the early years of the twentieth century – see p. 71) were influenced by science and the scientific method of establishing evidence. Many of the philosophers that we considered in the chapter on the theory of knowledge can therefore reappear in considering science, largely because scientific knowledge and its methods are such an important part of our general appreciation of what we know and how we know it.

In order to put these things into an historical perspective, however, we shall take a brief look at some of the philosophers who commented on, or were influenced by, science.

An historical overview

Within Western thought there have been two major shifts in the view of the world, and these have had an important influence on the way in which philosophy and science have related to one another. We may therefore divide Western philosophy of science into three general periods: early Greek and Mediaeval thought; the Newtonian world-view; and twentieth-century developments (although recognizing that such division represents a simplification of a more complex process of change).

EARLY GREEK AND MEDIAEVAL THOUGHT

In 529 CE the Emperor Justinian banned the teaching of philosophy in order to further the interests of Christianity. Plato had already had a considerable influence upon the development of Christian doctrines, and elements of his thought – particularly the contrast between the ideal world of the forms and the limited world of everyday experience – continued within theology. The works of Aristotle were preserved first in Byzantium and then by the Arabs, being rediscovered in the thirteenth century, when the first translations were made from Arabic into Latin.

In the thirteenth century, with thinkers like Thomas Aquinas (1225–74), Duns Scotus (1266–1308) and William of Ockham (c. 1285–1349), Greek thought began to be explored again in a systematic way. From that time, philosophy is very much a development of, or reaction to, the work of the Greeks.

Aristotle set out the different branches of science, and divided up living things into their various species and genera – a process of classification which became a major feature of science. He had a theory of knowledge based on sensations which depended on repetition:

sensations repeat themselves	→	**leading to perception**
perceptions repeat themselves	→	**leading to experience**
experiences repeat themselves	→	**leading to knowledge**

Thus, for Aristotle, knowledge develops out of our structured and repeated perception of evidence that comes to us from our senses – an important feature of the philosophy of science.

He also established ideas of space, time and causality, including the idea of the Prime Mover (which became the basis of the cosmological argument for the existence of God – see p. 161. He set out the four 'causes' (see p. 14), thus distinguishing between matter, the form it took on, the agent of change and the final purpose or goal for which it was designed. He considered a thing's power to be its potential. Everything had a potential and a resting place: fire rises up naturally, whereas heavy objects fall. Changes, for Aristotle, are not related to general forces like gravity (which belong to the later Newtonian scheme), but to the fact that individual things, by their very nature, have a goal.

Let us look at a few examples of the influence of Plato and Aristotle:

For Plato, the unseen 'Forms' were more real than the individual things that could be known through the senses. This way of thinking (backed by religion) suggested that human reason and its concepts of perfection were paramount, and that observation and experience were secondary.

Cosmology and astronomy give examples of this trend: Copernicus (1473–1543) and later Galileo (1564–1642) were to offer a view of the universe in which the Earth revolved around the Sun, rather than vice versa. Their view was opposed by those whose idea of the universe came from Ptolemy and in which the Earth was surrounded by glassy spheres – perfect shapes, conveying the Sun, Moon, planets in perfect circular motion. Their work was challenged (and Galileo condemned) not because their observations were found to be at fault, but because they had trusted their observations, rather than deciding beforehand what should be the case. Kepler (1571–1630) concluded that the orbit of Mars was elliptical, whereas all heavenly motion was thought to be perfect, and therefore circular.

These astronomers were struggling against a background of religious authority which gave Greek notions of perfection priority over observations and experimental evidence. In other words, the earlier mediaeval system of thought was deductive (it deduced what should be observed to happen from its pre-conceived ideas), in contrast to the later inductive method of developing a theory from observations.

Along with the tendency to look for theory and perfection rather than accept the results of observation, there was another, stemming from Aristotle. Following his idea of the final cause, everything was thought to be designed for a particular purpose. If something falls to the ground, it seeks its natural purpose and place in doing so. So, in a religious context, it was possible to say that something happened because it was God's will for it, or because it was designed for that purpose.

Insight
From this perspective, there was less interest in looking for a scientific principle or law to explain events in terms of 'efficient' causation.

THE NEWTONIAN WORLD-VIEW

The rise of modern science would not have been possible without the renewed sense of the value of human reason and the ability to challenge established ideas and religious dogma, which developed as a result of the Renaissance and the Reformation. But what was equally influential was the way in which information was gathered and sorted, and theories formed on the basis of it. Central to this process was the method of induction, and this was set out very clearly (and in a way that continues to be relevant) by Francis Bacon.

Bacon (1561–1626) rejected Aristotle's idea of final causes, and insisted that knowledge should be based on a process of induction, which, as we shall see later, is the systematic method of coming to general conclusions on the basis of evidence about individual instances that have been observed. He warned about 'idols' that tend to lead a person astray:

▶ *the desire to accept that which confirms what we already believe*
▶ *distortions resulting from our habitual ways of thinking*
▶ *muddles that come through our use of language (e.g. using the same word for different things, and then assuming that they must be one and the same)*
▶ *believing things out of allegiance to a particular school of thought.*

Bacon also pointed out that, in gathering evidence, one should not just look for examples that confirm a particular theory, but one should actively seek out and accept the force of contrary examples. After centuries of using evidence to confirm what was already known by dogma or reason, this was quite revolutionary.

The general view of the world which came about as a result of the rise of science is usually linked with the name of Isaac Newton (1642–1727). In the Newtonian world-view, observation and experiment yield knowledge of the laws which govern the world.

In it, space and time were fixed, forming a framework within which everything takes place. Objects were seen to move and be moved through the operation of physical laws of motion, so that everything was seen as a machine, the workings of which could become known through careful observation. Interlocking forces kept matter in motion, and everything was predictable. Not everything might be known at this moment, but there was no doubt that everything would be understood eventually, using the established scientific method.

Put crudely, the world was largely seen as a collection of particles of matter in motion, hitting one another, like billiard balls on a table, and behaving in a predictable way. It was thought that science would eventually give an unchallengeable explanation for everything, and that it would form the basis for technology that would give humankind increasing control over the environment, and the ability to do things as yet unimagined. Science became cumulative – gradually expanding into previously unknown areas; building upon the secure foundations of established physical laws.

Newton was a religious believer; he thought that the laws by which the universe operated had been established by God. But his god was an external creator who, once the universe had been set in motion, could retire, leaving it to continue to function according to its fixed laws. This view freed science from the need to take God into account: it could simply examine the laws of nature, and base its theories on observation rather than religious dogma.

With the coming of the Newtonian world-view, the function of philosophy changed. Rather than initiating theories about cosmology, the task of philosophy was to examine and comment on the methods and results of scientific method, establishing its limits. Kant, for example, argued that space, time and causality – the very bases of Newtonian science – were not to be found 'out there' in the world of independent objects, but were contributed by the mind. We saw things as being in space and time because that was the way our minds process the information given through the senses.

Hume pointed out that scientific laws were not true universal statements, but only summaries of what had been experienced so far. The method used by science – gathering data and drawing general conclusions from it – yielded higher and higher degrees of probability, but could never achieve absolute certainty.

Insight

Science always needs to be open to the possibility of contrary evidence – something utterly unexpected, requiring us to reconsider and perhaps modify our theories. Theories are therefore always provisional and limited.

Some aspects of philosophy related to this phase of science have already been examined (in Chapter 1). Hume's empiricism, for example, fits perfectly with the scientific impetus. At the beginning of the nineteenth century, William Paley's argument in favour of a designer for the universe (explained further on p. 163) reflects the domination of his world-view by the paradigm of the machine – a designer (God) is proposed in order to account for the signs of design in creation.

But not all philosophers supported Newton's fixed mechanical universe. Bishop Berkeley criticized Newton's idea that space and time are fixed. For Berkeley, everything (including matter and extension) is a matter of sensation, of human experience. Thus everything is relative to the person who experiences it, and there is no logical way to move from the relativity of our experience to some external absolute. In his own way, Berkeley anticipates the arrival of the third era for science and philosophy.

TWENTIETH-CENTURY DEVELOPMENTS

For most thinkers prior to the twentieth century, it was inconceivable that space and time were not fixed: a necessary framework within which everything else could take place.

Einstein's theories of relativity were to change all that. The first, in 1905, was the theory of *Special Relativity*, best known in the form of the equation $E = mc^2$. This showed that mass and energy are equivalent, and that (since energy was equal to mass multiplied by the speed of light squared) a very small amount of matter could be converted into a very large amount of energy. This, of course, is now best known for its rather drastic practical consequences in the development of nuclear weapons.

Einstein published the second theory, *General Relativity*, in 1916. It made the revolutionary claim that time, space, matter and energy were all related to one another. For example, space and time can be compressed by a strong gravitational field. There are no fixed points. The way in which things relate to one another depends upon the point from which they are being observed.

An example

Imagine you are looking out through space. You see two stars, which, although they may appear to you to be at the same distance, are in fact many light years apart. Suppose you see a change in one of those stars, followed by a change in the other. You might reasonably claim that one happened first, because from your perspective they occurred in a time sequence which, on Earth, would amount to one coming first and the other second.

But imagine that you are transported to a star that is beyond the second of the stars you have been observing. In this case you might see the second change first and the first change second. Clearly, the reason for this is that the time at which something 'happens' (or, strictly speaking, appears to happen) is related to the distance it is from you, because events only come to be observed after the light from them has travelled across space.

Of course, you could calculate which 'actually' happened first, from your perspective, if you knew the distances to the two stars. You could then calculate the extra length of time it took light to travel to you from the further star, and deduct that from the time difference between the two experienced events. But it would still be 'from your perspective', not absolute.

Modern physics and cosmology therefore offer a strange view of space and time, a view that is in contrast to that of Newton. We are told that the whole universe emerged (at the 'big bang') from a space-time singularity – a point at which all the matter of the present universe was concentrated into a very small point. Unlike an ordinary explosion, in which matter is propelled outwards *through* space, space and time were created at that moment, and space expanded as did the universe. If space could be represented by a grid of lines drawn on a balloon, then as the balloon is blown up, the grid itself expands, the balloon doesn't simply get more lines drawn on it.

The reason Newton's physics worked on the basis of fixed space and time was that he considered only a very small section of the universe, and within that section, his laws do indeed hold true.

Space and time are seen as linked in a single four-dimensional space–time continuum, and there is no fixed point from which to observe anything, for observer and observed are both in a process of change, moving through time and space.

Alongside relativity came quantum mechanics, which raised questions about whether events at the sub-atomic level could be predicted, and what it means to say that one thing causes another. Matter was no longer thought to be composed of solid atoms, but the atom itself was divided into many constituent particles, held together by forces. In the sub-atomic world, particles did not obey fixed rules. Their individual movements, while statistically predictable, were uncertain. Energy was seen to operate by the interchange of little packets or 'quanta', rather than by a single continuous flow. What had once been solid matter obeying fixed mechanical laws, could now be thought of as bundles of events open to a number of different interpretations depending on the viewpoint of the observer. Quantum mechanics is notoriously difficult to understand. A general view of it is that it works, so there must be something right about it, even if we don't understand it as a theory. What is certain is that quantum mechanics, however little understood, when combined with the theories of Relativity, rendered the old Newtonian certainties obsolete. Newton's laws of physics might still apply, but only within very limited parameters. Once you stray into the microscopic area of the sub-atomic, or the macroscopic world of cosmic structures, the situation is quite different.

Insight

A basic philosophical question: What can we mean by scientific 'truth' in such a strange, flexible and relativistic world?

A similar revolution has taken place within the understanding of living things. Through the discovery of DNA, the world of biology is linked to that of chemistry and of physics, since the instructions within the DNA molecule are able to determine the form of the living being.

In the twentieth century, therefore, philosophy engaged with a scientific view of the world that had changed enormously from the mechanical and predictable world of Newton. In particular, science started to offer a variety of ways of picturing the world, and cosmology – which had been dominated first by religious belief and Aristotle, and then by astronomy – was now very much in the hands of mathematicians. It became clear that the world as a whole was not something that could be observed; its structures could only be explored by calculation.

During much of the first half of the twentieth century, philosophy (at least in the United States and Britain) became dominated by the quest for meaning and the analysis of language. It no longer saw its role as providing an overview of the universe – it left that to the individual scientific disciplines. Rather, it adopted a supportive role, checking on the methods used by science, the logic by which results were produced from observations, and the way in which theories could be confirmed or discredited.

In other words

▶ *Up to the sixteenth century, Greek concepts, backed by religious authority, determined the general view of the world. Evidence was required to fit the overall scheme.*

> ▶ *In Newtonian physics, matter exists within a fixed structure of space and time, and obeys laws that can be discovered by 'induction' based on observation.*
> ▶ *The modern world view sees space and time as related to one another, and events as interpreted in the light of the observer's own position and methods of observation.*

Insight

In the first phase, philosophy seemed to determine content, in the second it offered a critique of method, and in the third it offered a clarification of concepts.

From evidence to theory: scientific method

In terms of the philosophy of science, the most important approach to gathering and analyzing information was the 'inductive method'. This was championed by Francis Bacon, and then by Thomas Hobbes (1588–1679) and became the basis of the Newtonian world of science. In its practical approach to sifting and evaluating evidence, it is also reflected in the empiricism of Hume (see p. 21). Indeed, it was the inductive method that distinguished 'modern' science from what had gone before, and brought in the first of the two major shifts in world view.

THE INDUCTIVE METHOD

This method is based on two things:

1 *The trust that knowledge can be gained by gathering evidence and conducting experiments, i.e. it is based on facts that can be checked, or experiments that can be repeated.*
2 *The willingness to set aside preconceived views about the likely outcome of an experiment, or the validity of evidence presented, i.e. the person using this method does not have a fixed idea about its conclusion, but is prepared to examine both results and methods used with an open mind.*

With the inductive method, science was claiming to be based on objectively considered evidence, and was therefore seen as in contrast to traditional religion and metaphysics, which was seen to be based on doctrines that a person was required to accept and which were backed up by authority rather than reason alone.

In practice, the method works in this way:

▶ *Observe and gather data (evidence; information), seeking to eliminate, as far as possible, all irrelevant factors.*
▶ *Analyze your data, and draw conclusions from them in the form of hypotheses.*
▶ *Devise experiments to test out those hypotheses, i.e. if this hypothesis is correct, then certain experimental results should be anticipated.*
▶ *Modify your hypothesis, if necessary, in the light of the results of your experiments.*
▶ *From the experiments, the data and the hypotheses, argue for a theory.*
▶ *Once you have a theory, you can predict other things on the basis of it, by which the theory can later be verified or falsified.*

It is clear that this process of induction, by which a theory is arrived at by the analysis and testing out of observed data, can yield at most only a high degree of probability. There is always the chance that an additional piece of information will show that the original hypothesis is wrong, or that it applies only within a limited field. The hypothesis, and the scientific theory that comes from it, is therefore open to modification.

Theories that are tested out in this way lead to the framing of scientific laws. Now it is important to establish exactly what is meant by 'law' in this context. In common parlance, 'law' is taken to be something which is imposed, a rule that is to be obeyed. But it would be wrong to assume that a scientific law can dictate how things behave. The law simply describes that behaviour, it does not control it (as Hume argued). If something behaves differently, it is not to be blamed for going against a law of nature, it is simply that either:

▶ *there is an unknown factor that has influenced this particular situation and therefore modified what was expected, or*
▶ *the law of nature is inadequately framed, and needs to be modified in order to take this new situation into account.*

Insight

To point out that all theories that are based on the inductive method are open to the possibility of modification is a *positive*, rather than a negative comment. This method is a hugely important feature of science, and one that delivers usable results.

FALSIFICATION

It may sound illogical, but science makes progress when a theory is falsified, rather than when it is confirmed, for it is only by rejecting and modifying a theory, to account for new evidence, that something better is put in its place. This view was argued very effectively by Karl Popper (1902–94), an Austrian philosopher from Vienna, who moved to New Zealand in 1937 and then to London in 1945, where he became Professor of Logic and Scientific Method at the London School of Economics. He was a socialist, and made significant contributions to political philosophy as well as the philosophy of science.

In his book *The Logic of Scientific Discovery* (1934, translated in 1959) Popper makes the crucial point that science seeks theories that are logically self-consistent, and that can be falsified. He points out that a scientific law goes beyond what can be experienced. We can never prove it to be absolutely true; all we can do is try to prove it to be false, and accept it on a provisional basis until such time as it is falsified.

This leads Popper to say that a scientific theory cannot be compatible with all the logically possible evidence that could be considered. It must be possible to falsify it. If a theory claims that it can never be falsified, then it is not scientific. On this basis, he challenged the ideas of both Marx and Freud.

In practice, of course, a theory is not automatically discarded as soon as one possible piece of contrary evidence is produced. What happens is that the scientist tries to reproduce that bit of contrary evidence, to show that it is part of a significant pattern that the theory has not been able to account for. Science also seeks out alternative theories that can include all the positive evidence that has been found for the original one, but also includes the new conflicting evidence.

An example

In Newtonian physics, light travels in a straight line. (This was confirmed over the centuries, and was therefore corroborated as a theory.)

But modern astronomy has shown that, when near to a very powerful gravitational field, light bends.

This does not mean that the Newtonian view was entirely wrong, simply that light does indeed travel in a straight line when in a uniform gravitational field. The older theory is now included within a new one which can take into account these exceptional circumstances.

Where you have a choice of theories, Popper held that you should accept the one that is not only better corroborated, but also more testable and entailing more true statements than the others. And that you should do this, even if you know that the theory is false. Since we cannot, anyway, have absolute certainty, we have to go for the most useful way of understanding the world that we have to hand, even if its limitations have already been revealed.

Insight

The implication of this would seem to be that science takes a pragmatic rather than an absolute approach to truth.

NEW EVIDENCE?

A theory should not necessarily be ignored just because present evidence fails to be conclusive, since we do not know what might come to light in the future. A theory may survive when it adapts to new situations yielding new evidence – a kind of **natural selection** in the scientific world.

A particularly appropriate example of this may be Charles Darwin's theory of natural selection. Darwin published *The Origin of Species* in 1859. He observed that within a species there were slight variations, most of which gave no particular benefit to the individual who displayed them. Sometimes, however, a beneficial variation gave that individual an advantage and, in a world of limited resources of food and habitat, the advantaged individual was more likely to survive to adulthood and breed. Hence, the beneficial variations would be passed on to a proportionately larger number of the next generation, and so on. Thus a competitive natural environment was doing exactly what a breeder of domestic animals would do in selecting and breeding individuals who showed particular qualities.

He presented natural selection as a process that he considered to be the best explanation for the variety of species that he had observed and catalogued.

Darwin thus claimed to have discovered the mechanism by which species evolve, and also an explanation of those features of each species which seem most appropriate to its own survival. His theory seemed to render obsolete the idea that the appearance of design in nature could only be explained by the existence of a designer God. In effect, natural selection explained how nature could design itself. Its implications were far beyond his areas of research. If species are not fixed, then everything is subject to change. To accept such an idea (with all its scientific, social, emotional and religious implications) on the basis of limited evidence was to take a great risk.

Insight

The theory of natural selection illustrates how a strictly inductive method of scientific argument, gathering and interpreting evidence, can then take an imaginative leap in order to grasp a more general theory.

But the debates that followed the publication of Darwin's theory were not simply about his perceived challenge to religious ideas, but about his interpretation of evidence. In particular, there did not seem to be adequate fossil evidence for a gradual evolution of species. In other words, the fossil evidence lacked sufficient 'halfway' stages that might illustrate the change from what appeared to be one fixed species to another. And, of course, weighing such evidence was an essential feature of the inductive method.

Today, we have evidence to support the theory of natural selection that was unavailable to Darwin. So, for example, in a book entitled *The Beak of the Finch* (1994), Jonathan Weiner described a 20-year study of finches on one of the Galapagos Islands, showing, for example, that in times of drought only those finches with the longest beaks could succeed in getting the toughest seeds, and therefore survived to breed. At the same time DNA studies of blood from various finches corresponded to their physical abilities and characteristics.

New evidence for survival of those best able to adapt to their changing environment is seen all the time in terms of medicine and agriculture. As soon as a pesticide appears to have brought a particular pest under control, a new strain is found which is resistant to it. Equally, in medicine, new strains of disease are appearing which are resistant to the available antibiotics. What is happening is that those examples of a pest or a disease which survive the onslaught of a pesticide or treatment, breed. The next generation is therefore resistant. These examples show the flexibility of nature: the present disease has been 'designed', not by some original designer but in response to existing treatments. We see an evolution of diseases over a space of a few years, mirroring the longer term evolution of species over millennia.

More generally, we now know that random genetic mutations are the cause of the tiny variations which form the basis of natural selection. Genetics therefore provides a whole new level of evidence. Analysis of the genetic make-up of each species is able to show how closely those species are related and may trace them back to common genetic ancestors.

There is no way that Darwin could have considered his theory from the standpoint of genetic mutation, or from the way in which viruses adapt and take on new forms, but such new areas of evidence may be used to corroborate a previously held theory, particularly where (as was the case with Darwin) the problem was not so much that his theory had been falsified as that there was a perceived lack of positive evidence.

Experiments and objectivity

Karl Popper argued that science was not subjective, in the sense of being the product of a single human mind, but neither was it literally objective, (i.e. a scientific law is not an external 'fact', but a way of stating the relationship between facts as they appear to us). Rather, it transcends the ideas of particular individuals, as does art, literature or maths. So how do the theories we devise, based on evidence and experiment, relate to what is 'out there' in the world?

The process of induction is based on the idea that it is possible to get hard evidence which does not depend upon the person who observes it. Indeed, from Francis Bacon onwards the theory has been that a scientist sets aside all personal preferences in assessing data. But can we observe nature without influencing it by our act of observing it, and how much of what we think of as evidence is contributed by our own minds?

The sensations that we have are not simply copies of external reality, they are the product of the way in which we have encountered that reality: colour is the result of a combination of light, surface texture and the operation of our eyes; space is perceived as a result of our brain linking one thing to another; time is a matter of remembering that some experiences have already taken place. Our experiences (and any theories based on them) are not independent facts, but the product of our ways of looking and thinking.

Kant argued that when we observe something, our mind has a contribution to make to that experience. Space, time and causality are all imposed on experience by the mind in order to make sense of it. Physics, since Einstein, has endorsed this relevance of the observer for an understanding of what it observed. As we saw above, neither space nor time is fixed, and movement is only perceived in terms of the change in position of one body in relation to another.

An example

I look out of the window of a stationary train at the train in the next platform. Suddenly, what I see starts to move. But is my train moving forward, or is the other train pulling away? Unless I feel a jolt, it will be a moment before I can decide between the two – and I will be able to do so only by looking beyond or away from the other train to some third object.

What is perceived transcends the individual perceiver, simply because the perception may be confirmed by others. Several people all witnessing the existence of a table in the room will confirm my own perception. In the same way, scientific evidence, repeated in various experiments, gives a trans-personal element of truth, even if the object being studied, and the way in which it is described, ultimately depend upon human perceptions.

Right, wrong or what?

The Newtonian world was at least predictable. A law of nature could be regarded as a fixed piece of information about how the world worked. That has now gone. We find that science can offer several equally valid but different ways of viewing the same phenomenon. There are no absolutes of space or time. Quantum theory is seen to work (results can be predicted on the basis of it) but without people understanding exactly why.

An example

Light can be understood in terms of particles or in terms of wave motions. They are two utterly different ways of understanding the same thing, but the fact that one is right does not mean that the other is wrong.

As laws and theories become established within the scientific community, they are used as a basis for further research, and are termed 'paradigms'. Occasionally there is a paradigm shift, which entails the revision of much of science. In terms of cosmology, the move from an Aristotelian (Ptolemaic) to a Newtonian world view, and then the further move from that to the view of Einstein, represents two shifts of paradigm.

Science offers a set of reasoned views about how the world has been seen to work up to the present. Taken together, the laws of science that are understood at any one time provide a structure within which scientists work; a structure which guides and, influences, but does not dictate how scientific research will progress. With hindsight, we can see philosophers and scientists boldly proclaiming the finality of their particular vision of the world just as the scientific community is about to go through a 'paradigm shift' as a result of which everything is going to be re-assessed.

An example

In 1899, Haeckel published *The Riddle of the Universe*. He argued that everything, including thought, was the product of the material world and was controlled by its laws. Everything was absolutely controlled and determined. Freedom was an illusion and religion a superstition. He was proposing scientific materialism, popularizing Darwin's theory of evolution, and sweeping away all earlier philosophy that did not fit his material and scientific outlook. For Haeckel, science had discovered just about everything there was to discover; there would be no more surprises. What would he have made of relativity, quantum theory, genetics or computing?

T.S. Kuhn, in his book *The Structure of Scientific Revolutions* (1962), described these paradigms as the basic *Gestalt* (or world view) within which science at any one time interprets the evidence it has available. It is the paradigm that largely dictates scientific progress, and observations are not free from the influence of the paradigm either.

What makes Kuhn's theory particularly controversial is that he claims that there is no *independent* data by which to decide between competing paradigms (since all data is presented either in terms of one paradigm or the other) and therefore there is no strictly logical reason to change a paradigm. This implies a relativism in science, which seemed to threaten the logical basis of the development of scientific theories, as expounded by Karl Popper.

The general implication of the work of Kuhn and others is that, if a theory works well (in other words, if it gives good predictive results), then it becomes a *possible* explanation: we cannot say that it is *the definitive or only one*.

In other words

▶ *Different theories can give an equally true explanation of the same phenomenon.*
▶ *A scientific theory is a way of looking: a convenient way of organizing experience, but not necessarily the only one. It is provisional. It is also part of an overall paradigm.*

Imre Lakatos (1922–74) particularly argued that science is generally carried out within research programmes, and is essentially a problem-solving activity. There are core theories within a research programme (without which the whole programme would fail) and a 'protective belt' of theories that are more open to modification, while continuing with the overall programme. Core theories are not simply abandoned at the first piece of contrary evidence. At any one time, there will be many research programmes on the go, and they are gradually modified in a way that is rather more subtle than a straight 'falsificationist' view might suggest.

But beyond that, there are other criteria for assessing theories. 'Instrumentalism' is the term used for the evaluation of a theory on the basis of whether or not it actually works in making valuable predictions. Hence a theory may be useful, even if we are unable to say whether or not it is right.

If one scientific theory continues to be regarded as 'right' (however provisional it may be) does this imply that alternative theories must

be 'wrong' or what? This is a question for the philosophy
of science: Can we say that something is 'right' in a world of
optional viewpoints?

> **Insight**
> In popular debate, a 'scientific' approach tends to suggest one
> leading to objective certainty. In practice, science is far more
> pragmatic and open-ended – and that is not its weakness,
> but its strength.

The social sciences

Humankind is clearly a valid object of study for science. When
Darwin published *The Origin of Species*, much of the controversy
that followed was generated because his theory of natural selection
applied to humankind as well as all other species, and that was seen
as particularly threatening of the special place accorded to the human
species in most traditional religious and philosophical thinking. In
more recent debates, Richard Dawkins (in *The Selfish Gene* and
elsewhere) examines the relationship between human behaviour
and life at the genetic level, where genes are inherently 'selfish',
in that their task is simply to promote survival and to reproduce
successfully. It is also possible to show that human behaviour can be
examined alongside, and in the same way as that of other species,
as Edward Wilson did in his controversial book *Sociobiology*.

There are, however, particular problems when science examines
humankind. First of all, there continues to be a widespread view
that science is basically determinist. In other words, setting aside the
subtleties and developments that we have already examined in this
book, it sees science as giving a single, fixed and empirically based
explanation of every phenomenon. On the other hand, the experience
of being human – the subjective side of what science examines
objectively – is of freedom, complexity, mixed motives and so on. In
spite of philosophers like Kant, who were quite able to see us as being
phenomenally determined (as seen by others) but noumenally free
(as experienced in ourselves), most people have found it difficult to

accept any scientific attempt to 'explain' human life at either a social or individual level.

On the other side of the argument, two disciplines in particular – sociology and psychology – have sometimes had their methodologies and findings challenged by the mainstream physical sciences. We shall therefore look at each of these briefly, to see what special issues they raise for the philosophy of science.

SOCIOLOGY

The scientific method relies on measurable data. Today, we are accustomed to statistical information about humankind, from life expectancy and income to our shopping preferences and voting intentions. But it was only in the nineteenth century that information began to be gathered and presented in the form of statistics. Before that, philosophers made observations about humankind in general, but were unable to move from those observations to produce scientifically based theories about society.

Most widely known of the early sociologists was Emile Durkheim (1858–1917). He analyzed regularities in society and formed theories to explain them. Although each individual was aware of a measure of freedom over his or her actions, the assumption upon which Durkheim worked was that there were social forces at work, as real as physical forces, which influenced behaviour. These forces put pressure on individuals to conform, and the number of individuals influenced would then show up in statistics.

Insight

Statistics tell me that, if I am male and under the age of 30, I am more likely than an elderly female to drink and drive, or take illegal drugs. But do those statistics actually influence me to do either of those things? I am free to choose, and so is everyone else. I can say, 'Well, life just happens to be like that!' But that is exactly what a sociologist is claiming, that certain features of human life can be quantified and examined in a scientific manner.

On the political side, Karl Marx (1818–83), as a result of researching social and political patterns in societies over history, formulated his theory (dialectical materialism) that social activity is based on people's material needs and the means of producing and distributing them. He saw evidence for a pattern within society, in which classes oppose one another, and thus drive forward a process of social and political change.

As has already been discussed, some thinkers (e.g. Popper, see p. 47) question whether Marxist theory should be considered to be genuine science, on the grounds that Marx appears to interpret evidence in the light of an overall theory, whereas Popper sees genuine science as always open to the possibility that a theory will be falsified and replaced.

Nevertheless, it is clear that sociology and political science are valid disciplines, operating using methods that are not that far removed from the physical sciences. They are based on the interpretation of data, gathered using the normal checks to obtain objectivity. One major difference between these disciplines and, say, physics is the scope for conducting experiments. Because human beings are involved, it is perfectly valid to collect data about their behaviour, but it is not considered ethical to subject them to intrusive testing that may cause them harm. Hence (in spite of the present interest in reality shows on television) it would not be acceptable to send a bunch of people into an extreme environment to measure who died first and from what!

PSYCHOLOGY

Sigmund Freud (1856–1939) was a hospital doctor with a particular interest in neuro-pathology, later setting himself up as a private practitioner for the treatment of nervous conditions, particularly hysteria. As is well known, he developed the method known as psychoanalysis in which, through dream analysis and free association, patients were encouraged to become aware of those experiences buried in their unconscious which were having a harmful effect on their conscious behaviour. So, for example, examining those who had compulsive washing routines, he sought the origin of the compulsion in buried childhood experience of uncleanness. Psychoanalysis worked on the assumption that, once the origin of a problem was discovered and articulated, it would lose its power, and the patient would be cured.

Psychoanalysis depends on the analytic skills of the practitioner. What the patient says is analyzed and given significance, and that analysis is done in the light of the overall theory and approach of the analyst. Notice here the old problem for the philosophy of science – which comes first, the data or the interpreting theory? Popper criticized Freud as much as Marx, on the grounds that their work did not have the scientific discipline that allowed their theories to be open to falsification.

Other branches of psychology are more in line with traditional scientific method. Behaviourism, for example, set up animal experiments, and thus produced data that could be analyzed in much the same way as in the physical sciences. However (as we shall see in Chapter 4) there are issues about the validity and scope of behaviourism as a way to understand human behaviour. By being more traditionally scientific in its method, it limited what it could examine. Measuring the ability of a rat in a box to learn how to press a lever in order to get food, is hardly likely to explain the sort of compulsive neuroses that interested Freud!

Cognitive science is a major area of research today, and we shall examine it again in Chapter 4. For now we only need to note the basic fact that the study of humankind, whether in sociology, psychology or cognitive science, presents a special set of problems for the application of traditional scientific method.

What counts as science?

At one time, an activity could be called 'scientific' if it followed the inductive method. On these grounds, the work of Marx could be called scientific, in that he based his theories on accounts of political changes in the societies he studied. Similarly, behavioural psychology can claim to be scientific on the basis of the methods used: observing and recording the responses of people and animals to particular stimuli, for example. So science is generally defined by method rather than by subject.

Popper criticized both Marx and Freud, not because he considered they failed to observe and gather evidence, but because of what he saw as their willingness to interpret new evidence in the light of their theories, rather than to allow that evidence to challenge or modify those theories. So how should we distinguish between science and what Popper called 'pseudo-science'?

An example

Astronomy is regarded as a science. Astrology, on the other hand, is not. This is because the former is based on observable facts, while the latter is based on a mythological scheme.

Except: suppose astrologers could show that there was a definite link between a person's star sign and his or her behaviour. Suppose the results of a very large number of studies indicated this. Would that prove that astrology was scientific?

On the face of it, it would probably depend upon who did the experiment; if it were an attempt to gather favourable information to support the previously held views, then it would not be acceptable. On the other hand, if it were gathered in a strictly objective way, by someone who genuinely wanted to know if the phenomena of star signs was relevant to human behaviour, then it might be claimed to be scientific.

But even if it were shown to have a scientific basis, astrology would only be termed a science if its practitioners subsequently used scientific methods of assessment and prediction.

Distinguishing features of science include the consistent attempt at the disinterested gathering of information and the willingness to accept revisions of one's theories. But what happens if one's conclusions are radically different from those of other scientists? This leads us to ask about the nature of authority within the scientific community.

Science and authority

With the rise of science in the seventeenth and eighteenth centuries, it was widely believed that the days of superstition and authority were over; everything was to be considered rationally. But has that always been the case with the discipline science?

Once a theory, or a method of working, has become established, the scientific world tends to treat it as the norm and to be rather suspicious of any attempt to follow a radically different approach. When Darwin introduced the idea of natural selection, or Einstein the theory of relativity, the radical changes in scientific outlook that they implied were seen by some as a threat to the steady accumulating of knowledge along the previously accepted ways of seeing the world. Although both were accepted, there was a pause for consideration.

Scientists may be considered to be 'heretics' within the world of scientific orthodoxy, if their views are radically different from those of the majority of their peers.

Since it is possible that there will be different but equally valid theories to account for phenomena, there will always be an element of debate within scientific circles. But are there limits to the range of views that can be accommodated within the scientific community?

New scientific work is presented to the world scientific community by being published, generally in one of the established 'peer reviewed' journals. In order to be accepted for publication, of course, it must be plausible as a piece of work, at least to those who are reviewing it. Once published, the theory may be evaluated by other scientists. The original experiments are repeated elsewhere to see if the same results can be obtained. Sometimes the results of attempting this are ambiguous; sometimes the attempt to repeat the experiment failed completely, and the validity and reliability of the original results are then called into question.

Scientists have to earn a living. Some are employed by universities and are therefore, in theory, free to explore their theories without external influence – other than the requirement that they show real advance in research in order to continue to attract funding. On the other hand, the funding for such research often comes from the commercial world, and is not, therefore necessarily totally disinterested.

Other scientists are employed within various industries. Their task is to find a scientific basis and make possible the enterprise which their industry seeks to promote. They are not engaged in 'pure' science (in the sense of a quest for knowledge, unfettered by its implications) but science put to the use of industry. Their task is halfway between science and technology – they seek a basis upon which a technology can be developed in order to achieve something that will then yield a profit.

An example

A scientist employed by a drugs company is hardly likely to keep his job if his conclusion is that the disease he is attempting to combat by the development of a new drug is best cured by drinking pure fruit juice!

He or she is therefore likely to try the following:

▶ *isolate the element within the fruit juice which actually effects the cure*

(Contd)

Commercial funding looks for new products and ideas for
developing those things in which it has a vested interest, and even
state funding favours those projects that promise economic benefit.
Philosophers like Bacon and Hume insisted that the quest for
knowledge should be a disinterested one. Indeed, the fact that a
scientist stands to gain a great deal from a particular conclusion to
his or her research might indicate that the results should be treated
with some caution. We have already seen that there are really no
facts that are free of interpretation and this flexibility, coupled with
a personal motive, makes the tendency to incline towards the most
favourable conclusion a real threat to impartiality.

FOR REFLECTION

What can be said about the world, and what cannot? In *Tractatus*
(see p. 71), Wittgenstein took the view that the function of language
was one of picturing the world and started with the bold statement,
'The world is everything that is the case' (*Tractatus* 1) and equates
what can be said with what science can show, 'The totality of true
propositions is the whole of natural science' (*Tractatus* 4.11).

It ends, however, with the admission that when it comes to the
mystical (the intuitive sense of the world as a whole) language
fails; we must remain silent. What is 'seen' in a moment of mystical
awareness cannot be 'pictured'. It cannot be expressed literally.

Wittgenstein points to other things that cannot be described –
the subject self (it sees a world, but is not part of that world) and
even death (we do not live to experience death). Wittgenstein is
thus setting limits to what can be said, and by implication, limits
to science.

His thought might prompt us to ask:

▶ *Is not modern cosmology a bit 'mystical'? Does it not seek to find images (including that of the 'big bang') by which to express events so unlike anything experienced on Earth, that literal language is of little use?*

▶ *Does science not sometimes require imaginative leaps beyond evidence, in the formation of new paradigms, within which detailed work and calculation can subsequently find its place?*

▶ *What is the place of intuition within the scientific process? Like an eye which sees everything other than itself, intuition may underpin much of the scientific endeavour without itself ever featuring directly.*

Science offers a very rich and exciting view of the world. Whether you start by considering the idea that matter is a collection of nuclear forces, rather than something solid and tangible, or whether you start with the idea that the universe is expanding outwards from the space-time singularity, creating its own space and time as it does so, modern science seems to contradict our common-sense notions. Yet, in doing so, it performs the valuable function of shaking us out of our ordinary assumptions and reminding us that the world is not as simple as may at first sight appear. In this, science acts rather like philosophy: challenging our assumptions and examining the basis of what we can say about reality.

In other words

▶ *Philosophy cannot determine what information is available to science: it cannot provide data.*

▶ *Philosophy examines the use of scientific data, and the logical processes by which this information can become the basis of scientific theories.*

▶ *Most importantly, philosophy can remind scientists that facts always contain an element of interpretation. Facts are the product of a thinking mind encountering external evidence, and they therefore contain both that evidence and the mental framework by means of which it has been apprehended, and through which it is articulated.*

Science is not confined to theoretical knowledge; it has practical consequences. Through the products of technology, science raises ethical issues – from genetic engineering to nuclear weapons – and this brings it into contact with another branch of philosophy to be considered later in this book: ethics. Science may show what is possible, and technology may make it possible, but that does not address the issue of whether the use of that technology is right or wrong. Just because you can do something does not mean that it is right to do it. Thus, whereas the philosophy of science is concerned with the validity of scientific method, science itself has implications in other areas of thought, including ethics and the philosophy of mind.

10 THINGS TO REMEMBER

1 *Science was originally called 'natural philosophy'.*

2 *Science is characterized by method, rather than by results.*

3 *Science is based on evidence and experiment, rather than pre-established theory.*

4 *The inductive method attempts to get objective conclusions from empirical data.*

5 *Science progresses as existing theories are falsified and replaced.*

6 *Science generally works within an accepted 'paradigm'.*

7 *There may be more than one valid theory to explain a phenomenon.*

8 *New evidence may validate previously neglected theories.*

9 *Theories are subject to peer review and acceptance by the scientific community.*

10 *Science is influenced by funding priorities and has ethical implications.*

3

Language and logic

In this chapter you will learn:

- *about the function of different forms of language*
- *about how language may be assessed and its claim verified*
- *about formal logic and the limitations of rational discourse.*

Language is the vehicle through which the ideas and concepts of philosophy are transmitted. It might be tempting therefore to assume that it has a necessary but secondary role, communicating what is already known. But that would be mistaken, for philosophical issues arise within, and often as a result of our language. A basic question in philosophy is, 'What do we mean by ... ?' which asks for more than a definition – it seeks to relate the thing we are interested in to the rest of our ideas and language. The language we use colours the way in which we think and experience the world.

It is therefore most unwise to philosophize without being aware of the role played by language. In looking at language, however, there are three quite different things to examine:

- ▶ the **philosophy of language** *(which looks at what language is, how it works, whether statements are meaningful and how it may be verified)*
- ▶ **linguistic philosophy** *(which is a way of doing philosophy through the analysis of problematic statements)*

▸ **logic** *(which examines the structure of arguments, in order to illustrate whether their conclusions can be shown to follow from their premises).*

Language and certainty

A key question for the study of language is **'verification'**. How can you show that a statement is true?

▸ *Do you set out bits of evidence that correspond to each of the words used? (An empiricist might encourage you to do that. A reductionist might say that your statement was nonsense unless you could do it!) This assumes that language has a picturing or pointing function.*
▸ *Is a statement 'true' if its logic is sound? If so, does its truth also depend on some sort of external evidence?*

The distinction between 'synthetic' and 'analytic' statement has already been made. But language is complex: an average line of poetry, a joke, a command, a piece of moral advice or the whispered endearments of lovers can quickly dispel any simple theory of verification. We need to move on from 'Is it true?' to the broader issue of 'What, if anything, does it mean?'

In examining the quest for certainty in Chapter 1, we looked at Descartes (who cannot doubt his own existence as a thinking being) and at the empiricist approach. We also saw the way in which Kant identified the contribution of the mind to our process of understanding the world, and went back to Plato, noting the way in which, for him, the world of appearances is but a shadow play, and that reality is in the world of 'Forms'. If we do not know exactly what the world is like, how can we know if our language reflects it accurately?

Probably the greatest influence in shaping modern life is science, which (as we saw in Chapter 2) is based on observation of the world, and uses empirical data to form hypotheses. With the obvious success of science, it was very tempting for philosophers to see science as in some way a paradigm for the way in which knowledge as a whole could be gained.

As science is based on observation, each claim it makes is backed up with reference to data of some sort. Without data, there is no science. The language used by science is therefore justified with reference to external objects. It 'pictures' them. A statement is true if it corresponds to what has been observed, false if it does not so correspond. But can this test be applied to all language?

LOGICAL POSITIVISM

Ludwig Wittgenstein (1889–1951), an Austrian who did most of his philosophy in Cambridge and studied under Bertrand Russell, was deeply impressed by the work done in mathematics and logic by Gottlob Frege (1848–1925), Russell and A. N. Whitehead, with whom Russell had written *Principia Mathematica*, a major work attempting to establish the logical foundations of mathematics. These thinkers had argued that logic and mathematics were objective, not subjective; that is, they described features of the external world, rather than simply showing ways in which the mind worked.

Wittgenstein suggested that philosophical problems would be solved if the language people used corresponded to the phenomenal world, both in terms of logic and the evidence for what was being said. In the opening statement of his hugely influential book *Tractatus* (1921), he identifies the world with the sum of true propositions: 'The world is all that is the case', but he has to acknowledge that there are therefore certain things of which one cannot speak. One of these is the subject self: 'The subject does not belong to the world; rather it is a limit of the world.' Another is the mystical sense of the world as a whole. Whatever cannot be shown to correspond to some observable reality, cannot be meaningfully spoken about.

Insight

> Wittgenstein's early approach to language (he was to change his view later, as we shall see) presented it as a precise but narrowly defined tool for describing the phenomenal world.

His ideas were taken up by the Vienna Circle, a group of philosophers who met in that city during the 1920s and 1930s. The approach they took is generally known as **logical positivism**. Broadly, it claims that:

▶ *Analytic propositions tell us nothing about the world. They are true by definition, and therefore tautologies. They include the statements of logic and mathematics.*
▶ *Synthetic propositions depend on evidence. Therefore there can be no necessary synthetic propositions.*
▶ *Metaphysics and theology are literally 'meaningless' – since such statements are neither matters of logic (and therefore true by definition – a priori) nor are they provable by empirical evidence.*

Moritz Schlick, one of the Vienna Circle, argued that 'the meaning of a statement is its method of verification'. This became known as the 'Verification Principle'.

Logical positivism was promoted by the British philosopher A. J. Ayer (1910–89) in an important book entitled *Language, Truth and Logic* (1936). In that book he asks: 'What can philosophy do?' His answer is that it certainly cannot tell us the nature of reality as such – in other words, it cannot provide us with metaphysics. If we want to know about reality we have to rely upon the evidence of our senses.

He therefore argued that philosophy cannot actually give new information about anything, but has the task of analysis and clarification. It looks at the words people use and analyzes them, showing their logical implications. By doing so, philosophy clarifies otherwise muddled thought.

He argued that every genuine proposition, capable of being either true or false, should be either a tautology (in other words, true by definition) or else an empirical hypothesis (something which makes a claim that can be verified by experience). He therefore considered all metaphysics to be meaningless, for its claims involved statements that were neither capable of empirical verification, nor true by definition.

Of course, there are other kinds of meaning, but Ayer is concerned with statements which claim to have 'factual meaning'. In other words, if experience is not relevant to the truth or falsity of a statement, then that statement cannot claim to have factual meaning, whatever else it may claim by way of meaning of significance for the person making it.

Ayer distinguished between two forms of what can be called the Verification Principle:

1 *A proposition is said to be verifiable and have meaning if and only if its truth may be established in experience. This is the strong form of the Verification Principle, as originally proposed by Moritz Schlick: meaning and verification are identical.*

An example of the strong form

'There are three people in the next room.'

Meaning: If you go into the next room, you will see three people there.

2 *A proposition is said to be verifiable if it is possible for experience to render it probable, or if some possible sense experience would be relevant to determining whether it was true or false. This weaker version was the one Ayer himself favoured. Clearly, it is not always possible to get factual evidence – about the past, for example, or about events predicted to happen in inaccessible places. Where evidence is simply not available, it was thought important at least to be able to specify what sort of evidence would count for or against the factual truth of such a statement.*

An example of the weaker form

'Within the universe there are other planets supporting life.'

Meaning: If you were able to examine every planet in the universe, you would find others with life on them. Although we have not been able to detect signs of carbon-based life like our own as yet, such a discovery would be able to show that the statement is true. The statement is therefore factually 'meaningful'.

Statements are meaningless if there is nothing that would count for or against them being true. On this basis, much of what passes for religious language, or aesthetics, or morality, would be categorized as 'meaningless', because none of these things can be specified in terms of concrete facts that can be checked by observation.

If the only meaningful statement is one that is in the form of an empirical proposition, there is really nothing more to say. Ayer accepts that statements may be emotionally significant for him, but not literally significant – but it is literal significance which is taken to be the basis of certainty.

However, there are two fundamental problems with logical positivism and its verification principle:

1 *How do I know that what I think I see is actually there? I could ask other people to look, checking if they see the same thing. But that would never actually prove that the object was there – for there is no way of getting beyond the sense experiences to the thing-in-itself. However many bits of evidence I get, I can never have absolute proof that there is an external thing being observed: we could all be mistaken.*

Insight

In other words, if you base your certainty on evidence, you should also be aware that evidence is never certain!

2 *How do we verify the statement: 'The meaning of a statement is its method of verification?' Is it synthetic? If so, what is the evidence for it? What evidence could count against it? Or is it analytic? If so then the word 'meaning' is logically the same as 'method of verification' and the theory doesn't say anything.*

This second criticism sounds plausible, but is actually based on a false notion of what the Verification Principle claimed to do. It never claimed to be a factual proposition, rather it set out a policy for evaluating propositions which claimed to be factual, and that is a very different matter. After all, at a road junction a sign may tell you to turn right, but the sign itself does not turn to the right! An instruction is not the same thing as a statement of fact.

The key thing about logical positivism was that it represented a particularly strong form of empiricism and a particularly narrow form of language. The service it rendered philosophy was that, by arguing that a wide range of propositions was 'meaningless', it forced philosophers to think again about the way in which we use language. Whereas the logical positivists had concentrated on a simple 'picturing' view of language, it was soon realized that language can be meaningful in terms of many other functions (for example: expressing feelings; giving commands; stating preferences). In this way, by reacting against the logical positivists, it became widely recognized that a more sophistical view of the function of language needed to be developed.

That said, the Verification Principle is a valuable check, to make sure that statements about personal preferences or commands do not parade themselves as though they were straightforward empirical statements of fact.

Interestingly, towards the end of his life (as illustrated by the interview extract on p. 26), Ayer was to admit that his thought had moved on since the time of writing *Language, Truth and Logic* (accepting that one might communicate aesthetic experience, for example); but that book remained an important touchstone for a particular view of language and approach to philosophy.

Few today would want to take on the bold claims of meaning and certainty of the logical positivists or Ayer, since philosophy has in general recognized the far more flexible nature of language, but they came from a period when science and mathematics were generally thought to provide suitable images of clarity and precision, and therefore became models of an approach to which ordinary language was pressed to conform.

But where does that leave general statements about the way the world is?

Language and perception

In what sense can a proposition be known to be true? In the Introduction, we saw that statements could be true by definition or true by experience. The former included statements of mathematics. Once the words were known, the truth or falsity of a statement followed automatically.

But as we looked at statements based on experience, we found other problems. First of all, there is the uncertainty about any experience: it might always be mistaken or interpreted differently. Secondly, there is the way in which we have to use general words in order to describe particular things:

▶ *Imagine a situation in which there were no general words. How would you describe a tree without the word 'tree', or without the words 'green', 'tall' or 'thick', etc.? Each of these words, unlike a proper name, has a meaning which can be applied to a whole variety of individual things – indeed, learning a language is about learning the whole range of general terms which we can put together in order to describe particular things.*
▶ *Do these general terms refer to things that exist, or are they simply 'names'? Does 'goodness' exist, or is it just a name for certain kinds of things of which I approve? We saw this reflected in differences between Plato and Aristotle, and in the realists/nominalists debate.*

- *In looking at logical positivism, we saw a philosophy that was based on the 'picturing' function of language. Statements had meaning only if they reflected evidence (or potential evidence) from the world of the senses.*
- *But how far can we trust our perception? And is perception the same thing as sense data?*

It's all a matter of interpretation

There are a number of examples of drawings that can be interpreted in a number of different ways. Here is a simple example:

Do you see the profiles of two people facing one another, or do you see an elegant chalice?

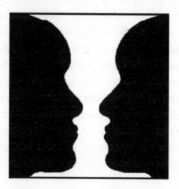

- *Try switching your perception from one to the other – notice the mental effort involved.*
- *Is there any difference between the one and the other perception – difference, that is, in what is actually being seen?*

Such visual games illustrate the ambiguity of all experience. As you make the mental effort to shift from one interpretation of what you see to the other, you are discovering the reality of 'experience as' – that all experience requires an element of interpretation.

Notice also that the way you see the thing as a whole will
subsequently influence your perception of each individual
part: you no longer see a nose, but part of the chalice's stem;
no longer chins, but a base.

Here is the dilemma facing any empirical method of verification
for language:

▶ **If** *all experience involved 'experiencing as'*
▶ **And** *if two people may therefore interpret the same data
  differently*
▶ **How** *do you decide between them or verify the truth
  of what they say?*

Note

It seems curious that, in logical positivism, philosophy was
developing a narrow view of meaning (that of picturing items of
sense data) at the very time when science was starting to realize
that there can be two different and incompatible ways of viewing
things, both of which can be considered correct, as with the wave
or particle theories of light.

Knowledge and language

As far as philosophers in the Anglo–American tradition were
concerned (see Chapter 8 for the different approach taken by
Continental philosophy), for much of the twentieth century,
philosophy was dominated by the discussion of language. Indeed, there
was a feeling that this was all that philosophy was about – everything
else being sorted out by sciences or politics or sociology. Philosophy,
rather than having any specific content, was an activity, and that
activity was to do with the sorting out of words and their meaning.

So philosophy was given a role rather like that of an indigestion tablet, something necessary in order to purify the system and enable comfort and efficiency to return. *Philosophy, according to that view, would help every other subject by clearing away its linguistic confusions.*

Early in the twentieth century, as we previously saw, the logical positivists argued that the meaning of a statement was its method of verification. This view attempted to purge language of all that could not be reduced to sense experience. Metaphysics was out, and ethics was little more than the expression of a preference.

By the 1950s this view of language was becoming broader. Wittgenstein (who, in the earlier phase of his work, had espoused this radically reductionist approach to language) broadened his view, and accepted that language could take on different functions, of which straight description of phenomena was only one. This allowed greater flexibility, and recognized that the expression of values and emotions, the giving of orders and making of requests, were all valid uses of language. His keynote was that language was a 'form of life' and that, to understand it, it had to be observed in use.

He described the different uses of language as 'language games'. Just as a game, such as chess, can only be appreciated once the rules for moving the various pieces are understood, so language can only be understood within its context; words have meaning that is related to their function in the 'game'. This is not to trivialize language (it is not a 'game' in that sense), but to recognize that language is a tool for doing something – a tool that is based on rules that are understood by those who use it.

At this point, philosophers seemed to be catching up with common sense, and abandoning the purity of the unchallengeable statement as the goal of meaning. To know the meaning of a statement, you have to see it in its context and understand what it is intended to achieve. In Chapter 6 we shall be examining different tasks that language can perform in the field of ethics. What we need to recognize at this point is that language is neither simple nor transparent.

▶ *People (hopefully) think before they speak.*
▶ *They may also perceive before they think.*

Therefore

▶ *What they say reflects the nature of thought and of perception.*
▶ *Language is therefore only as simple and straightforward as the thought and perception that produced it.*

Add intuition, emotion, existential angst and the general confusions of human life, and the resulting language is very complex indeed.

▶ *It may perform many different functions.*
▶ *It may play many different games.*
▶ *We may not even be aware of the implications of what we are saying, which is to return to Plato, who in his dialogues portrays Socrates as a man who is constantly asking people what they mean, and thereby exposing their confusions and opening up the way to greater clarity.*
▶ *Without language we cannot have metaphysics or epistemology: indeed, we cannot have philosophy, civilization, culture or other distinctively human features of life.*

Linguistic philosophy

While the logical positivists were analyzing statements in terms of their verification through sense experience, other philosophers – notably, G. E. Moore (1873–1958) and J. L. Austin (1911–60) – were investigating the ordinary use of words. Along with the broader approach taken by Wittgenstein, this led to the view that ordinary speech was an activity that could be analyzed to show its internal logic and implications, and that such analysis would clarify meanings and therefore solve philosophical problems.

This approach, known as 'linguistic philosophy', became a dominant feature of philosophy in the 1940s and 1950s. In Chapter 4 we shall see that one of the most controversial books on the Philosophy of Mind at the time was entitled *The Concept of Mind*, and offered a radical view of mind based on the analysis of ordinary language.

And here is the key to what linguistic philosophy was about: it worked on the assumption that philosophical problems came about because of the ambiguities and confusions of normal speech. Once that speech could be analyzed and its confusions exposed, new insights and clarity would emerge.

Linguistic philosophy therefore redefined the task of philosophy in terms of the clarification of language. We see linguistic philosophy having a significant influence on the philosophy of mind (in asking what we mean when we use words like 'mind' or 'person'), or ethics (where moral statements can be considered in terms of recommending a course of action, for example). It is a way of doing philosophy, and it is not the same as the philosophy of language, which asks questions about how language develops, what it does and how it relates to those things which it describes or brings about, and how it is learned.

Insight

As a student, I found linguistic philosophy clever but frustrating – it was all to do with the subtleties of meaning and apparently nothing to do with life. That has largely changed, with philosophy engaging directly with issues in ethics, politics and personal identity, rather than simply analyzing the language used.

Formal logic

Logic is the branch of philosophy which examines the process of reasoning. When you start with a set of premises and reach a conclusion from them, the process of doing so is called **deductive logic**. An argument is *valid* if it is impossible for the conclusions to be false if the premises are true. An argument can be valid even if the premises are false (and therefore the conclusion is false); just because you are mistaken, it does not mean that your reasoning is not logical. An argument where the premises are true and the logic is valid is *sound*.

Note

Deductive logic differs from the 'inductive' method of reasoning used by science. The inductive method starts with evidence and concludes that (on the balance of probability) this or that is to be expected in the future. A conclusion reached by that method is always open to be revised if there is new evidence. Deductive logic is not about evidence; it is the formal and abstract way of looking at the structure of an argument.

Logic has a long history. In Plato's dialogues we find Socrates debating with various people. He invites them to put forward propositions and then analyzes their implications and the arguments they have used. His argument often takes the form of, 'If B follows from A, and B is clearly wrong, then A must also have been wrong.'

But the main influence on logic for 2,000 years was Aristotle. He set down the basic features of deductive logic, in particular the **syllogism,** in which major and minor premises lead to a conclusion.

The most quoted piece of logic ever, has to be the syllogism:

All men are mortal.
Socrates is a man.
Therefore Socrates is mortal.

This can be expressed as:

All As are B.
C is an A.
Therefore C is B.

From the basic syllogism, we can go on to explore the forms of *inference* – in other words, what can validly follow from what.

Some principles of logic appear quite obvious, but are crucially important for clarifying arguments. William of Ockham (1285–1349), a logician who commented on Aristotle, is best known for his argument that one should not multiply entities unnecessarily. In other words, given a number of possible explanations, one should incline towards the simplest. This is generally known as *Ockham's Razor*.

Logic is often able to highlight common errors. One of these is known as the *argumentum ad ignorantiam*, which is to argue for something on the grounds that there is no evidence *against* it, whereas to establish that something is the case, one needs to show evidence for it.

In other words

There may be no evidence that someone did not commit a particular crime, but that cannot be offered as proof that he or she did commit it. If this basic feature of logic were overlooked, the justice system would be in deep trouble. Notice that an *argumentum ad ignorantiam* may sometimes be slipped into a popular discussion of the paranormal: there is no evidence to show that extra-terrestrials were not the cause of some phenomenon, therefore, in the absence of any other explanation, we can take it that they were!

Logic can become very complex, with parts of an argument depending on others: 'if not this, then that, but if that then something else ... '. Clearly, it would be cumbersome to write out all the elements of each argument in order to examine the logic involved.

To overcome this problem, formal logic uses an artificial form of language. This language uses sets of letters, A, B, C, etc., to stand for the various component premises and conclusions, and also a set of signs to act as connectives. These signs stand for such logical steps as 'and', 'or', 'it is not the case that', 'if ... then' and 'if and only if'.

This use of artificial languages is particularly associated with the German philosopher and mathematician Gotlob Frege (1848–1925).

Example

The connective 'if ... then' is shown by an arrow pointing to the right. The conclusion (therefore) is shown as a semi-colon.

Take this argument:

I have missed the train. If I miss the train I arrive late at work. Therefore I shall arrive late at work.

We can formalize this by using the letter 'A' for 'I have missed the train' and 'B' for 'I will arrive late at work'.

Rewritten, the argument becomes:

A (A → B); B

An important feature of logic is that it breaks down each sentence into its component parts and makes clear the relationship between them. So formal logic helps to clarify exactly what is and what is not valid. Arguments set out in this way become very complex indeed, and there are a large number of unfamiliar signs used for the various connectives. If you pick up a copy Russell and Whitehead's famous *Principia Mathematica* or browse through *The Journal of Symbolic Logic* you will see page after page of what looks like advanced mathematics or complex scientific formulae. For the uninitiated, it is extremely difficult to follow!

MATHEMATICS

Much work on logic has been done by mathematicians, and that is not surprising, since mathematics, like logic, works on premises and rules. Two philosophers already mentioned, Frege and Russell, independently came to the conclusion that the rules of mathematics could be shown to be elementary logic, and that it should therefore be possible to *prove* the basis of mathematics. In their work, developed by Russell in *Principia Mathematica* (published in three parts, 1910–13), mathematics becomes an extension of logic, and in theory (although not in practice, because it would take far too long to set down) all mathematical arguments could be derived from and expressed in logical form.

Earlier, we saw that statements may be categorized as synthetic (depending on experience and therefore uncertain) and analytic (known directly and therefore certain). Now where does mathematics fit into this scheme?

A classic example of an analytic statement is $2 + 2 = 4$. One does not have to check numerous examples to come to the conclusion that their sum will always be 4 and never 5. This is true in general of mathematics; it is a matter of logical deduction and certainty. But does that mean that mathematics is true only in the mind? Is it not the case that two things, added to another two things in the external world, will always make four? If this is so, then things in the 'real' world can be understood through mathematics and logic; *it has to do with actual relationships, not simply with mental operations.*

Insight
If this were not so, how is it that theories about the origin of the universe come from professors of mathematics?

Perhaps, like so many other issues, this can be traced back to Plato. He held that numbers, or geometrical shapes such as triangles or squares, were all perfect; you don't get 'almost square's or a 'nearly 2' in mathematics. But in the real world, nothing is quite that perfect. He therefore held that mathematics is about objects known through the mind rather than the senses, objects which (like his 'Forms') belonged to a world different from the one we experience. Hence, mathematics could be known a priori, with a certainty impossible with things in this world.

Predictably, Aristotle countered this with the claim that mathematical concepts were abstractions and generalizations, based on things experienced. The debate between the Platonic and Aristotelian views has been very influential in the history of mathematics, as in so many other areas of philosophy.

The philosophy of mathematics is a major area of study, beyond the scope of this book. All we need to note is the close relationship between mathematics and logic. Debate continues into whether arithmetic can validly be reduced to 'set theory' and whether mathematics as a whole can fully be reduced to logic and, if so, what the value is in making such a reduction.

IN DEFENCE OF THE ILLOGICAL

Just because Frege saw that mathematics was based on logic, and logic is concerned with the structure of language, it does not follow that all language is (or should be) presented with mathematical precision, any more than the logical positivists succeeded in eliminating all statements that could not be empirically verified. At the very end of *Tractatus*, Wittgenstein pointed out that there were some things of which one had to remain silent. In other words, they were beyond the scope of meaningful propositions, validated with reference to sense experience. But that has not stopped people speaking of them.

Language performs a great variety of functions, and its meaning is given by its function. When we move on to examine Continental philosophy – including existentialism and postmodernism – we shall be exploring questions about the meaning that do not fit the more narrow parameters of analytic philosophy. We have to be prepared to explore the fact that a statement can communicate something of importance, even if – by the standards of an Aristotelian syllogism – it is illogical.

This is not to make a value judgement, simply to point out that logical argument is not the only form of meaningful language.

10 THINGS TO REMEMBER

1   *Logical positivism sought to model all meaningful language on science, picturing the world.*

2   *It saw religious, ethical and aesthetic language as factually meaningless.*

3   *The strong form of the Verification Principle identifies meaning with the method of verification.*

4   *The weak form equates meaningfulness with the ability to specify what could count as evidence.*

5   *Perception (and the language in which it is expressed) depends on interpretation.*

6   *Wittgenstein later argued that meaning was shown by use.*

7   *Wittgenstein also argued that meaning was given within the rules of a 'language game.'*

8   *Linguistic philosophy seeks to solve problems by clarifying language.*

9   *Formal logic analyzes arguments using a shorthand notation.*

10 *Language need not be logical in order to be meaningful.*

4

The philosophy of mind

In this chapter you will learn:
- *some theories about how our minds relate to our bodies*
- *about artificial intelligence and how it compares with human thought*
- *about how we get to know ourselves and one another.*

It was on a dreary night of November, that I beheld the accomplishment of my toils. With an anxiety that almost amounted to agony, I collected the instruments of life around me, that I might infuse a spark of being into the lifeless thing that lay at my feet. It was already one in the morning; the rain pattered dismally against the panes, and my candle was nearly burnt out, when by the glimmer of the half-extinguished light, I saw the dull yellow eye of the creature open; it breathed hard, and a convulsive motion agitated its limbs.

Frankenstein, 1818

Thus Mary Shelley describes the moment of triumph and disaster for Victor Frankenstein in her novel. He had sought the origin of life by a process of analysis; dissecting the human body and exploring its various components. He had observed the changes that take place on death, the corruption of the various organs, and had longed to reverse that process, to bring life back to the dead. Then he collected the 'materials' for his experiment – all the various bits of human anatomy – and fashioned them into a human-like creature. Eventually he finds the secret of their animation, and in that horrifying moment, the creature which he has fitted together comes to life. (In Shelley's novel details of this process are not given, but later film treatments of the Frankenstein story have generally focused on electricity, the spark of life being brought about by the sparks of electrical discharge.)

Released into the world, the 'creature', not fully human and shunned by society, nevertheless develops human emotions, reasoning and skills. Filled with both tenderness and rage, longing for a mate of his own kind and murderously angry with Frankenstein for creating him thus, he asks 'Who am I?'

The 'philosophy of mind' (sometimes called 'philosophical psychology'), is that branch of philosophy which undertakes the Frankenstein-like task of analyzing bodies, minds and persons, dissecting them and attempting to re-animate them, in order to understand the nature of intelligent life.

As you read this book, your eyes are scanning from left to right, your fingers turn the pages, your brain is consuming energy, taking oxygen from its blood supply, tiny electrical impulses are passing between brain cells. All that is part of the physical world, and can be detected scientifically. How does all that relate to the process of reading, thinking, learning and remembering? And how do both relate to personal identity?

If, as the result of an accident, I were to have an arm or leg amputated, I should refer to the detached member as 'my arm' or 'my leg', not in the sense that I owned it, but that I regarded it as part of myself, a part which I must now do without. In the same way, I can list all the parts of myself: my hair, my face, my body, my mind, my emotions, my attitudes. Some of these will be parts of my mental make-up, others will be parts of my physical body.

Where in all this is the real 'me'?

▶ *Am I to be identified with my physical body?*
▶ *Am I my mind?*
▶ *Could I exist outside my body?*

- *If so, could I continue to exist after the death of my body?*
- *Is my mind the same thing as my brain?*
- *If not, then where is my mind?*
- *Can I ever really know other people's minds, or do I just look, listen and guess what they're thinking?*
- *What about computer-created artificial intelligence?*

These are just some of the questions that are explored within the philosophy of mind. Its issues relate to biology, psychology, sociology, computer science, and all aspects of human thought, memory, communication and personal identity.

Ancient minds: Plato and Aristotle

We have already looked at Plato's idea of the 'Forms' – the eternal realities by which we are able to understand and categorize the particular things that we encounter. He argued that, since they are eternal and cannot be known through the senses, we must have had knowledge of them prior to birth, and hence that there is an eternal element to the self. But, if so, how is it related to the physical body?

It is possible to trace a development in Plato's thinking on this through the various dialogues, and it is clear that he wanted to take into account both knowledge of the eternal realities and also the fact that individuals are shaped by the environment into which they are born – so the self cannot be entirely separate from the body.

In *The Republic*, Plato describes the self by way of analogy with a city. Just as a city has workers who produce its goods and services, the military who organize and defend it, and an elite of philosopher-guardians who rule it, so the self has three parts: the physical body with its appetites, the spirited element which animates and drives it, and the thinking mind that rules it. For Plato, the ideal is to have the appetites held in check by the active faculties, which are in turn guided by reason. In other words, he sees the ideal human life as integrating its three distinct elements in a hierarchy.

Aristotle's approach was very different. He rejected Plato's idea of the immortal self, but he was equally critical of the idea that the self was some kind of material substance. His great work on this is *On the Soul* (*De Anima*). Aristotle argued that everything had both physical substance and form (or essence). The form of something is what makes it what it is. To use his own example, you take some wax and give it a particular shape by using a mould or stamp. How does the shape relate to the wax? There is no shape without wax. But, at the same time, the shape is not the same thing as the physical wax that forms it. In the same way, Aristotle sees the self (or soul) as the form or essence of the physical body. It is not something that is separable from the body (you don't have a shape if you don't have any wax), but it is not the same thing as the body. To use another of Aristotle's analogies, an eye is not the same thing as 'seeing', but you cannot see without an eye, and if the eye cannot 'see', then it is not an eye – for the essence of an eye is 'seeing'.

Naturally, both Plato and Aristotle have far more to say about the nature of the self, but this contrast between the two of them sets the agenda for much later debate about the relationship between the self and the physical body. However, their views have been overlaid by that of another philosopher to whom we must now turn – Descartes.

'I think, therefore I am'

In looking at the theory of knowledge, we found that Descartes – using the method of systematic doubt in his quest for certainty – could doubt everything except his own existence as a thinking being. Hence his key statement: 'I think, therefore I am.' This provided him with a starting point from which to build up knowledge. But it also created an absolute distinction between the physical body (which is extended in time and space and which can be known to the senses), and the mind (which is not extended, and which has one function – to think).

So, while Plato can speak of a physical body, with an animating self, ruled by a thinking self, and while Aristotle sees the self as that which gives form and purpose to the physical body, Descartes absolutely pulls apart the physical and the mental – the one is in the world of space and time, the other is not.

In the next section we shall examine the general question of the relationship between mind and body, an issue with which the philosophy of mind was much preoccupied from the time of Descartes up to the second half of the twentieth century. In doing this we will need to return again to both Plato and Descartes, since they both argued for a form of **dualism**. However, in looking at the various forms of dualism, it is worth keeping the historical perspective in view – Cartesian dualism is not the same as that of Plato, and it is only with developments in cognitive science in the latter part of the twentieth century that we return to a broader appreciation of the complexity of the mind/body issue which – following Descartes – had been focused on the single 'problem' of how a non-physical mind could influence a physical body.

The relationship between mind and body

Philosophy has explored a whole range of possible relationships between mind and body. At one extreme there is the view that what we call 'mind' is simply a way of describing the physical body and its activities (**materialism** and **behaviourism**), at the other is the rarer idea that everything is fundamentally mental (**idealism**). Between these is the view that both bodies and minds have distinct but related realities (**dualism**). How exactly they are related is a further problem, and so our consideration of dualism has many sub-theories.

MATERIALISM

A materialist attempts to explain everything in terms of physical objects, and tends to deny the reality of anything that cannot be reduced to them. So, for a materialist, the mind or 'self' is nothing more than a way of describing physical bodies and their activity. We may experience something as a thought or an emotion, but in fact it is *nothing but* the electrical impulses in the brain, or chemical or other reactions in the rest of the body.

Note

This 'nothing but' is an example of the philosophical approach known as '**reductionism**' – the view that the reality of each thing lies in its simplest component parts, rather than the whole phenomenon of which they are parts. Reductionism would suggest, for example, that:

▶ *music is nothing but a set of vibrations in the air*
▶ *a painting is nothing but a collection of coloured dots on canvas*
▶ **so** *a person is nothing but a brain, attached to a body and nervous system.*

The 'nothing but' distinguishes materialism from other theories, for nobody would deny that, in some sense, a person is related to a brain, in the same way as a symphony is related to air movements. The essential question is whether or not it is possible to express what a 'something more' might be, if the materialist position seems inadequate.

Points to consider:

▶ *Apply electrical shocks to the brain, and the personality can be affected. (This is the basis of a form of treatment for severe depression, simulating epileptic fits.)*

▶ *A person who suffers brain damage is no longer the same. In severe cases he or she may not appear to be a person at all, but merely a living body, devoid of all the normal attributes of mind.*

Do these examples confirm the materialist view?

For reflection

You see people waving to you and smiling.

▶ *Does this indicate that they are friendly? That they know you? That they have minds as well as bodies? That they have freely chosen to act in that way? That they have previously recognized you, had friendly thoughts towards you, and therefore decided to wave?*

▶ *Let us analyze what is actually happening as you look at one of those people:*
  ▷ *You see an arm moving.*
  ▷ *Within that arm, muscles are contracting.*
  ▷ *The contraction is caused by chemical changes, brought about by electrical impulses from the brain.*
  ▷ *The electrical activity in the brain has caused the impulses.*
  ▷ *That activity depends on consuming energy and having an adequate oxygen supply via the blood.*
  ▷ *Nutrition and oxygen are taken in from the environment.*
  ▷ *And so on, and so on …*

(Contd)

> ▶ The act of waving is explained in terms of a material chain of cause and effect. That chain is, for practical purposes, infinite – it depends upon the whole way in which the universe is constructed. There is no point in that chain for some 'mind' to have its say. The world, as we experience it through the senses, appears to be a closed system, within which everything is totally determined by physical causes and conditions.

Behaviourism is the term used for the rather crude materialist theory that mental phenomena are in fact simply physical phenomena. Crying out and rubbing a part of the body is what pain is about. Shouting and waving a fist is what anger is about. All mental states are reduced by the behaviourist to things that can be observed and measured.

Insight

Behaviourism developed out of the desire for a scientific approach to the mind that could involve measurement and experiment. Rats in cages learned to press a lever to get food, and dogs to salivate at the bell rung before its arrival. Behind behaviourism lay the thought that human minds too could be controlled by adjusting their environment and by conditioning.

The problem is that we experience a difference between a sensation or thought and the physical movement or the words that result from it. I can think before I speak, or before I write, but for a behaviourist there is nothing other than the words or the writing. To know a feeling, for a behaviourist, one must observe behaviour. This might be a plausible theory if one is observing rodents in a cage, but becomes more problematic when human beings are concerned. One can, for example, observe a brilliant performance by an actor – and one knows it to be a brilliant performance because it gives an illusion of (but is clearly not the same as) the expression of genuine emotions and views. But how, if everything is reduced to what is being observed, can one ever even contemplate the idea of being fooled by someone else about their real feelings? We shall examine this and related problems later in this chapter.

IDEALISM

George Berkeley's idealist theory of knowledge has already been considered in Chapter 1 (see p. 19). All that we know are the ideas in our mind, and we have to infer the physical world from them. What we speak of as 'body' is simply an aggregation of mental facts that are our interpretation of the data that emerge from our sense organs.

A criticism of the idealist approach might be that, although we may not be certain of the existence of matter, for all practical purposes we have to assume it. However much our knowledge of other people is the result of our interpretation of the sense impressions we receive, we are forced by common sense to infer that there really are people with minds and bodies like our own. One of the key problems of a strictly idealist approach is that it leads to **solipsism** – the view that we are unable to know other minds, forever locked in the lonely contemplation of our own sense experience. Perhaps understandably, idealism has not been a popular approach to the issue of how mind and body are related.

DUALISM

If neither the materialist nor the idealist position convinces you by its account for the relationship between mind and body, the answer may be sought in some form of dualism: that mind and body are distinct and very different things. Each is seen as part of the self, part of what it means to be a person, but the question then becomes: How do these two things interact?

This question has a long history. Plato, in *Phaedo*, argued for the immortality of the soul on two grounds:

1 *That the body was composite, and was therefore perishable, whereas the mind was simple, and therefore imperishable.*

2   *That the mind had knowledge of the universals – the eternal
    Forms (such as 'goodness' or 'beauty') – but its experience
    during this life is of individual events and objects. Hence Plato
    argued that the soul itself must be immortal, having existed
    in the realm of the Forms before birth, and thus also able to
    survive the death of the body.*

Few people today would wish to take up these arguments in the
form that Plato presented them. But they persist in two widely
accepted features of the mind/body question:

1   *That the mind is not within space/time and not material – and
    thus that it should not be identified with its material base in
    the brain.*
2   *That the mind functions through communication – it is not
    limited to the operations of a single particular body, i.e. the
    mind is not subject to physical limitations, and is related to a
    network of transpersonal communication.*

For reflection

Where does our conversation take place? Within my mouth?
Within yours? Somewhere in the space between us? Or is a
conversation not related to space in the same way as physical
bodies? We know that a conversation is going on in a room, for
example, which gives a broad physical location, but not a specific
one. Try asking where the internet is located and you start to run
into exactly the same problems. Every piece of information is
actually contained on some physical computer somewhere, but
the overall effect is of a reality that is not physically limited.

Descartes' starting point in the quest for knowledge, 'I think,
therefore I am', implied a radical distinction between the world of
matter, known to the senses, and the mental world, known (at least
in one's own case) directly. They are two different realms, distinct

but interacting. The mind, for Descartes, is able to deflect the flow of physical currents in the nervous system, and thus influence the mechanical working of the physical body. For Descartes, there has to be a point of interaction, for in all other respects he considers the material world to be controlled by mechanical forces, and without a mental component to make a difference, there would be no way in which a mental decision to do something could influence that otherwise closed mechanical world.

One danger here is to imagine the mind as some kind of subtle, invisible body, existing in the world of space and time, yet not subject to its usual rules of cause and effect. This, of course, is a rather crude caricature of what Descartes and other dualists have actually claimed.

Insight

It is also an important caricature, having been used by Gilbert Ryle in *The Concept of Mind* (1949), an influential book for an understanding of the mind/body issue, where he called the Cartesian dualism the 'official view' and labelled the mind 'the ghost in the machine'.

The essential thing for Descartes is that mental reality is not empirical and therefore not in the world of space. The mind is not located in the body – it may be related to the body, but is not some occult alternative set of physical causes and effects. It is therefore a matter of debate whether Ryle was justified in calling Descartes' view 'the ghost in the machine', although a popular form of dualism may well give that impression.

Forms of dualism
EPIPHENOMENALISM
This view is that the brain and nervous system are so complex that they give the impression of individuality and free choice. Although totally controlled by physical laws, we therefore 'seem' to have an independent mind. This is the closest that a dualistic view comes to materialism. The essential thing here is that the mind does not influence the body – the mind is just a product of the complexity of the body's systems.

The various things that I think, imagine, picture in my mind are epiphenomena. They arise out of and are caused by the electrical impulses that move between brain cells, but they are not actually part of that phenomenon, they are above (epi-) them.

For reflection

When does epiphenomenalism start to become thinkable?

Imagine a robot, programmed by a computer. A simple version could be the source of amusement, as it attempts to mimic human behaviour. But as the memory capacity of the computer is increased, the process of decision making in the program is so complex that an observer is no longer able to anticipate what the robot will select to do, and the robot (via the computer) gradually starts to take on a definite personality or character of its own. In this case the character that starts to emerge is seen to be a product of the computer's memory, and hence it would be an epiphenomenon. (We shall examine artificial intelligence later in this chapter.)

INTERACTIONISM

Most forms of dualism claim that the mind and the body are distinct but act upon one another. For example, if you have tooth decay (a bodily phenomenon) it will lead to pain (a mental experience); the body is affecting the mind. Equally, if you are suddenly afraid, you may find yourself breaking out in a cold sweat and start to shake; the mind is affecting the body. Although they interact, the mind and body remain distinct and appear self-contained. Thus (to take up the example of the person waving) an interactionist would not try to claim that there was some break within the series of causes that led to the arm waving. The physical world remains a closed system within the body, but *the whole of that system is influenced by the mind*, and responds to its wishes.

But how exactly is this interaction to come about? Here are some theories:

Occasionalism:

On the occasion of my being hit over the head with a cricket bat, there is a simultaneous but uncaused feeling of pain! The two systems (physical and mental) do not have a direct causal connection. The philosopher Malebranche suggested that whenever he wanted to move his arm, it was actually moved by God.

Pre-established harmony:

The physical and mental realms are separate and independent processes. Each appears to influence the other, whereas in fact they are independent but running in harmony. This view was put forward by Geulincx, a Flemish follower of Descartes. It is also found in Leibniz, who holds that ultimately everything is divisible again and again until you arrive at monads – simple entities without extension, and therefore mental. These monads cannot act upon one another, for each develops according to its own nature. But a complex being comprises countless monads. How do they all work together to produce intelligent activity? Leibniz argued that there must be a pre-established harmony, organizing the otherwise independent monads. As far as human persons are concerned, Leibniz holds that there is a dominant monad (a soul) and that God has established that the other monads, which together form the complex entity that is a person, work in harmony with it.

Note

'Pre-established harmony' may seem to be one of the most bizarre of the mind–body theories, but for Leibniz it served a very specific purpose, and one which has important implications for

(Contd)

both metaphysics and the philosophy of religion. Leibniz was concerned to preserve the idea of **teleology** (i.e. that the world is organized in a purposeful way) in the face of the mechanistic science and philosophy of his day.

If everything is locked into a series of causes and totally determined by them, what room is left for a sense of purpose or for God? Leibniz' answer is that the individual monads of which everything is comprised do not actually affect one another. Rather, God has established a harmony by which they can work together.

DOUBLE ASPECT THEORY

This is the view, sometimes called the 'identity hypothesis', that the ideas a person has, and the operation of bits of his or her brain, are simply *two aspects of the same thing*. Thinking is thus the inner aspect of which the outer aspect is brain activity.

Insight

Perhaps we could use an analogy and say that music is the inner cultural aspect of which sound waves of particular frequencies are the outer physical aspect.

Of course, if the identity hypothesis is correct, there is a problem with freedom. Brain activity, like all physical processes, is limited by physical laws and is in theory predictable. But if mental events are simply another aspect of these physical events, they must also be limited by physical laws. If all my action is theoretically predictable, how can I be free?

Spinoza argued that everything is both conscious and extended; all reality has both a mental and a physical aspect. The mind and body cannot be separated, and therefore there can be no life beyond this physical existence. Spinoza also held that freedom was an illusion, caused by the fact that we simply do not know all the real causes of our decisions.

Survival?

The relationship between body and mind has implications for the idea that human beings might survive death.

If Plato was right to think that the soul was eternal, then its existence does not depend upon the physical body, and it is therefore at least logically possible for it to survive the death of the body. Similarly, Descartes' dualism of extended body and thinking mind at least leaves open the possibility of survival, since the mind is separate from the body, and cannot be reduced to anything physical.

However, if one accepts a materialist or behaviourist view of the self, it would make no sense to speak of a self that existed separately from a body, or survived physical death, since the self is an aspect of bodily activity. The only possibility would be to redefine death in some way, so that it allowed for some form of physical existence to continue, but that would beg the whole question about survival of death, since 'death' in the normal sense of the word would not have occurred.

From the religious point of view, belief in life after death is linked to two other fundamental ideas:

1 *There is a deeply held view that there should be some appropriate compensation, good or bad, for what a person has done during his or her life. All religious traditions have some element of reward or punishment, whether externally imposed (as in Western religions) or self-generated (as the 'karma' of Eastern traditions).*

2 *There is also a sense that human life somehow goes beyond the confines of a fragile human body, expressed in the idea that 'This cannot be everything: there must be something more.'*

Neither of these constitutes evidence for survival of death. What they do show is the appropriateness of such belief for a religious person, and the reasons why he or she might hold to it in the absence of evidence.

In terms of the religious perspective on survival, we should note that there are three different possibilities: immortality, resurrection and reincarnation.

Immortality implies that there is a non-physical element to the self that can exist independently of the physical body with which it is presently associated. This presupposes a dualist view of the mind/body relationship, and does not strictly speaking require belief in God, since a natural immortality can be argued as a logical consequence of dualism.

Resurrection, the Christian view, is that the soul is not naturally immortal, and that the whole person – body and mind – dies, but is then raised to life by God and given a new body. This view depends on a prior belief in God, assumes that individuality requires some sort of body in order to express itself, but raises many questions about the nature of an embodied future life. If that future life is to be endless, then what age is a person in such a future life? A body, after all, can vary from baby to old age. Would a resurrected child become the adult that he or she never was? Would I, in such a life, recognize my grandfather as a young man, and would he recognize me as an old one? This issue, of course, begs all the questions about knowledge of other minds and so on.

Reincarnation, particularly associated with Hindu philosophy, sees the soul as distinct from the body, and as able, at death, to move on to take up another physical body. Personal qualities and dispositions move on from life to life, expressed through a sequence of physical incarnations. Rather like the idea of resurrection, this assumes dualism (since the self that moves on is not the same as the physical body), but still considers the self to require some form of physical body in order to live.

....

Insight

Although illogical, the need to accommodate belief in an afterlife is without doubt a significant factor in shaping some people's view of the nature of the self. Materialism is really only an option for those who take a secular, atheist or a Buddhist view.

....

The concept of mind

Gilbert Ryle suggested, in *The Concept of Mind* (1949), that to speak of minds and bodies as though they were equivalent things was a '**category mistake**'. To explain what he meant by this he used the example of someone visiting a university and seeing many different colleges, libraries and research laboratories. The visitor then asks, 'But where is the University?' The answer, of course, is that there is no university over and above all its component parts that have already been visited. The term 'university' is a way of describing all of these things together – it is a term from another category, not the same category as the individual components.

In the same way, Ryle argued that you should not expect to find a 'mind' over and above all the various parts of the body and its actions, for 'mind' is a term from another category, a way of describing bodies and the way in which they operate. This, he claims, is the fundamental flaw in the traditional dualistic approach to mind and body (which he attributes to Descartes and calls the 'ghost in the machine'):

> **When two terms belong to the same category, it is proper to construct conjunctive propositions embodying them. Thus a purchaser may say that he bought a left-hand glove and a right-hand glove, but not that he bought a left-hand glove, a right-hand glove and a pair of gloves …. Now the dogma of the Ghost in the Machine does just this. It maintains that there exist both bodies and minds; that there occur physical processes and mental processes; that there are mechanical causes of corporeal movements and mental causes of corporeal movements. I shall argue that these and other analogous conjunctions are absurd; but, it must be noticed, the argument will not show that either of the illegitimately conjoined propositions is absurd in itself. I am not, for example, denying that there occur mental processes. Doing long division is a mental process and so is making a joke. But I am saying that the phrase 'there occur mental processes' does not mean the same sort of thing as 'there occur physical processes', and, therefore, that it makes no sense to conjoin or disjoin the two.**

The Concept of Mind, Peregrine Books, 1949, p. 23

For Ryle, talking about minds is a particular way of talking about bodies and their activity. Remember, however, that Ryle is primarily concerned with language – his book is about what we mean when we speak about the 'mind'. What he shows is that, in ordinary language, mental terms actually describe activities performed by the body, or are at least based on such activities. We speak about the mind of another person without claiming to have any privileged information about their inner mental operations.

Clearly, we can get to know another person but, if Ryle is correct and there is no 'inner' self to be found, in what does the personality consist? His answer is in terms of 'dispositions'. These are the qualities that make me what I am; the propensity to behave in a particular way in a particular situation; the sort of beliefs and knowledge that habitually inform my actions and words.

If I say that someone is 'irritable' I do not mean that I have some privileged access to an 'irritability factor' in their mind. I just mean that, given a situation that is not to his or her liking, he or she is likely to start complaining, sulking, etc. In other words, the irritability is simply a way of describing a disposition.

Thus, for Ryle, the ascription of mental predicates (clever, etc.) does not require the existence of a separate, invisible thing called a mind. The description 'clever' may indeed refer to the way in which something is done but, equally, cleverness cannot be defined simply in terms of that action. What is clever for one person might not be so for another, and the mental description refers more to the way in which the individual person habitually relates to the world, and the expectation a person would have of him or her, rather than some special quality of an action that makes it clever.

A small child is 'clever' if it learns to stagger to its feet and totter a few paces forwards before collapsing down on the ground again. The same is not claimed for the drunk who performs a similar set of movements. If Ryle wishes to dismiss 'the ghost in the machine' he must equally dismiss 'the ghost in the action', for mental predicates refer to, but are not defined by, individual actions.

One particular difficulty with identifying a mental phenomena with physical actions is illustrated by the idea of pain.

▶ *I may shout, cry, hold the afflicted part of my body; I may scream and roll on the ground, curl up, look ashen. But none of these things is actually the same thing as the pain I am experiencing. The pain is indicated by them, but not defined by them.*
▶ *I may watch an actor performing all the things listed above. But because he or she is acting, I do not imagine that there is any actual pain.*
▶ *Yet, if being in pain is actually identified with those things (as Ryle implies), then the actor is in pain.*

Comment

Much modern debate on the mind/body issue has been prompted by Ryle's critique of dualism. One feature of his work that one should keep in mind is that his approach is linguistic. He asks what it means to ascribe mental predicates. The question remains, of this or any similar approach, whether the meaning of the mental predicate is the same as its method of verification. I can verify my description of someone as clever by observing and listening to him or her. But is the information I receive in that way identical to what I mean by cleverness? Or is cleverness hinted at by, but not defined by, such information?

A 'place' for mind?

A basic question for mind/body, as for many other areas of
philosophy: Can something exist if it does not have a place within
the world of space and time?

It is clear, for example, following Ryle, that there is no place
for a 'self' or 'soul' alongside the body. Everything to which
language about the mind refers has its own place in the world –
the clever action, the kindly word – and he is surely right to claim
that the words 'clever' and 'kindly' here would not refer to some
occult substance, but to the way in which particular deeds are
performed.

But the dualist is not actually saying that the mind exists
physically outside the body. The dualist position is that the
mind is not extended, that it does not exist within time and
space. We have returned therefore to the fundamental
philosophical issue of reductionism. Consider any piece
of music:

▶ *It comprises a sequence of sound waves within the air.*
▶ *There is no music apart from those sound waves. For even if
I have a tune running in my head (a problematic thing for any
philosopher to say) what I am doing is recalling that pattern
of sound waves.*

- ▶ *All the qualities of music (its ability to move one emotionally, its sense of beauty, of completeness, its ability to calm) have as their source that series of sound waves.*
- ▶ *The language a musician uses to describe a piece of music is quite different from the language a physicist uses to describe sound waves.*
- ▶ *There is no hidden, secret music that exists alongside the sound waves – rather, the sound waves are the physical medium through which music is generated.*
- ▶ **Therefore** *it really should not be too difficult to see that the brain, along with the nervous system and all the physical activities (including speech) that it controls, is the physical medium through which a mind expresses itself.*

There have been many subtle variations on the problem of how the body and mind are related, but most of them can be seen, in one way or another, to be a result of an attempt to express the interconnectedness and yet distinctness of physical and non-physical reality.

What is clear from recent neurophysics is that the brain is extremely complex, that it controls not just the autonomic nervous system, but also those elements that we describe as personality or mind.

It is equally clear that an essential feature of the mind is communication. It is difficult to see how one could describe a mind that did not communicate – and in communicating, by words, facial expressions, writing, the qualities of that mind are shared. It is no more sensible to try to analyze an isolated human brain in the hope of discovering the seeds of cultural history, than it is to take a Stradivarius apart in order to discover why a violin concerto can be so moving!

BACKGROUND NOTES

A person's view on the mind/body issue depends on his or her general view of the world and knowledge of it. It is possible to trace the debate through the history of philosophy. For example:

- *Plato sees the soul as eternal, trapped in a limited material body.*
- *Aristotle sees the soul as the 'form' of the body (everything for him has both substance and form), giving it unity.*
- *For Descartes ('I think therefore I am') the mind is primary.*
- *Hume said (in his 'Treatise on Human Nature'): '... when I enter most intimately into what I call myself, I always stumble on some particular perception or other, of heat or cold, light or shade, love or hatred, pain or pleasure. I never can catch myself at any time without a perception, and never can observe any thing but the perception.' Hume, an empiricist, cannot see a general 'self' because he cannot step outside the world of phenomena, which is his starting point for all knowledge.*
- *Kant argues that humans are phenomenally conditioned but noumenally free, therefore the mind is beyond the categories that apply to sense experience.*

There is also a tradition which puts the mind quite beyond what can be known. So, for example, Wittgenstein, at the end of the *Tractatus*, says: 'The subject does not belong to the world, but it is a limit of the world.' In other words, from the standpoint of empirical evidence, I do not exist. As I experience it, the world is everything that is not me, although it includes my own physical body.

Insight

It is also possible to see the self as a process, rather than an entity – a process that unfolds as personal history, mapping out moments of personal significance. To follow up on this idea, see my book *Me* (listed in the Further reading section).

Neurones and computers

In *The Astonishing Hypothesis: The Scientific Search for the Soul* (1994), the scientist Francis Crick asked how it is that, if the brain is a machine made up of nerve cells and neurones, it can also take on the functions of what we know as mind: appreciating colour, telling jokes, thinking through problems. He argued that the brain had 'awareness neurones', which were the physical basis of mind, and that the 'soul' was physically located in the head, and therefore that research into brain activity would eventually reveal the processes which we call consciousness.

In suggesting this, Crick was rejecting two common conceptions. The first (from a dualistic standpoint) is that the soul or mind is not physically located in the body but is external, and may therefore be able to survive the death of the body. The second is the 'homunculus' idea: that the soul is distinct from the brain, but located inside the head, like a person within a person.

Instead, he argued that a complex structure has characteristics that go beyond those of its component parts. (So, for example, a city has a character over and above those of its individual citizens.) Therefore the 'soul', or mind, is the product of the interactions of the billions of brain cells. The human brain is, after all, the most complex thing known in the universe. Most of it controls the various functions that keep us alive, but he suggested that other parts of the brain could be involved with consciousness.

Notice what can and cannot be claimed by taking Crick's approach. 'Awareness neurones', once identified, could be recognized as the physical basis of mind, in exactly the same way that DNA is the physical and chemical basis of life. (Crick was awarded a Nobel Prize in 1962 for his part in the discovery of DNA.) Since the unique set of characteristics of any physical body is given in its DNA, we can identify an individual through its analysis. But that does not mean that the physical body is 'nothing but' a DNA code; the code is simply the set of instructions for building that unique body. In the same way, the most that Crick's quest for 'awareness neurones' might show is the physical location of mental activity. It cannot explain it.

In other words

▶ *Our DNA does not show where we live, or what experiences we have had. It makes us unique, it enables all the cells in our body to grow*

> *and work together, but it does not make us a 'person'. Traces of it*
> *in body tissue can identify us and show basic characteristics, but it*
> *cannot describe what we are like as living beings. Life is based on DNA;*
> *but life is not the same thing as DNA.*
> ▶ *Similarly, 'consciousness neurones' could not be 'you' any more than*
>   *your DNA is 'you'.*

Clearly, since Crick wrote about 'consciousness neurones', much progress has been made in terms of the mapping of brain function. We now know far more precisely which parts of the brain are involved in thinking, monitoring sensations and controlling activity. Nevertheless, with every advance in neuroscience, there is the temptation to resort to his argument and suggest that we are about to find the physical 'mind'. The logic of the argument does not suggest that it is possible to do so. The firing of neurones in my brain is one level of activity, thinking is quite another; the fact that the latter depends on the former does not imply that the two are identical.

Insight

In *Consciousness Explained* and other popular books on this subject, Daniel Dennett, taking a materialist position, suggests that, at some point in the future, a perfect neuroscience will tell us all we need to know about the mind. My own view is that it will tell us nothing more than we know now about who we are as persons – it will simply show which neurones fire when we think, experience or do various things.

AI AND NEURAL COMPUTING

To appreciate how the brain might be thought to create the mind, one can look at two different areas of computer science:

▶ *Artificial intelligence (AI) uses computers to perform*
  some of the functions of the human brain. It works on
  the basis of knowledge and response, the computer stores
  memories and is programmed to respond to present
  situations which correspond to them. It can, for example,

recognize words, and can respond to them. The bigger the computer memory, the more 'lifelike' this form of artificial intelligence becomes.

▶ *Neural computing goes about its task quite differently. It tries to produce a computer which actually works like a human brain – recognizing things, forming mental images, even dreaming and feeling emotions. A neural computer, although very simple by comparison, is like a brain in that it programmes itself and learns from its environment.*

Some scientists claim that AI holds the key. The human brain, they argue, comprises about 100 million memories and a few thousand functions. All you need, in a sense, is raw computing power. On the other hand, this is never going to be that easy, because attempting to match the human brain – the most complex thing known in the universe – will take an enormous amount of computer power.

This view is countered by those who claim that neural computing holds the key to an understanding of the 'mind', since a neural computer can take on characteristics that are normally regarded as human. Human brains are not programmed, they just learn, and that is also the defining feature of neural computing.

In other words

AI is the attempt to store and reproduce the workings of already developed brains (of those who programme the computers); neural computing is the attempt to get a simple artificial brain to 'grow' in intelligence.

The difference between AI and neural computing highlights a feature of Ryle's argument in *The Concept of Mind*. Ryle made the distinction between 'knowing that' and 'knowing how'. He argued that to do something intelligently is not just a matter of knowing facts, but of applying them – to use information, not just to store it. To do something skilfully implies an operation over and above applying ready digested rules. To give one of Ryle's examples, a clock keeps time, and is set to do so, but that does not make it intelligent. He speaks of the 'intellectualist legend', which is that a person who acts intelligently, first has to think of the various rules that apply to his or her action, and then think how to apply them (thus making 'knowing how' just part of 'knowing that' – knowing the rules for action as well as the facts upon which that action is based).

Ryle claims that when, for example, we make a joke, we do not actually know the rules by which something is said to be funny. We do not perform two actions, first thinking of the rules, and then trying to apply them. Rather, we simply say something that, in spite of not knowing why, actually strikes us as funny.

The same could be said for a work of art, literature or musical composition. The second-rate composer follows all the established rules and applies them diligently. He or she produces art that follows fashion. The really creative person does not follow rules, producing work that may be loathed or controversial, but nevertheless may be said to be an intelligent production, since it attempts to express something that goes beyond all previous experience or rules. This is a kind of 'knowing how': knowing how to perform creatively.

Now, if a computer is fed with sufficient information, it 'knows that'. It can also follow the process that Ryle calls the 'intellectualist legend' – it can sort out the rules and apply them to its new data. What it cannot do – unless we claim that it suddenly 'takes on a life of its own' – is to go beyond all the established (programmed) rules and do something utterly original.

By contrast, a neural network responds to each new experience by referring back to its memory of past experiences. In this way, it learns in the immediate context of its experience, not by predetermined rules. Everything is judged (by the neural network as well as by the human being) in terms of past experiences and responses, so that its understanding of the world is constantly changing. Its understanding is based on the relationships between events, not on rules.

Some philosophers, while accepting that the brain is the origin of consciousness, are suspicious of the computer-view of consciousness. John Searle of the University of California, Berkeley, believes that consciousness is part of the physical world, even though it is experienced as private and subjective. He suggests that the brain causes consciousness in the same sense that the stomach causes digestion. The mind does not stand outside the ordinary physical processes of the world. On the other hand, he does not accept that this issue will be solved by computer programs, and has called the computer-view of consciousness a 'pre-scientific superstition'.

While some hold that consciousness is really a higher order mental activity (thinking about thinking: being self-conscious) others claim that it is really a matter of the brain recognizing and relating the various sensations received by the body. So, for example, Professor Roger Penrose of Oxford (in *The Emperor's New Mind*, 1989) argued that it would be impossible to create an intelligent robot because consciousness requires self-awareness, and that is something that a computer cannot simulate. He argues that consciousness is based on a 'non-algorithmic' ingredient (in other words, an ingredient which does not depend on an algorithm – a set of rules).

For consideration

A robot would not need self-awareness in order to carry out actions intelligently, merely a set of goals to be achieved. So, for example, a chess program can play chess and beat its own creator, but it only knows what constitutes winning at chess, not the significance of playing the game.

Such discussions of artificial intelligence and neural networking take us well beyond the old mechanistic view of the universe, and therefore away from the kind of mind/body dualism that was introduced by Descartes. Intelligent activity is more likely to be seen now as a feature of complexity and of relationships. If something is complex enough, and if its operation is based on a constantly changing pattern of relationships between its memory components, then it appears to evolve in a personal and intelligent way; it takes on character.

Chinese writing

A most graphic way of exploring the difference between being able to handle and manipulate information (which a computer can do very efficiently) and actually understanding that information (which, it is claimed, a computer cannot) was given by the philosopher John Searle (in his 1984 Reith Lectures, *Minds, Brains and Science*):

You are locked in a room, into which are passed various bits of Chinese writing, none of which you can read. You are then given instructions (in English) about how to relate one piece of Chinese to another. The result is that you are apparently able to respond in Chinese to instructions given in Chinese (in the sense that you can post out of the room the appropriate Chinese reply), but without actually understanding one word of it. Searle argues that this is the case with computers; they can sort out bits of information, based on the instructions that they are given, but they cannot actually understand the information they are given.

The philosopher Hubert Dreyfus has given a criticism of AI based on an aspect of the philosophy of Heidegger (see p. 251). Heidegger (and Dreyfus) argued that human activity is a matter of skilful coping with situations, and this presupposes a 'background', which is all the facts about society and life in general that lead us to do what we do. Now AI, according to Dreyfus, attempts to reduce this 'background' to a set of facts ('know-how' is reduced to 'know-that'). But this is an impossible task, because there is an ever-growing number of facts to be taken into account; for practical purposes the number of background facts is infinite. Also, a person has to select which of those facts are relevant to the decision in hand, and the rules for deciding which are going to be relevant then form another set of facts that might also be infinite. It is therefore impossible to provide enough rules and facts to fill out the whole background to any human decision, and this is, according to Dreyfus (see Dreyfus and Dreyfus, *Mind over Machines*, 1986), a problem which will continue to be formidable for AI.

For reflection

It seems to me that artificial intelligence is basically a modern computerized form of Frankenstein's experiment! It is assembling 'materials' (in this case memory, processing power and the data upon which it is to work) in the hope that it will find the key to make this become a thinking being, a self. So far, the AI limbs have started to twitch, but the monster has not taken on human form!

and a comment ...

Over the last two decades, there has been a phenomenal rise in the power and sophistication of computers and in the way they are used, not least in connection with the internet, with its huge impact on commerce, communication and society. Much of what was written in this section appeared in the first edition of this book and reflected the situation in the mid 1990s. However, reviewing it fifteen years later, it seems that the fundamental issues concerning the relationship between computing and the human mind remain much the same, and those early arguments are still valid in our more computer-sophisticated environment.

Knowing me, knowing you

We now turn to some implications of the mind/body problem, particularly those that affect individuals in terms of their self-understanding, identity and knowledge of other people.

FREE WILL

Freedom of the will is a major feature in the mind/body debate. If, as a materialist or even a epiphenomenalist would claim, the mind is simply a by-product of brain activity, and if that brain activity, being part of a material world is, in theory, totally predictable, then there is no such thing as free will. We appear to be free only because we do not understand the unique combination of causes which force us to make our particular decisions. We are pawns of fate – if all causes were known, we would have no freedom and no responsibility for what we (erroneously) call our 'mental' operations.

In effect, the issue here is exactly the same as '**determinism**' within the broader scope of the philosophy of science. We live in a world of cause and effect. If causality is universal (or if, as Kant, we believe that the mind automatically assumes that it is) then it provides a closed loop of explanation for everything that happens. Human beings and their choices, being part of the physical world, come within that loop.

Insight

There is a danger here of falling into a fallacy that the philosopher Henri Bergson called 'retrospective determinism'. Just because something has happened we are tempted to assume that it had to happen, and therefore search backwards for its necessary causes. This is not a sound argument for determinism, because it has already ruled out the possibility of genuine chance and spontaneous creativity before it starts.

Yet many people would want to argue that freedom and morality are an essential part of what it means to be a human individual. We are not robots, even sophisticated ones. Our role in the world is proactive, not reactive. We shape the world as much as we are shaped by it. From this perspective, it is difficult to see the mind as 'nothing more than' a by-product of brain activity.

DISEMBODIED CONSCIOUSNESS

Clearly, it is only logical to believe that the mind or self can exist outside the body or survive the death of the body if you take a dualist view of the mind/body relationship – since if the mind is a product of, or inevitably bound up with the physical body (and particularly the brain), it could have no disembodied existence.

Quite apart from general religious beliefs about life beyond death, there is plenty of evidence for strange phenomena concerning the dead – such as the sighting of ghosts, or speaking with the dead at a séance – but such evidence is always open to interpretation, and a person who takes a strictly materialist standpoint will always find an explanation for the experience that does not stray towards the paranormal. Many would argue that a person who is recently bereaved or for whom the possibility of contacting the dead is highly charged emotionally, is hardly going to be able to give an objective and detached account. So while the evidence for life beyond death may be plentiful, it is unlikely to be objective or scientific.

Another form of disembodied consciousness concerns so-called 'out of body' experiences. These are generally associated with times of personal crisis or physical danger, while having an operation, for example. Some people have the sense that they have left their physical body 'down there' on the operating table, and are able to move away from it, observing what is happening to it as though watching from a distance.

About one in three people who come near to death in this way report a 'near-death experience', so it is not a rare phenomenon, nor is it limited to people of any particular set of religious or other beliefs.

An example

I was in a great deal of discomfort and pain. Suddenly, the sounds of the ward – the nurses bustling about, women laughing, the babies crying – all disappeared, and I just floated gently away from my bed, sideways at first, then up.

I know it sounds extraordinary, but I knew that I was dying. It was extraordinary, because all the pain and discomfort disappeared and I was conscious of light surrounding me, and I was warm – it was a beautiful feeling.

But then I thought of my mother, with whom I have a very strong bond, and I remember thinking that I can't do this to my mum. I made a conscious effort to return to my body, which I did – with a great jolt, as if I'd been thrown back. And immediately all the pain returned.

Sunday Telegraph, 30 January 1994, p. 11

Such experiences can be investigated to see if they can represent a genuine spatial removal from the physical body, or if they are simply a product of the imagination. If they were proved to be literally true, it would suggest that the mind/body relationship is dualistic, and that – even if related closely to what is happening in the brain – the mind cannot be simply identified with the brain. Others, however, would suggest that it is exactly the sort of oxygen starvation that the brain may suffer in approaching death that leads to these unusual experiences.

As in all cases where we try to evaluate the experience of individuals, a useful test is that which Hume applied to the accounts of miracles (see p. 176): Which is more likely, that the event actually happened as reported, or that the person reporting it is mistaken?

KNOWLEDGE OF OTHER MINDS

In a strictly dualistic view of bodies and minds, you cannot have direct knowledge of the minds of others. You can know their words, their actions, their writings, their facial and other body signals, but you cannot get access to their minds. For a dualist, knowledge of other minds therefore comes by analogy. I know what it is like to be me. I know that, when I speak, I am expressing something that I am thinking. Therefore, I assume that, when another person speaks, his or her words are similarly the product of mental activity.

From Ryle's point of view there is no problem. There is no 'ghost in the machine'; what we mean by 'mind' is the intelligent and communicative abilities of the other person. If I know his or her actions, words, etc., then I know his or her mind; the two things are one and the same.

Returning to an earlier question

What is the difference between an actor who is playing the part of a person in pain, and someone who is actually in pain?

If I say that the one *really* feels pain, while the other only appears to feel pain, do I not assume that there is some non-physical self which exists over and above the actual grimaces and moans that lead me to describe the person as being in pain?

But is it possible to know another mind directly? What about telepathy? Here we have the difficulty of knowing how to evaluate a phenomenon the validity of which may be challenged, and for which there is, at present, no scientific explanation. But actually, if we are considering what we understand by the self of mind, it makes little difference whether telepathy works between minds that are distinct from their respective bodies, or whether there is some as yet unexplained way in which brains manage to communicate with one another. So, in itself, it does not help us to decide between a materialist or a dualist position.

Of course, if what you are is not a fixed entity but a process – if you are your personal history of the things you have said and done – then knowing you is simply (although far from simple!) a matter of getting to know you by being with you, listening to what you say and the descriptions of your thoughts, watching your habitual responses to life, getting to anticipate your wishes.

Insight

This suggests that the self is not a hidden, unknowable entity, but the ongoing story of you as an individual, responding to your world, developing a pattern of values, interests and relationships that you can think about, describe and share with others.

In other words

Other minds can be known by:

▶ *observing bodies (e.g. Ryle)*
▶ *by analogy with myself (the dualist's position)*
▶ *by telepathy (if this is accepted as a proven phenomenon)*
▶ *because of the phenomenon of language (how could there be communication, unless there were minds with which to communicate?)*
▶ *by observing ongoing patterns of behaviour, relationships and stated wishes (getting to see what is important for that person, as a living intelligent being).*

Knowing oneself is rather different, in that we are immediately aware of our own thoughts, whereas the thoughts of others come to us via their words, gestures and appearance. This has led some people to argue that we can know only our own mind, and are therefore radically alone, surrounded by bodies in which we have to infer that there are other minds similar to our own.

Such a lonely view is termed **solipsism**, and this is the fate of those who think of the soul or mind as a crude, unknowable 'ghost', as caricatured by Ryle.

In practice, we actually get to know other people by observation, by considering what they say or write, and by judging how they deal with life. We can question them, in order to clarify their likes and dislikes, for example. But in the end, we still depend upon our own observation.

An example

I ask someone, whom I have invited to dinner that evening, if he likes strawberries. He replies that he does.

▶ *If he is telling the truth, and I believe him, then I know at least one thing about his own private tastes.*

▶ *He could, however, be saying that he likes them in order to be polite (seeing that I am returning home with a punnet of strawberries in my hand when I ask him the question). I need to ask myself if, in my past experience of him, he is someone who is straightforward about his views, or if he is always anxious to please and agree with people. If the latter is the case, then I am really no nearer knowing if he really does like strawberries.*

▶ *I could observe him at the dinner table that evening. Does he savour the strawberries, or swallow them quickly? Does he appear to be enjoying himself, or does he suddenly turn rather pale and excuse himself from the table?*

▶ *Do I subsequently observe him buying and eating strawberries?*

This is a simple example of weighing up the evidence for a person's private sensations. It would become far more complex if the question were, 'Did you have a happy childhood?' In this case, there are profound psychological reasons why the immediate response may not be the correct one. Indeed, such is the way in which the unconscious mind affects the conscious, that the person may not actually know if he was or was not happy. Moments of trauma may have been blocked off and unacknowledged. The whole process of psychotherapy is one of gradually unpicking the things that a person says, in the light of their actual behaviour and physical responses.

Knowledge of other minds is therefore a process of assessment, based on observation. It is not instantaneous (if it were, most therapists would starve!). It is constantly open for revision.

I meet up with a friend whom I have not seen for 20 years.

▶ *Do I now treat this senior executive as though he were still the scruffy 15-year-old I once knew, with unchanged tastes and habits? If so, we are unlikely to renew our friendship!*
▶ *I have to learn anew – check what remains of old views, check what has changed, ask about life's experiences and their impact.*

Notice the assumption that I make in all this: that I am getting to know another person as a communicating subject. I do not explore his brain, nor seek for any occult 'soul'. I simply recognize that he is a person who has views, feelings, thoughts, experiences, and that he can communicate them. That process of communication means that getting to know another person is a two-way process. It depends upon my observation and enquiries, but also upon the willingness of the other person to be known. Without the person's co-operation, even a very experienced psychotherapist would find it extremely difficult to get to know that individual's mind. You can build up a profile – he is this sort of person with those sort of interests – but you cannot get much of an idea of the person as a unique, rounded individual. Psychologists advising the police can suggest the sort of person who might have committed a particular crime, based on their experience of similar people, especially in the case of those with severe mental disturbance. But they cannot point to a particular individual.

Contrast this with knowledge of yourself:

▶ *It is instantaneous. As soon as I stop to reflect, I can say if I feel happy or not.*

► *It is based on sensation, not observation. I do not have to listen to my own words, or look at my facial expressions in a mirror in order to know if I am enjoying myself. I have immediate sensations of pleasure or pain.*

BUT:

► *It is not certain. Although my knowledge of myself is more reliable than the knowledge of anyone else, I may still be mistaken. If it were not so, we could never become confused about ourselves, for we would know and understand both our experiences and our responses to them. Adolescence would be negotiated smoothly, mid-life crises would never occur, psychotherapists and counsellors would become extinct. Alas, the process of knowing oneself is probably more complex than knowing another person.*

In knowing myself, I have two advantages over others:

1 *I have memory. This means that my own knowledge of events and my response to them is more immediate and detailed than the accounts given by others, although my memory may let me down, and (in the case of traumatic experiences) things may be repressed because they are too painful to remember. In such a case, for example of trauma in childhood, another person may have a clearer memory of what happened and of my response at the time than I have myself.*
2 *I can deliberately mislead others about my feelings and responses. Generally speaking, except for cases of strong unconscious motivation, I do not mislead myself.*

PERSONAL IDENTITY

There are many ways of identifying yourself:

► *son or daughter of –*
► *a member of a particular school, university, business*

- *a citizen of a country, member of a race*
- *an earthling (if you happen to be travelling through space, this might become a very relevant way of describing yourself).*

At various times, each of these will become more or less relevant for the purpose of self-identity. Relationships establish a sense of identity, and the closer the relationship, the more significant will be its influence on the sense of self. Aristotle held that friendships were essential for a sense of identity.

An example

Walking down a street in London, I am not likely to think of myself first and foremost as British (unless, of course, I am near a famous building, and am surrounded by foreign tourists). Yet if I travel to a far-flung and inaccessible part of the globe, I might well say, 'I'm British' as one of the first means of identifying myself.

- *In general, self-identification is made easier by emphasizing those things by which one differs from others around one at the time.*
- *Those who are fearful of having their individuality exposed tend to 'blend in' with a crowd, giving themselves an 'identity' in terms of shared values. In practice, this leads to group identity, not individual identity.*

In practice, identity is not a matter of body or mind only, but of an integrated functioning entity comprising both body and mind. Of course, once the process of analysis starts, it is difficult to find a 'self' that is not at the same time something else – but that is exactly the reason why identity is not a matter of analysis.

- **Analysis** *shows bits and pieces, none of which is 'you'.*
- **Synthesis** *shows the way in which body, mind and social function all come together in a unique combination – and that is 'you'.*

Identity is therefore a matter of synthesis, not of analysis. *You are the sum total, not the parts.*

Reflecting on location

▶ *Are your thoughts physically contained within your head, just because they originate in brain activity?*

▶ *Where are your friendships located? In your head? In the heads of your friends? Somewhere in space between the two? In a level of reality that does not depend on space, if there is such a thing?*

▶ *Think of a chat show on radio. The programme is put together by a team of people. It is broadcast across hundreds, perhaps thousands of miles. The words of the host spark off thoughts in the minds of thousands of listeners. Some respond and phone in to the programme. Where is this whole phenomenon of the chat show located? If it does not have a single physical location, what does that say about personal identity and personal communication? Can it be that our identity is not contained within a physical location, but is formed by networks of significance?*

Is it possible, in thinking about mind as the prime way of defining a self or person, to ignore the importance of physical identity? Consider therefore a world in which we were all physically identical:

▶ *You would not know if someone was young or old, male or female.*

▶ *You would not know if the person facing you were a relative, a friend, a stranger or an enemy.*

▶ *Other people would fail to recognize you, would have to ask who you are. Your name would probably mean nothing to them. You would be most unlikely to know if you had ever seen them before.*

How would society or relationships be able to develop in such a world? Physical differences are the starting point of recognition and shared experience. A world of clones is likely to be a world devoid of relationships.

More than once in this chapter we have turned to the idea of an actor, and the distinction between acting and reality. This is also relevant for an understanding of 'persons'. For example, Aldo Tassi, writing in *Philosophy Today* (Summer 1993), explored the idea of a persona (or mask) that an actor puts on. The actor projects a sense of self – the self who is the character in the play. In doing so, the actor withdraws his own identity. In the theatre, the actor can go off stage and revert to his own identity. In the real world, Tassi argues, we create a character in what we do, but we can never step outside the world to find another self 'off stage'. He refers back to Aristotle, for whom the soul is the substantial form of the body, but substance for Aristotle was not a static thing. The soul is not superadded to the body in order to make the body a living thing; rather, the body gets both its being and its life from the 'soul'. Tassi says: 'Consciously to be is to project a sense of oneself, that is to say, to "assume a mask".'

Insight

Personal identity, if Tassi is right, is dynamic rather than static; it is acted out and developed; it does not exist in terms of static analysis.

For reflection

Frankenstein's monster takes on character as the novel unfolds. It is not there in the inanimate materials from which he (or it) is fashioned. Do we ever achieve a definitive 'character' of our own? Can we maintain multi-personalities without moving in the direction of schizophrenia?

There is much that can be explored in terms of 'persons'. In recent philosophy this has been brought to attention by the work of

P. F. Strawson (1919–2006), a British philosopher known particularly for his work on the nature of identity, and for his exposition and development of the philosophy of Immanuel Kant. In 'Persons', an article first published in 1958, and '*Individuals*', 1959, he argued that the concept of 'person' was prior to the popular analysis of it as an animated body, or an embodied mind. Rather, a person is such that both physical characteristics and states of consciousness can be ascribed to it. The concept of a 'person' has many practical and ethical implications:

▶ *In what sense, and at what point, can an unborn child be called a person?*
▶ *An unborn child has a brain, but cannot communicate directly. Is such communication necessary for it to be called a full human being? (Consider also the case of the severely handicapped. Does lack of communication detract from their being termed 'people'?)*
▶ *Does a baby have to be independent before being classified as a person? If so, do we cease to be human once we are rendered totally dependent on others, for example, on the operating table?*
▶ *What is the status of a person who goes into a coma?*

Insight
Morality depends on a sense of personal identity and therefore needs to take such issues into account.

MEMORY

Memories are personal, and they are also influential. You are what you are because you have learned from the past – and that learning depends on memory. A person who has lost his or her memory finds it difficult to function, is constantly surprised or bewildered by the response of others who claim long-established friendship or hatred. Our responses are determined by our memories.

Hume saw memories as a set of private images running through one's head. It follows that, if I say I have a memory of a particular thing, nobody else can contradict me, because nobody else has access to that particular bit of internal data. But what if one thinks that one remembers something and then is shown that it would not be possible, for example, that I remember the Second World War, only to find that I was born after it was over? I would have to admit that my memory was faulty, or perhaps that a war film had lodged such vivid images in my mind that I genuinely believed that I had lived through it. I remember the image clearly enough, and am not lying about it, but what I have forgotten is the origin of that image, the original experience (on film, in this case, rather than in reality).

Memory errors can sometimes be countered by the idea that the person imagined an event rather than remembered it. Again, there is no doubting the mental image, what is at doubt is the origin of that image.

Great feats of memory require sifting through the many facts and images that are habitually available to us, to more specific events: remembering a place leads to remembering a particular person who was seen there, which then leads on to remembering any suspicious actions that he or she may have made. The feature of such memory is that it is revealed bit by bit; something that was previously forgotten is now remembered because another memory has triggered it. Following serious crimes, an identically dressed person is sometimes sent to retrace the steps of the victim, hoping that it may trigger off a memory in a passer-by.

But just because we may have privileged access to our own memories, does not mean that we are infallible. Four people, giving accounts of the same dinner party, may all provide quite different versions of events. Our memories are selective, providing us with recall of those sense experiences which are deemed significant, and ignoring those that are not.

Memory also serves to develop the 'background' of our actions and thoughts (to use Heidegger's term). Faced with a choice in the present, my memory searches for similar experiences in the past, and the memory of them will influence the choice I now have to make. In this sense, memory is an ever-growing means of self-definition.

Cognitive science

Much of what we have been discussing in this chapter is related to the traditional mind/body problem, which developed out of the radical dualism of Descartes and the issues raised by it. By the latter part of the twentieth century, however, these problems (without necessarily being resolved) were set in a new and broader context which is generally known as cognitive science.

Cognitive science is an umbrella term for a number of disciplines which impinge upon ideas of the self or mind:

▶ *We have already considered the impact of computers on our understanding of mental process, and the development of Artificial Intelligence and neural networking.*
▶ *Neuroscience is now able to map out the functions of the brain, identifying areas that are associated with particular mental or sensory processes.*
▶ *Pharmacology is able to control behaviour by the use of drugs, bringing a whole new chemical element into our understanding of behaviour.*
▶ *There is an increased awareness of the influence of food additives and environment in influencing mental activity; how we feel may well reflect what we eat and drink.*

▶ *Clinical psychology looks at the way an individual's mind functions, taking into account both its conscious and unconscious workings.*

Clearly, there is no scope within this present book for examining all these disciplines. All we need to be aware of is the way in which science today is far more flexible in its approach to the mind than would have been the case a century or more ago.

Science needs data upon which to work. In the case of mental operations, one approach has been to examine the physical equivalent of the mental operation – generally in terms of brain function. Another has been to allow mental operations to provide their own physical data. For example, the behaviourist approach to gathering data was to set up experiments that involved actions and responses, and then measure those responses. Can this boxed rat learn – by rewarding it every time it does the right thing – to press a button in order to get food?

A key term here is **functionalism**. This approach sees mental operations as the way in which intelligent life sorts out how to react to the stimuli it receives. Let us take a crude example. If I put my hand on something hot, my body receives the sensation of burning. My mind then becomes aware of the pain, remembers that, if the hand is not removed from the heat, damage is likely to be done, and therefore decides that I should withdraw my hand. Muscles contract, the hand is withdrawn, and the pain subsides. We may not be able to tell exactly which neurones, firing in the brain, were responsible for each step in that operation. What we do know, however, is the mental functions that were performed. Mind is what mind does.

A functionalist reflection

I own several corkscrews. One is fairly straightforward; screw it into the cork, hold the bottle and pull upwards. Another, once

(Contd)

screwed in, uses a lever function and is pulled from the side. The most sophisticated has arms that grip round the side of the bottle, and so on.

These are all corkscrews, not by virtue of how they operate, or what they look like, but simply by virtue of their function. Whatever gets a cork out for you is your corkscrew!

Does it make any difference if an action is performed by a computer or by a human brain? We may not appreciate the difference in the mechanics by which each performs the operation, but the function is the same. There is a gap (usually referred to as the 'Leibniz' gap') in our knowledge, because we cannot see the point at which the physical and the mental interact. But does that matter, provided that we understand how the mental and physical function together?

Hence, a functionalist is able to produce what amounts to a map of the mind; a map that shows the different functions that the mind performs. What it cannot do, and argues that it is not necessary to do, is to wait to find out what each physical or electrical component does in the chain of events, before the significance of the mental function can be appreciated.

INTENTIONALITY

The idea of intentionality predates cognitive science, but is relevant to the broad range of issues that it considers. It originated in the work of the nineteenth-century psychologist Franz Brentano (1838–1917) and influenced the philosopher and psychologist William James (1842–1910). Intentionality, put simply, is the recognition that every perception and every experience is directed towards something. I do not just experience the shape of an apple before me, but I experience it as something to eat. In other words, mental functions shape and interpret what we experience – and we cannot have experience except as experience 'of' something.

Experience is about living in the world, relating to it, getting what we need from it, influencing it. It is not a separate and detached play of passing sense data. The mind takes an 'intentional stance' towards what it experiences.

Linking ideas

One may trace lines of thought from intentionality, through functionalism and (via William James) pragmatism, and even – as far as language is concerned – through the later developments of Wittgenstein's thought. We are not passive observers of the world. That is not why we have developed sense organs and brains. We have senses and minds in order to function, to find tools around us by which we can survive in a hostile environment or enjoy a comfortable one. Mind and thought is about relating and doing; when we observe, we do so with intentionality; our senses are judged by the function they perform in our life; and we take a pragmatic view of their operations. Wittgenstein said that, in order to understand it, one should look at how language is used, what function it plays in life. The same could be said of mind: intentionality, functionalism and pragmatism all suggest that we will only understand mind by considering what it does, not by standing back and trying to analyze what it is.

A 'personal' postscript

The mind/body issue, perhaps more than any other, illustrates the problem of the analytic and reductionist approach to complex entities. Frankenstein got it wrong! The analysis and reassembling of the components of a human being, whether it be a crude autopsy to hunt for the elusive 'soul', or the sophisticated attempt to reproduce the process of thinking with the aid of computers, is, I am convinced, unlikely to produce more than a caricature of a human person.

The experience of being a thinking, feeling and reflecting person is not susceptible to analysis, because it is not *part of* the world we experience. Wittgenstein was right in saying that the self was the limit of the world, rather than part of it.

Nor is the self a fixed entity. Hume could never see his mind except in the procession of thoughts that passed through it. From birth to death, there is constant change, and our thoughts of today shape what we will be tomorrow.

Insight

Throughout life, we leave our imprint on the world around us: words we speak, actions we perform, roles we assume. It is these that form our changing story, and define our character from moment to moment.

Even our process of reflection, the most private of activities, is dependent upon the outside world. It is extremely difficult to experience something with absolute simplicity or purity, for we immediately categorize it and understand it 'as' something. We cannot help doing that, because the way we think is shaped by our common language, common culture and the whole range of ideas and experiences that we share with others. As soon as we explain ourselves, we are engaged in a social activity; private language is meaningless.

Philosophers and scientists tend to think – that is their job, but it is also their problem! They search around in the mental jungle for ideas, concepts, theories and evidence. Hence they find it difficult to locate the self or explain its nature, for they launch into an analysis, using the product of mind in order to try to define the nature of mind itself. They focus in upon that which focuses in upon itself focusing in upon itself, and so on. In the spiral of analysis, the self becomes elusive and vanishes.

By contrast, those who *meditate*, who still the mind until it is gently focused on a single point, become aware of something very different. The self becomes empty, becomes nothing and everything at the same moment. There is no separate 'self' waiting to be discovered, only an ongoing process of thinking, experiencing and responding. Returning to the world of everyday experience, however, the 'self', as we conventionally understand it, continues its ever-changing patterns of thought, feeling and response. Without some idea of self we could not function nor relate to others; we may not know exactly what it is, but we know we cannot make sense of people and relationships without it.

Insight

The mind (as a separate, definable thing) is a convenient illusion, a shorthand term we use for the ongoing personal process of experiencing, thinking and responding that is our life as an intelligent being.

10 THINGS TO REMEMBER

1 *Materialism generally identifies the mind with (and restricts it to) activity in the brain.*

2 *Dualism sees the mind as non-physical, but has problems showing how it interacts with the body.*

3 *The idea of life beyond death depends on a dualist view of the mind.*

4 *Computers replicate brain function but not the experience of consciousness.*

5 *Knowledge of other minds is problematic for a dualist.*

6 *We define ourselves by ways in which we differ from others.*

7 *The experience of personal identity depends on memory.*

8 *Neuroscience shows how specific brain activity relates to elements of thought and experience.*

9 *'Functionalism' is the term for studying what the mind does, rather than what it is.*

10 *The self is a process, rather than a fixed entity.*

5

The philosophy of religion

In this chapter you will learn:
- **about religious experience and how it may be described**
- **about the arguments for the existence of God**
- **about miracles, the problem of evil and other key issues.**

In Western thought, the philosophy of religion is concerned with:

▶ *Religious language: what it means, what it does and whether it can be shown to be true or false.*
▶ *Metaphysical claims (e.g. that God exists): the nature of the arguments by which such claims are defended, and the basis upon which those claims can be shown to be true or false.*

In addition to these basic areas of study, there are many other questions concerning religious beliefs and practices which philosophy can examine:

▶ *What is faith? How does it relate to reason? Is it ever reasonable to be a religious 'fundamentalist'?*
▶ *What is 'religious experience' and what sort of knowledge can it yield?*
▶ *Is the universe such as to suggest that it has an intelligent creator and designer?*

- *Are miracles possible? If so, could we ever have sufficient evidence to prove that?*
- *Is belief in a loving God compatible with the existence of suffering and evil in the world?*
- *Can psychology explain the phenomenon of religion?*
- *Is life after death possible? If so, what difference does it make to our view of life?*

Faith, reason and belief

Is religious belief based on reason? If it were, it would be open to change, if the logic of an argument went against it. However, experience tells us that most religious people hold beliefs that, while they may be open to reasonable scrutiny, depend on a prior commitment or wish to believe, and therefore belief may persist in the face of reasonable criticism.

Within Christianity, there is a tradition – associated particularly with the Protestant Reformation and Calvin – that human nature is fallen and sinful, and that human reason is equally limited and unable to yield knowledge of God. Belief in God is therefore a matter of faith, and any logical arguments to back that belief are secondary.

Note

The last sentence speaks of belief 'in God' and not just belief 'that God exists'. That is a crucial difference, and we shall return to it on p. 171. Belief 'in' something implies an added element of commitment and valuation. One might, after all, believe 'that' God exists, but think that such belief is quite trivial and of no personal significance, which is not what believing 'in' something is about.

The quest for certainty is sometimes termed **foundationalism** – the attempt to find statements that are so obviously true that they cannot be challenged. We have already seen that Descartes came to his incontrovertible statement 'I think, therefore I am.' Some modern philosophers of religion, notably Alvin Plantinga, argue for a 'Reformed Epistemology'. That is, a theory of knowledge that, like the theologians of the Reformation, is based on basic beliefs that are self-evident to the person who holds them, even if they are not open to reasoned argument. An example of this would be the belief that the universe is designed by God, based on a sense of wonder and beauty. We shall look at the 'design argument' on p. 163; what is different here is that Plantinga thinks that such belief is not a logical conclusion to an argument, but is held *prior to* engaging with that argument.

A related idea is **fundamentalism**. Originally used as a term for those who wished to set aside the superficialities of religion and return to its fundamental principles, it is now more commonly used for those who take beliefs, as they are found in the Bible or the Qur'an for example, in a very literal and straightforward sense and apply them without allowing them to be challenged by reason. A basic problem with this is that the scriptures were written using particular language and in a particular context, and if statements are taken literally and out of context, the original intention of the writers may be lost. Of course, the fundamentalist would not accept this, believing that the words of scripture are given directly by God and are therefore not open to any form of literary or contextual analysis.

That something more than logic is needed if we are to understand the nature of religious statements was highlighted by the Danish philosopher Søren Kierkegaard (1813–55). He argued that a 'leap of faith' was necessary, and that it was not so much the content of a belief that made it religious, but the way in which it is believed – with subjectivity and inwardness.

PASCAL'S WAGER

Blaise Pascal (1623–62) put forward what must count as one of the saddest pieces of logic ever employed within the philosophy of religion. His *Pensées* were published posthumously in 1670. In them, Pascal battles (as did his contemporary Descartes) with the implications of **scepticism** – the systematic challenging of the ability to know anything for certain. Pascal was a committed Catholic and wanted to produce an argument that would both justify and commend belief.

To appreciate the force of his argument, you need to be aware that his view of human nature was rather bleak: without God's help, people were inherently selfish, and would only do what seemed to be in their own self-interest. He also believed that non-believers would see the life of religion as one which would limit their freedom, and would therefore appear to go against their self-interest. His famous 'wager' is an attempt to counter this view.

His starting point is that reason alone cannot prove that God exists; to believe or not believe therefore involves an element of choice. Which choice is in line with enlightened self-interest, and therefore likely to appeal to the non-believer? His argument runs like this:

▶ IF *I believe in God and he does indeed exist, I stand to gain eternal blessings and life with God after my death.*
▶ IF *I believe in God and he does not exist, all I lose is any inconvenience of having followed the religious life – inconvenience that he considers negligible.*

However:

- ▶ **IF** *I do not believe in God and he does indeed exist, I stand to suffer eternal punishment in hell, banished for ever from his presence.*
- ▶ **IF** *I do not believe in God and he does not exist, I have lost nothing, but gained some benefit from not having had to lead a religious life.*

On balance, therefore, Pascal claims that self-interest suggests that it is best to believe in God and follow the religious life!

Insight

Many philosophers would challenge the idea that one can choose to believe; one either does or one does not, anything else is pretence.

I called this the saddest piece of logic because it takes a rather grim view of God (as one who will punish or reward according to a person's belief), and a less-than-attractive view of the religious life (regarding it as a mild inconvenience, rather than something of value and enjoyable in itself). Fear of hell may drive people to believe; but that is hardly wholehearted belief in God.

Comment

Pascal saw people as caught between dogmatism and doubt, and hoped that he had found a way to overcome the latter without imposing the former. My personal view is that he ended up with the worst of both worlds – self-deception motivated by self-interest!

For the rest of this chapter we shall be looking at reasoned argument concerning religious ideas. However, both in terms of the religious experience and religious language, we shall need to recognize that faith and the religious beliefs associated with it are often rather more complex than the intellectual assent to propositions.

Religious language

If you describe a religious event or organization, the language you use need not be especially religious. Consider the following:

The Pope is the Bishop of Rome.
The Jewish religion forbids the eating of pork.

The first of these is true by definition, since 'Pope' is a title used for the Bishop of Rome. The second can be shown to be true by looking at the Jewish scriptures. (It would not be made invalid by evidence that a non-practising Jew had been seen eating a bacon sandwich, for the moral and religious rules remain true, even if they are broken.)

Provided that the terms are understood, such descriptive language presents few problems.

Religious people themselves use language in a variety of ways. They may pray, give thanks, hold moral discussions and – most importantly – make statements about what they believe. The problem is that these belief statements sometimes make claims about things that go beyond what can be known of the ordinary world that we can experience and examine scientifically. We have already seen that some philosophers want to dismiss all metaphysics as meaningless, and along with it they would therefore discard most statements of religious belief.

But here's the problem. Religious statements are not (or should not be taken as) bad science, so, if we are to take religion seriously, it should not be equated with superstition. Hence, in order to understand religious beliefs, we need to examine the character of religious language and the function that it performs.

One way of expressing a distinctive flavour of religious language is to highlight the difference between 'how?' questions and 'why?' questions. Science answers 'how?' questions by explaining how individual parts of the world relate to one another. But religion asks 'why?'; not 'how does the world work?' but 'why is there a world at all?'

A 'why?' question asks about meaning and purpose. It cannot be answered in terms of empirical facts alone. This is illustrated by a story by John Wisdom (1904–93), a professor of philosophy at Cambridge from 1952 to 1968, and also at Virginia and Oregon.

Two explorers come across a clearing in the jungle. It contains a mixture of weeds and flowers. One claims that it is a garden and that there must be a gardener who comes to tend it; the other disagrees. They sit and wait, but no gardener appears, they set up various means of detecting him, but still nothing.

One explorer continues to deny that there is a gardener. The other still claims that there is a gardener, but one who is invisible and undetectable. But – and this is the central point of the argument – how do you distinguish an undetectable gardener whose activity is open to question, from an imaginary gardener or no gardener at all?

Insight

Of course, there is another relevant question: What difference does it make to you if you choose to see the clearing as a garden? In other words, how might your view of life be changed by seeing the world as controlled by a loving God (whether or not such a God exists)?

As originally presented, this story was used to show that a good idea could die the death of a thousand qualifications. In other words, when all obvious qualities that the gardener might have are eliminated, nothing of any significance remains. But the story also illustrates the idea of a **blik** – a particular 'view' of things. In the story, the same evidence is available to the two explorers, but they choose to interpret it differently. We have our own particular blik and interpret everything in the light of it. It can be argued that religious belief is just one such blik; one way of organizing our experience of the world. As such it is no more or less true than anyone else's blik, and every argument ends with someone saying: 'Well, if that's the way you want to see it …'

Insight

That's fine, until you want to argue that your blik is right and another person's is wrong. Then – with no factual evidence to decide between them – you have a problem.

THE PERSONAL ASPECTS OF LANGUAGE

In *Religious Language* (1957), the British theologian I.T. Ramsey pointed out that there were elements of both discernment and commitment in religious statements. They were not simply detached, speculative comments. Although they include facts, they are far more complex than that. He makes the essential point that the word 'God' is used to describe a reality about which the believer feels strongly and wishes to communicate.

We should therefore distinguish between the philosopher who examines arguments for the existence of God in an objective and disinterested way, and the religious believer who uses 'God' to express a sense of direction, purpose and meaning which comes through religious and moral experience.

Arguments for the existence of God can be seen as:

▶ *discussions about something which may or may not exist*
▶ *indications of what it is a religious believer is talking about when he or she speaks of 'God'.*

Ramsey uses the terms *models* and *qualifiers* to explain the way in which religious language differs from ordinary empirical language. A 'model' is like an analogy – an image that helps a person to articulate that which is rather different from anything else. For example, if God is called a 'designer', it does not imply that the religious believer has some personal knowledge of a process of design carried out by God, simply that the image of someone who designs is close to his or her experience of God. Contrariwise, having offered the 'model', it is then important for the religious believer to offer a 'qualifier' – God is an 'infinite' this or a 'perfect' that – the model is therefore qualified, so that it is not mistakenly taken in a literal way.

In other words

▶ Religious language is sometimes simply descriptive (e.g. of religious activities).
▶ When it expresses beliefs it may be:
  ▷ a particular way of looking at the world (a 'blik')
  ▷ based on personal commitment (not simply a matter of speculation).
▶ Since it is not simply a statement of fact, to be checked against evidence, such religious language is 'meaningless' from the point of view of logical positivism (see p. 71)

Religious experience

If nobody had religious experiences, there would be no basis for the idea of a 'god', nor would there have been any reason for religions to have developed. So what is it that makes an experience religious?

The nineteenth-century religious writer and philosopher Schleiermacher described religious awareness in terms of a 'feeling of dependence' and of seeing finite things in and through the infinite. This was rather like mystical experience – a sudden awareness of a wider dimension, which throws new light on the ordinary world around us. What Schleiermacher was trying to express was that religion was not a matter of dogma or logic, but was based on a direct experience of oneself as being small and limited, against the background of the eternal. It was also an identification of the self with the whole: a sense of belonging to the whole world. Feelings like that are destroyed by logic; they are not the result of reasoning but of intuition.

Rudolph Otto, in *The Idea of the Holy* (1917), argued that the religious experience was essentially about the *mysterium tremendum*, something totally other, unknowable; something that is awesome in its dimensions and power; something which is also attractive and fascinating. He outlined a whole range of feelings ('creeping flesh'; the fear of ghosts; the sense of something that is uncanny, weird or eerie) to illustrate that this encounter is with something that is quite other than the self; threatening, but at the same time attractive and of supreme value.

However unusual and special such an encounter with the 'holy' might be, it can only be described by using words that have a rational, everyday meaning – language which, if taken literally, does not do justice to the special quality of the experience. Many words seemed to describe the feelings and express ideas that were close to this experience of the 'holy' (goodness, wonder, purity, etc.) but none of them was actually about the holy itself. This set of words that attempts to describe the holy are (to use Otto's term) its **schema**. The process of finding words by means of which to convey the implications of the holy is **schematization**. Religious language is just such a schema, whereas the 'holy' itself is an a priori category; in other words, the holy cannot be completely described or defined in terms of the particular experiences through which we encounter it. It is conveyed by means of these terms but is always elusively beyond them and cannot be contained by them.

Insight

The holy cannot be fully explained, only experienced, and its 'religious' interpretation is optional.

Examples

1 *You feel overwhelmed at the sight of a range of snow-capped mountains looming above you. Their sheer size and bulk, contrasting with your own minuscule body, give you a 'tingle', a sense of wonder, a sense that, faced with this scene of absolute and almost terrifying beauty, your life cannot ever be quite the same again. You then try to describe the experience to a cynical friend. You cast around for suitable words. You cannot convey that 'tingle', unless, as a result of your description, he or she too can start to sense 'the holy'.*

2 *You watch a horror movie on television. You know that the parts are played by actors, that there is artificially constructed scenery. Yet, for all that, you feel the hairs bristle on the back of your neck, you may even feel a shudder, your heart may beat faster. Because of what you are seeing on the screen, and in spite of all the rational explanations, you are sensing something that is 'beyond' that immediate experience.*

Otto's idea of schematization is important for understanding the nature of the philosophy of religion, and suggests that it is always a secondary activity. Philosophy examines the rational concept by means of which the prime experience is schematized. The proofs of the existence of God are, following this way of thinking, not proofs of the actual existence of a being which is known and defined as 'God', but are rational ways of expressing the intuition about 'God' that comes as a result of religious experience.

Thus, the idea of God as the designer of the universe is not open to logical proof but is a schema, i.e. think what it would be like if this whole world had been designed for a particular purpose, with everything working together as it should: that (according to this schema) is something akin to what it means to believe in God.

Notice that this also applies to language. Following the idea of models and qualifiers, the model is the result of the schema (God is like this or that) but that it is then qualified to show that it is not simply a literal description (e.g. the all-perfect ... or the absolute ...).

We can see, therefore, that the pattern of religious language and the analysis of religious experience point in the same direction – that of an experience and a level of reality which transcends, but springs out of the literal, the empirical or the rational. All of these things can suggest the object of religious devotion, but none can define or describe it literally.

TRANSCENDENCE

One way of describing religious experience is in terms of 'transcendence' – that an experience goes beyond ordinary perception to give some sense of what is 'beyond' or 'absolute' even if that cannot be described in itself. Clearly, great works of art, or a beautiful landscape, or simply the awesome power of nature (whether benign or threatening) can give rise to a sense of transcendence. But there is a fundamental question with which the philosophy of religion needs to deal. Just because an experience is transcendent – just because it gives that sense of awe, or wonder, or a new view of oneself – does that imply that there has to be a transcendent *object* of which we become aware? If not, it might be possible to have the same transcendent experience that inspires the believer, but to have it entirely within a secular context. This is explored in a chapter entitled 'Transcendence without God' by Anthony Simon Laden in *Philosophers without Gods* (ed Louise Anthony, 2007).

Does God exist?

We shall look at some traditional arguments for the existence of God, and the problems they raise. But first we need to have some working idea of what is meant by the word 'God'.

Since we are concerned with Western philosophy, the relevant concepts have come from the Western theistic religions – Judaism,

Christianity and Islam. For these, God may be said to be a supreme being, infinite, spiritual and personal, creator of the world. He is generally described as all-powerful (having created the world out of nothing, he can do anything he wishes) and all-loving (in a personal caring relationship with individual believers). Although pictured in human form, he is believed to be beyond literal description (and is thus not strictly male, although 'he' is generally depicted as such).

Some terms

- Belief in the existence of such a god is **theism**.
- The conviction that no such being exists is **atheism**.
- The view that there is no conclusive evidence to decide whether God exists or not is **agnosticism**.
- An identification of God with the physical universe is **pantheism**.
- The belief that God is within everything and everything within God (but God and the physical universe are not simply identified) is **panentheism**. (Although this term is used by some theologians, most interpretations of theism include the idea of everything being 'within' God; indeed, if he is infinite, there is nothing which is external to him.)
- The idea of an external designer God who created the world, but is not immanent within it, is **deism**.

There is a problem with taking the idea of the existence of God too literally. Thomas Aquinas (whose arguments we shall be examining) described God as being *supra ordinem omnium entium* – beyond the order of all beings. In other words, God is not a being who might or might not exist somewhere; indeed, he is not *a* being at all. So we should not be tempted (as are some evangelical atheists) to assume a crude idea of God and then show that there is no evidence for his existence. On those terms, Aquinas and most serious religious thinkers down through the centuries would certainly have qualified as atheists. The meaning of God is far more subtle than that.

In his *Critique of Pure Reason* (section A, 590–91), Kant argued that there could be only three types of argument for the existence of God:

1 *based on reason alone*
2 *based on the general fact of the existence of the world*
3 *based on particular features of the world.*

They are called the **ontological**, **cosmological** and **teleological** arguments. He offered a critique of all three, and introduced a fourth one: the moral argument.

Insight

Before getting into these arguments, one thing needs to be absolutely clear. God does not and cannot exist in the sense that anything else can be said to exist. God is neither part of the universe nor somehow 'outside' the universe. The question is: what (if anything) is God if he does not exist in that sense?

THE ONTOLOGICAL ARGUMENT

The ontological argument for the existence of God is not based on observation of the world, or on any form of external evidence, but simply on a particular definition of the meaning of 'God'. In other words, it offers a definition of God that implies that he must exist.

This argument is of particular interest to philosophers because it raises questions about language and metaphysics which apply to issues other than religious belief.

The argument was set out by Anselm (1033–1109), Archbishop of Canterbury, in the opening chapters of his *Proslogion*. He makes it clear that he is not putting forward this argument in order to be able to believe in God, but that his belief leads him to understand God's existence in this particular way, a way which leads him to the conclusion that God must exist.

Religious experience leads him to speak of God as *aliquid quo nihil maius cogitari possit* – that which nothing greater can be thought. This does not mean something that just happens to be physically bigger, or better, than anything else – it is the idea of 'perfection', or 'the absolute', the most real thing (*ens reallissimum*).

In the second chapter of *Proslogion*, the argument is presented in this way:

> *Now we believe that thou art a being than which none greater can be thought. Or can it be that there is no such being, since 'the fool hath said in his heart, "There is no God"'? [Psalm 14:1; 53:1] But when this same fool hears what I am saying – 'A being than which none greater can be thought' – he understands what he hears, and what he understands is in his understanding, even if he does not understand that it exists. For it is one thing for an object to be in the understanding, and another thing to understand that it exists ... But clearly that than which a greater cannot be thought cannot exist in the understanding alone. For if it is actually in the understanding alone, it can be thought of as existing also in reality, and this is greater. Therefore, if that than which a greater cannot be thought is in the understanding alone, this same thing than which a greater cannot be thought is that than which a greater can be thought. But obviously this is impossible. Without doubt, therefore, there exists, both in the understanding and in reality, something than which a greater cannot be thought.*

(translation: as in *The Existence of God*, John Hick, Macmillan, 1964)

In other words

Something is greater if it exists than if it doesn't. If God is the greatest thing imaginable, he must exist. I may paint an imaginary masterpiece, but that only means I imagine that I paint a masterpiece. In fact, since it does not exist, it is no better than my actually existing 'inferior' paintings. A real masterpiece must always be better than an imaginary one!

One of the clearest criticisms of this argument was made by Kant (in his *Critique of Pure Reason*) in response to Descartes, who had maintained, in his version of the argument, that it was impossible to have a triangle without its having three sides and angles, and in the same way it was impossible to have God without having necessary existence. Kant's argument may be set out like this:

- ▶ **If** *you have a triangle*
- ▶ **Then** *it must have three angles (i.e. to have a triangle without three angles is a contradiction)*
- ▶ **But** *if you do not have the triangle, you do not have its three angles or sides either.*

In the same way, Kant argued:

- ▶ **If** *you accept God, it is therefore logical to accept his necessary existence*
- ▶ **But** *you do not have to accept God.*

To appreciate the force of Kant's argument, it is important to remember that he divided all statements into two categories – analytic and synthetic (see Introduction):

- ▶ **Analytic statements** *are true by definition.*
- ▶ **Synthetic statements** *can only be proved true or false with reference to experience.*

For Kant, statements about existence are synthetic; definitions are analytic. Therefore, the angles and sides of a triangle are necessary because they are part of the definition of a triangle. But that says nothing about the actual existence of a triangle – necessity (for Kant) is not a feature of the world, but only of logic and definition.

Kant gives another way of expressing the same idea. He says that *existence is not a predicate*. In other words, if you describe something completely, you add nothing to that description by then saying 'and it has existence'. Existence is not an extra quality, it is just a way of saying that there is the thing itself, with all the qualities already given.

Norman Malcolm (in *Philosophical Review*, January 1960) pointed out that Kant's criticism failed in an important respect. You can either have a triangle or not, but (on Anselm's definition) you simply cannot have no God, so the two situations are not exactly parallel.

For Anselm, then, 'God' is a unique concept. This was something that he had to clarify early on, in the light of criticism from Gaunilo, a fellow monk, who raised the idea of the perfect island, claiming that, if Anselm's argument were true, then the perfect island would also have to exist. Anselm rejected this. An island is a limited thing, and you can always imagine better and better islands. But he holds that 'a being than which a greater cannot be thought' is unique. If it could be thought of as non-existent, it could also be thought of as having a beginning and an end, but then it would not be the greatest that can be thought.

This is another version of the argument that he had already introduced in Chapter 3 of the *Proslogion*:

> **Something which cannot be thought of as not existing ... is greater than that which can be thought of as not existing. Thus, if that than which a greater cannot be thought can be thought of as not existing, this very thing than which a greater cannot be thought is not that than which a greater cannot be thought. But this is contradictory. So, then, there truly is a being than which a greater cannot be thought – so truly that it cannot even be thought of as not existing.**

In other words, Anselm claims that necessary existence is implied by the idea of God. But he goes one step further. In Chapter 4 of *Proslogion*, he asks how the fool can still claim that God does not exist, and concludes:

> **For we think of a thing, in one sense, when we think of the word that signifies it, and in another sense, when we understand**

*the very thing itself. Thus in the first sense God can be
thought of as non-existent, but in the second sense this is quite
impossible. For no one who understands what God is can think
that God does not exist ... For God is that than which a greater
cannot be thought, and whoever understands this rightly must
understand that he exists in a way that he cannot be non-existent
even in thought.*

So what did Anselm mean by speaking of God as 'that than which
none greater can be thought'?

In another work, *Monologion*, he spoke of degrees of goodness
and perfection in the world, and that there must be something that
constitutes perfect goodness, which he calls 'God', which causes
goodness in all else. This idea of the degrees of perfection was
not new. Aristotle had used this idea in *De Philosophia*, and it is
also closely related to Plato's idea of forms. Anselm's idea of God
comes close to Plato's 'Form of the Good'.

There are several philosophical points to be explored here (which
is why this argument has been set out at greater length than others
in this book).

A silly example

You have a classroom full of pupils, and are told that it is
'Class 1A'. Where is the 'class'?

▶ *You ask each of the pupils in turn, but each gives only his or her name.*
▶ *You conclude that 'Class 1A' does not exist.*

This is what is called a **category mistake**. Class 1A is real, and comprises
the pupils – but there does not exist anything that is 'Class 1A', which is
not also something else, namely a particular pupil (see also p. 105 for the
category mistake expounded in Ryle's *The Concept of Mind*).

This suggests that different categories of things can be equally real,
but cannot be set alongside one another. Similar problems arise when

we try to set an ideal alongside the particular examples of which it is the ideal. So, to continue our example, you may have in your mind the idea of 'the perfect pupil'. However good a particular pupil might be, you could always imagine one that was just a little better. But 'the perfect pupil' exists in a different category from individual pupils and therefore does not appear in the class. But if you had no idea of what a perfect pupil might be like, there would be no way of judging between one pupil and another. 'The perfect pupil' can be seen as a necessary concept in order to make any sense of putting the pupils in some sort of rank order.

Similarly, for Anselm, if there were no idea of perfection, there would be no criterion for judging between one thing and another. Even if our judgements are entirely subjective, we need to have some concept of perfection in order to make them.

Some might see putting pupils in order of merit as politically incorrect, arguing that 'the perfect pupil' is a dangerous idea, since all are equally good, each in his or her own way! But if you remove ideals, how do you assess anything? Perhaps 'that than which a greater cannot be thought' is an absolute which enables us to compare and give value to things.

The class of pupils can illustrate a second point: a comparative or superlative term is not a quality, but simply shows a relationship.

To say that a pupil is the tallest in the class is not a fixed quality that a particular pupil has, but is simply a way of comparing sizes. You do not eliminate the idea of 'the tallest pupil' by amputation – the amputee might be demoted, but immediately there would be some other pupil who qualified as 'the tallest'. What is more, that pupil would not have grown at all since he or she was second tallest! There is no additional height, just a new relationship. So:

▶ *'the perfect ... ' is in a different category from individual things*
▶ *'the perfect ... ' is not simply the top of a series of individual things.*

This is like the idea of Plato's 'cave', which we considered in
Chapter 1. What was taken for reality by those in the cave was,
in fact, only a set of shadows, cast because of light coming from
behind them. The wise man, although not able to see the source
of the light directly, yet knows that it is there beyond the entrance
to the cave – the 'Form of the Good'. Something of the same can
be said of this argument. The 'greatest thing' for Anselm is an
intuition, necessitated by seeing lesser values as merely shadows or
copies of something greater.

This approach to the ontological argument was taken by Iris
Murdoch, the well-known novelist and Oxford philosopher, in
her book *Metaphysics as a Guide to Morals* (1992). She held that
an argument about necessary existence can only be taken in the
context of this Platonic view of degrees of reality. She pointed out
that what the proof offers is more than a simple logical argument,
for it points to a spiritual reality that transcends any limited idea of
God. It is also something that goes beyond individual religions:

*An ultimate religious 'belief' must be that even if all 'religions'
were to blow away like mist, the necessity of virtue and the
reality of the good would remain. This is what the Ontological
Proof tries to 'prove' in terms of a unique formulation.*

p. 427

And this, she claimed, is a necessary part of our understanding of life:

*What is perfect must exist, that is, what we think of as
goodness and perfection, the 'object' of our best thoughts,
must be something real, indeed especially and most real, not as
contingent accidental reality but as something fundamental,
essential and necessary. What is experienced as most real in*

our lives is connected with a value which points further on.
Our consciousness of failure is a source of knowledge. We are
constantly in process of recognizing the falseness of our 'goods',
and the unimportance of what we deem important. Great art
teaches a sense of reality, so does ordinary living and loving.

p. 430

In other words

▶ *If we simply think of the ontological argument in terms of 'existence is a predicate' then Kant was probably right, and Anselm wrong – for to say that something 'exists' is quite different from anything else that can be said about it.*

▶ *Anselm's argument also shows that some idea of 'the greatest that can be thought' is a necessary part of the way we think, since, every time we ascribe value to something, we do so on the basis of an intuition of that which has supreme value.*

▶ *At its heart, the ontological argument is about how we relate the ordinary conditioned and limited things we experience to the idea of the perfect, the absolute and the unconditioned – and that is a key question for philosophy.*

THE COSMOLOGICAL ARGUMENTS

Thomas Aquinas (1225–74) was probably the most important philosopher of the mediaeval period, and has certainly been the most influential in terms of the philosophy of religion. He sought to reconcile the Christian faith with the philosophy of Aristotle, which in the thirteenth century had been 'rediscovered' and was being taught in the secular universities of Europe.

Aquinas presented five ways in which he believed the existence of God could be shown. They are:

1 *The argument from an unmoved mover.*
2 *The argument from an uncaused cause.*
3 *The argument from possibility and necessity.*

4 *The argument from degrees of quality.*
5 *The argument from design.*

The fourth of these has already been considered, for a version of it came in Anselm's *Monologion*. The last will be examined in the next section. For now, therefore, we need to look at the first three, which are generally termed 'cosmological arguments'.

These arguments are based on the observation of the world, and originate in the thinking of Aristotle, whom Aquinas regarded as *the* philosopher. The first may be presented like this:

- ▶ *Everything that moves is moved by something.*
- ▶ *That mover is in turn moved by something else again.*
- ▶ **But** *this chain of movers cannot be infinite, or movement would not have started in the first place.*
- ▶ **Therefore,** *there must be an unmoved mover, causing movement in everything, without itself actually being moved.*
- ▶ *This unmoved mover is what people understand by 'God'.*

The second argument has the same structure:

- ▶ *Everything has a cause.*
- ▶ *Every cause itself has a cause.*
- ▶ **But** *you cannot have an infinite number of causes.*
- ▶ **Therefore,** *there must be an uncaused cause, which causes everything to happen without itself being caused by anything else.*
- ▶ *Such an uncaused cause is what people understand by 'God'.*

The third argument follows from the first two:

- ▶ *Individual things come into existence and later cease to exist.*
- ▶ **Therefore,** *at one time none of them was in existence.*
- ▶ **But** *something comes into existence only as a result of something else that already exists.*
- ▶ **Therefore,** *there must be a being whose existence is necessary – 'God'.*

One possible objection to these arguments is to say that you might indeed have an infinite number of causes or movers. Instead of stretching back into the past in a straight line, the series of causes could be circular, or looped in a figure of eight, so that you never get to a first cause, and everything is quite adequately explained by its immediate causes. This image of circularity does not really help us to understand the force of Aquinas' argument, for it is unlikely that he was thinking of a series of causes (or movers) stretching into the past. His argument actually suggests a hierarchy of causes here and now. Every individual thing has its cause: Why should the whole world not have a cause beyond itself? You could therefore argue that within a circular series of causes, each individual cause would be caused by its neighbour, but what then is the cause of the whole circle of causes? If the world itself had such a cause, that cause too would require a cause, for it would have become part of the known world. The philosopher Kant argued that causality is one of the ways in which our minds sort out the world – we impose causality upon our experience. If Kant is right, then an uncaused cause is a mental impossibility.

A rather different objection came from Hume. He based all knowledge on the observation of the world. Something is said to be a cause because it is seen to occur just before the thing that is called its effect. That depends on the observation of cause and effect as two separate things. *But*, in the case of the world as a whole, you have a unique effect, and therefore cannot observe its cause. You cannot get 'outside' the world to see both the world and its cause, and thus establish the relationship between them. If, with Hume, you consider sense impressions as the basis of all knowledge, then the cosmological proofs cannot be accepted as giving proof of the existence of a God outside the world of observation.

Perhaps this gives a clue to a different way of approaching these cosmological arguments. If we follow them in a literal and logical way, they do not prove that there is an uncaused cause or unmoved mover. But they show how a religious person may use the idea of movement or cause to point to the way in which he or she sees God – as a being that in some way stands behind yet causes or moves everything; something beyond and yet involved with everything.

Note

Although Aquinas' is the best-known version of the cosmological argument, it was not the first. An argument from the existence of the universe to its first cause, known as the *Kalam Argument*, was put forward by the Muslim scholars al-Kindi (ninth century) and al-Ghazali (1058–1111).

THE ARGUMENT FROM DESIGN

Although Aquinas has a form of this argument, the clearest example of it is that of William Paley (1743–1805). He argued that, if he were to find a watch lying on the ground, he would assume that it was the product of a designer, for, unlike a stone, he would see at once that it was made up of many different parts worked together in order to produce movement, and that, if any one part were ordered differently, the whole thing would not work. In the same way he argued that the world is like a machine, each part of it designed so that it takes its place within the whole. If the world is so designed, it must have a designer whose purpose is expressed through it.

Insight

Purpose is acting with a particular intention. Aristotle saw purpose in everything – the striving to fulfil its proper nature. Descartes saw purpose as limited to intelligent human beings, with the material universe following impersonal laws of nature. Both Aquinas and Kant saw elements of purpose and design within the universe, suggesting that nature itself was capable of revealing to us some overall explanation in terms of design.

This argument, reflecting the sense of wonder at nature, was most seriously challenged by the theory of evolution. Darwin's 'natural selection' provided an alternative explanation for design, and one that did not require the aid of any external designer. At once, it became possible to see the world not as a machine, but as a process of struggle and death in which those best adapted to their environment were able to breed and pass their genes on to the next generation, thus influencing the very gradual development of the species. Adaptation in order to survive became the key to the development of the most elaborate forms, which previously would have been described as an almost miraculous work of a designer God.

Actually, the challenge of natural selection was anticipated in the work of Hume, who set out a criticism of the design argument some 23 years before Paley published his version of it. He argued that, in a finite world and given infinite time, any combination of things can occur. Those combinations that work together harmoniously can continue and thrive, those that do not will fail. Therefore, when we come to observe the world as it is now, we are observing only those that *do* work, for those that don't are no longer there to be observed. The implication of this is that we observe a world populated by survivors, but that does not mean that it is so ordered by an external designer; it is merely the result of a long period of time and endless failures.

Insight

Notice that the most this argument can claim is that the world shows features of design. Whether that is a natural phenomenon, or one caused by some external agency is a secondary matter. And even if you accept the latter possibility, you then have to ask if such an external 'deist' idea of God is adequate for religion. On the other hand, the sense of awe at the 'design' of the world is a source of 'religious' experience.

THE MORAL ARGUMENT

Kant believed that the traditional arguments could never prove the existence of God, and therefore hoped to go beyond them by presenting an understanding of God based on faith rather than reason. He did this by examining the idea of moral experience, and in particular the relationship between virtue and happiness. In an ideal world they should follow one another – that, if there is a 'highest good' to which a person may aspire morally, doing what is right (virtue) should ultimately lead to happiness. But clearly, there is no evidence that virtue automatically leads to happiness. Why then should anyone be moral?

Kant started from the fact that people do have a sense of moral obligation: a feeling that something is right and must be done, no matter what the consequences. He called this sense of moral obligation the **categorical imperative,** to distinguish it from a 'hypothetical imperative' (which says: 'If you want to achieve this, then you must do that').

In *The Critique of Practical Reason,* Kant explores the presuppositions of the categorical imperative. What do I actually believe about life if I respond to the absolute moral demand? (Not what must I rationally accept before I agree with a moral proposal, but what do I actually feel to be true, rationally or otherwise, in the moment when I respond to the moral imperative?) He argued that three things – God, freedom and immortality – were **postulates** of the practical reason. In other words, that the experience of morality implied that you were free to act (even if someone observing you claimed that you were not), that you would eventually achieve the result you wanted (even if you would not do so in this life, as when someone sacrificed his or her own life), and that, for any of this to be possible, there had to be some overall ordering principle, which might be called 'God'.

Insight

In effect, Kant turned the old arguments on their head. If all we know are the phenomena of our experience, speculative metaphysics cannot give us evidence that God exists. On the other hand, our minds need the idea of God in order to make sense of our moral experience.

The way in which Kant saw the world obliged him to go beyond the traditional arguments for the existence of God. After all, if the idea of causality is imposed on external reality by our own minds, how can it become the basis for a proof for the existence of God? We can only know things as they appear to us, not as they are in themselves:

▶ **If** *we contribute space, time and causality to our understanding of the world*
▶ **Then** *to argue from these to something outside the world is impossible*
▶ *God, freedom and immortality are therefore not* in *the world that we experience, but have to do with* the way in which *we experience the world*
▶ *In other words,* God is a 'regulative' concept (part of our way of understanding) not a 'constitutive' concept (one of the things out there to be discovered).

In other words

▶ *The cosmological and design arguments suggest that there are features of the world which lead the mind to that which goes beyond experience: What is the cause of everything? Why is the world as it is?*
▶ *The moral argument suggests that we all have an intuition of God (along with freedom and immortality) every time we experience a sense of absolute moral obligation.*
▶ *Even if these arguments are not conclusive, they do indicate the sort of thing a religious person is thinking about when he or she uses the word 'God'.*

THE MEANING OF 'GOD'

In considering all the arguments about the existence of God, it might be worth keeping the whole exercise in perspective by reminding ourselves that the sort of 'god' whose existence might or might not be the case is not what many people term 'God' anyway. Of course, this was the basis of the ontological argument, but it is relevant to consider it in the context of the modern American theologian, Paul Tillich. In his *Systematic Theology* (Vol. I, p. 262), he says:

> **The question of the existence of God can be neither asked nor answered. If asked, it is a question about that which by its very nature is above existence, and therefore the answer – whether negative or affirmative – implicitly denies the nature of God. It is as atheistic to affirm the existence of God as to deny it. God is being itself, not a being.**

This reinforces what has been implied throughout the ontological and cosmological arguments: that what is being claimed is not the existence of one entity alongside others, but a fundamental way of regarding the whole universe. It is about the structures of 'being itself' (to use Tillich's term) not the possible existence of a being.

The arguments explored so far in this chapter presuppose a generally accepted idea of what 'God' means. Earlier we looked at a basic idea of 'God', but let us now take it a little further.

Insight

The problem is that, in popular devotion and a literal reading of scriptures, God appears not just as a separate entity, external to the world and the individual, but as one that has human characteristics – a being who might or might not exist. For many people, it is difficult to switch from this image to an understanding of 'God' as a word used to describe reality itself as we experience it.

The most stringent test of the meaning of a statement is that given by logical positivism (see p. 71). Under this set of rules, a statement has a meaning if it pictures something that can be verified by sense experience. If no evidence is relevant to its truth, a statement is meaningless.

When we turn to language about God, such verification is not possible. Most definitions of 'God' are such as to preclude any explanation in terms of what can be directly experienced. This would lead a strict logical positivist to say that statements about God are meaningless.

The broader perspective – as illustrated by Wittgenstein's view of language as a 'form of life' (see p. 79) – seeks to understand language in terms of its function. Religious language finds its meaning in terms of what it does. So, for example, 'God' (for a religious believer) is not simply the name of some external object, about whose existence there could be a debate. Such a 'god' would not be adequate religiously, and to prove his existence would not significantly contribute to religious debate.

In other words

▶ **If** *you prove that God 'exists' in a way that would satisfy a logical positivist (i.e. testable by empirical evidence)*
▶ **Then** *'God' becomes part of the world*
▶ **So** *he is no longer 'God'.*

So you might call yourself a theist, but a religious person would be more likely to say that your belief was no more than idolatry. It is also worth remembering that idolatry is not simply a matter of worshipping a physical image. A person may claim to believe in 'God' when in fact he or she actually believes in a particular idea of God, not the source of reality itself. That is a very common form of idolatry. Indeed, many religious wars come about when conflicting ideas are elevated to divine status, and people feel the need to defend them as though they were defending 'God' himself, which – in the broader perspective – does seem a particularly silly thing to try to do!

This is an important thing to keep in mind, because it might be possible to see the arguments for the existence of God as either succeeding or failing to give definitive proof of the objective existence of an entity to which the name 'God' can be given.

This is simplistic, and is only part of the issue. More important is to ask what part such arguments play in the religious perception of the believer.

Generally speaking, the arguments show the sort of place the idea of God has in terms of the perception of the world – to say that he is uncaused cause, or the designer of the world, is to locate God in the realm of overall meaning and purpose. Such convictions are a 'blik' that is unlikely to be changed (but could be strengthened) by the traditional arguments.

'BEING ITSELF' AND 'ULTIMATE CONCERN'

Let us return for a moment to the theologian Paul Tillich, whose idea of 'being itself' was mentioned earlier. Tillich insisted that religious ideas could only be expressed by way of symbols. A symbol is something that conveys the power and meaning of the thing it symbolizes, in contrast to a sign, which is merely conventional. He argued that the religious experience has two elements: the material basis (the actual thing seen, which could be analyzed by science) and the sense of ultimate value and power that it conveys, which makes it 'religious'.

For him there were two essential features to the God that appears through religious experience or a religious symbol:

1 *That God is 'being itself' rather than a being. In other words, an experience of God is not an experience of something that just happens to be there, an object among others, but is an experience of life itself, of being itself, an experience which then gives meaning to everything else.*
2 *That God is 'ultimate concern'. This implied that 'God' could not be thought of in a detached and impartial way. For the religious believer, God demands total attention and commitment, covering all partial concerns, all other aspects of life. This sense of God as the most important thing in life is seen in the nature of religious experience.*

▶ *You cannot describe God literally (all language must be symbolic).*
▶ *God is not a being among others, he is 'being itself'.*
▶ *God is the name for what the religious person encounters in a way that is personal and demanding, not casual or detached.*

Language about 'God' need not be religious. You can have a statement about the structure of the universe which includes the idea of God, but that does not make it religious, only cosmological. In order for something to be religious, it has to use religious language in a way that reflects religious experience and/or religious practice. There are two other distinctive features of religious language:

1 *Martin Buber, the Jewish philosopher (1876–1965), introduced the important distinction between 'I–Thou' and 'I–It' language. 'I–Thou' language is personal, while 'I–It' is impersonal. Religious language is about an I addressing a Thou, not speculating about an It.*

2 *The distinction is often made between* 'believing that' *and* 'believing in'. *You believe* **that** *something is the case if you rationally hold it to be so. At the same time, it may be of no personal interest to you at all. You believe* **in** *something if you are personally committed to it. The essential limitation of the arguments for the existence of God is that they attempt to show that it is reasonable to believe that God exists, rather than to show why people believe in God.*

Insight

Take Wittgenstein's advice – don't just ask about a word's meaning, look at how it is used.

To sum up ...

We have looked at the nature of religious language and religious experience, the traditional arguments for the existence of God, and have therefore started to examine what the word 'God' can mean. The essential points are:

▶ *the inadequacy of literal, empirically based language to express 'God'*
▶ *the limitations of logical argument to encompass religious intuition.*

We have seen that religious language:

▶ *is a 'schema' by which a person may seek to convey the inexpressible*
▶ *is symbolic, not literal.*

Furthermore, religious experience may involve:

▶ *a sense of the unity of everything, and of oneself being at one with everything (mysticism)*
▶ *a sense of a presence of something quite extraordinary – terrifying, uncanny, fascinating, mysterious*
▶ *a sense of the absolute rightness of something (Kant's categorical imperative)*
▶ *a general sense of the wonder of nature*
▶ *a personal experience, resulting in a sense of value and commitment.*

We now turn to some key issues in the philosophy of religion: whether the world is created and designed by God; miracles; the problem of evil; and whether life after death is possible. We shall also look briefly at explanations of religion offered by sociology and psychology. In all these topics it is important to recognize that philosophy uses rational arguments in order to assess the truth of beliefs that people may hold for deeply personal reasons. This is not to negate the value of beliefs that are held for non-rational reasons, but simply to assess whether or not it is appropriate to try to justify such beliefs rationally.

The origin and design of the universe: religion or science?

Clearly, the origin and the nature of the universe are topics to be examined by science. There is broad agreement that, as far as we can judge at present, some form of 'big bang', whereby the known universe has expanded out of a space-time singularity, is the most likely theory for the origin of the world as we know it, and that – on Earth – there has been an evolution of species along the general principles of natural selection. Naturally, because these are scientific theories, they are open to be revised and perhaps eventually could even be replaced although, given the weight of evidence, that seems unlikely.

But from what we have seen from an outline of religious experience, and also from our brief look at the cosmological arguments (p. 161) and the argument from design (p. 163), it is clear that a sense of the wonder at the nature of the universe is a very common feature of religious awareness, and has given rise to the arguments for the existence of a creator and designer god.

The problem is that, once God is given a role in the origin and design of the universe, any alternative scientific theories that explain the same things without requiring any supernatural agency, may be seen as threats to religious belief. Hence, at a superficial level, religion would seem to have a vested interest in the failure of science to give a complete explanation of the universe. On the other hand, it is clear that many scientists – in the past and also today – do hold religious beliefs and certainly do not see their scientific work as in any sense incompatible with them.

So we need to ask: Are the religious and scientific approaches to these topics compatible?

In *The Blind Watchmaker*, Richard Dawkins makes the point that the argument for the world being made by an intelligent designer is based on the assumption that complexity cannot arise spontaneously. How then can an organized and complex designer exist without further explanation and cause? Surely, it is just as easy to accept that the complex organization of the world can appear spontaneously as it is to accept that a complex designer can appear spontaneously. But his central theme is that the process of natural selection gives us a mechanism which explains how complexity can arise from original simplicity. Once you accept that, there is no need to look for an external cause for design. Dawkins' point is not that belief in a creator can be disproved; rather, he shows that the idea is superfluous. This has been the principal threat to religious belief in a designer-god, ever since Charles Darwin put forward the theory of natural selection – for that theory put forward the first genuinely independent explanation of the appearance of design.

But this argument does not deny the sense of wonder at the beauty and complexity of the world. Indeed, Dawkins himself (in *Unweaving the Rainbow*) expresses amazement at what can arise from what is basically a mathematical sequence. Light and colour is no less impressive for being susceptible to scientific analysis.

Insight

The difference is that the religious person is likely to ascribe its origin to an external deity, whereas the atheist (whether scientist or not) accepts it as beautiful in itself, without seeking any external cause.

The fundamental question therefore is:

▶ *Can the world (in theory, if not in practice) provide us with an explanation of itself?*
▶ *If it can, this aspect of religion appears superfluous.*

If it cannot, is that because:

▶ *Our minds are incapable of understanding any overall cause for that within which we are immersed?*

Or

▶ *The explanation can only come through religious intuition (or the direct revelation of God) rather than through human reason and science.*

But this assumes that, for both scientist and religious believer, the world is such as to display design and intelligence. That can be challenged. One of the key nineteenth-century criticisms of the 'argument from design' came from J. S. Mill. He argued that the world was not a particularly benign place, and that evolution (for he was writing after Darwin's theory had been published) progressed only at the price of immense suffering.

It is clear that any objective assessment of nature is going to reveal the scale of suffering, as species prey on one another in the struggle to survive. If design were the product of an intelligent and loving God, why all this suffering? This leads into two related issues that may be addressed in the philosophy of religion – whether God, if he exists, can and does intervene selectively in the operating of the world through miracles, and whether a rational argument can show the compatibility of a omnipotent and loving God with the fact of suffering and evil.

Insight

Even Kant, who saw logical problems with the argument from design, nevertheless said that it deserved to be treated with great respect, saying that it gave life to the study of nature. In other words, it suggested that the world was a fascinating and wonderful place, worthy of our attention. And that is an inspiration for science, as much as for a this-worldly theology.

Miracles

The cosmological arguments for the existence of God were an attempt to lead the mind from an understanding of the physical world to a reality that lay behind it and was responsible for it. The arguments led from ordinary movement and causes to the idea of an unmoved mover or uncaused cause. But Western theistic religions have tended to go beyond this, and have claimed that the action of God can be seen in particular events, which may be called miracles.

Initially, we will be looking at miracles in terms of events for which it is claimed that there is no rational or scientific explanation. This is not the only type of miracle, and it raises some religious questions, but it will suffice as a starting point.

If you want to find an argument against this idea of a miracle, the logical place to look is among those philosophers who take an empiricist position, for an empiricist will want to relate everything to the objects of sense experience, and this is precisely what is not possible if an event is to be a miracle in the particular sense that we are considering. A critique along these lines is given by Hume.

Hume examines the idea of miracles in the tenth book of his *Enquiry Concerning Human Understanding*. His argument runs like this:

▶ *A wise man proportions his belief to the evidence; the more evidence there is for something, the more likely it is to have been the case.*
▶ *Equally, the evidence of other people is assessed according to their reliability as witnesses.*

He then turns to the idea of miracles and offers a definition.

▶ *A miracle is the violation of a law of nature.*
▶ **But** *a law of nature is the result of a very large number of observations.*

He therefore argues:

A miracle is a violation of the laws of nature; and as a firm and unalterable experience has established these laws, the proof

against a miracle, from the very nature of the fact, is as entire as any argument from experience can possibly be imagined. Why is it more probably that all men must die; that lead cannot, of itself, remain suspended in the air; that fire consumes wood, and is extinguished by water; unless it be, that these events are found agreeable to the laws of nature, and there is required a violation of these laws, or in other words, a miracle to prevent them? Nothing is esteemed a miracle if it ever happen in the common course of nature ... The plain consequence is ... That no testimony is sufficient to establish a miracle, unless the testimony be of such a kind, that its falsehood would be more miraculous, than the fact, which it endeavours to establish.

In other words, it is always more likely that the report of a miracle is mistaken, than that a law of nature was actually broken, for the evidence against the miracle will always be greater than the evidence for it.

For Hume, the only way in which, on balance, a miracle could be accepted, is if it would be a greater miracle if all the evidence for it were to be proved mistaken, than if a law of nature were broken. In practice, that rules out miracles, although strictly speaking it does not preclude a miracle, it simply says that *there can never be sufficient evidence* for a wise man to accept it as such.

Hume's argument is based on the assumption (which we accepted at the opening of this section) that a miracle is a violation of a law of nature; in other words, that the event is inexplicable in terms of present scientific knowledge. But is that necessarily the case for an event to be a miracle?

Take the example of a 'black hole' in the middle of a galaxy. It is a violation of what are generally called 'laws of nature' (according to Newtonian physics). Yet it is not seen as a miracle, merely an extreme case, which suggests that the existing 'laws' of physics need to be modified to take it into account.

We therefore have to ask a further question: *What distinguishes a miracle from a rare or unique occurrence?*

Generally, in order to be termed a miracle, something needs to be seen as fitting into a scheme which displays positive purpose. If a life is saved, against all expectations, that may be regarded as a miracle by those for whom that life was dear. If a person suddenly drops dead, his or her friends are unlikely to call it a miracle. However, the long-lost relative, who had no emotional connection with the deceased, and who is suddenly saved from financial ruin by an unexpected legacy, may well find it miraculous.

Therefore, a unique occurrence (for instance, a previously unobserved event in a distant galaxy) would not be called a miracle unless it had some personal relevance and apparent sense of purpose. Equally, an ordinary event – in other words, one for which there is a perfectly reasonable explanation – may still be regarded as a miracle if its timing is right, or it has particular significance. Thus the long-lost relative just mentioned might find that the legacy arrives at the same time as a final demand for payment of some impossibly large debt. Not that it has happened, but that it has happened *now*, is the remarkable thing.

Insight

With a miracle, it's not so much what happened, but *why*. If the world is an impersonal mechanism, any sense of purpose suggests the deliberate choice of an agent. The problem, without direct evidence, is proving either purpose or agent.

UNIQUE OR UNIVERSAL?

There is an important sense in which the idea of the miraculous and that of the cosmological and design arguments work against one another. The whole essence of the earlier arguments is that the world is structured in a way that displays an overall purpose. Those arguments only work on the basis of regularity, for only in regularity does the sense of design and purpose appear. Yet the literal idea of a miracle violates that regularity, introducing a sense of arbitrariness and unpredictability into an understanding of the world which therefore undermines the cosmological structures.

In other words

You can't have it both ways. *Either* God is seen to exist because the world is a wonderful, ordered place, *or* his hand is seen in individual events because the world is an unpredictable, miraculous place. It is not reasonable to try to argue for both at once, since the one appears to cancel out the other!

The problem of evil

In its simplest form, the problem can be stated like this:

▶ **If** *God created the world*
▶ **And** *if God is all-powerful and all-loving*
▶ **Then** *why is there evil and suffering in the world?*

Conclusion:

▶ **Either** *God is not all-powerful*
▶ **Or** *God is not all-loving*
▶ **Or** *suffering is either unreal, necessary or a means to a greater good*
▶ **Or** *the whole idea of an all-loving and all-powerful creator God was a mistake in the first place.*

An important book setting out suggested answers to this problem is *Evil and the God of Love* (1966) by John Hick (b. 1922), a philosopher and theologian notable for his contribution to the problem of evil and also to the issue of religious pluralism. In that book he gives two main lines of approach, the Augustinian and the Irenaean:

1 *The Augustinian approach is named after St Augustine (354–430), and reflects his background in neo-Platonism. In Plato's thought, particular things are imperfect copies of their 'forms'. Imperfection is a feature of the world as we experience it. The Augustinian approach to evil and suffering is to say that evil is not a separate force opposing the good, but is a lack of goodness, a deprivation. The world as we experience it is full of imperfect copies, and suffering and evil are bound up with that imperfection.*

   But Augustine had a second line of argument, coming from the Bible and Church teaching, rather than from Plato. The biblical account of the Fall of the Angels and of Adam and Eve in the Garden of Eden led to a 'fallen' state for all creation. Because of human disobedience, the world is a place of suffering rather than innocent bliss. Hence moral suffering (the pain caused by humans) can be seen as a consequence of the sin, and natural evil (earthquakes, tsunami, diseases and the like) can be seen as a just punishment for sin.

2 *The Irenaean approach is named after Bishop Irenaeus of Lyons (c. 130–c. 202). It presents the idea that human life is imperfect, but having been made in the image of God, human beings are intended to grow and develop, aspiring to be what God intended them to be. Through free will and all the sufferings of life, people have an opportunity to grow and learn. Without a world in which there is both good and evil, that would be impossible:*

> **How, if we had no knowledge of the contrary, could we have had instruction in that which is good? ... For just as the tongue receives experiences of sweet and bitter by means of tasting, and the eye discriminates between black and white by means of vision, and the ear recognizes the distinctness of sounds by hearing; so also does the mind,**

receiving through the experience of both the knowledge
of what is good, become the more tenacious in its
preservation, by acting in obedience to God ... But if any
one do shun the knowledge of both kinds of things, and
the twofold perception of knowledge, he unaware divests
himself of the character of a human being.

Irenaeus, *Against Heresies* iv, xxxix.1, quoted in Hick, Fontana, 1968

In other words, it is only by having a world in which there is both good and evil that we can have moral choice and develop spiritually. In this way, Irenaeus can justify the presence of natural evil, for a world that includes sickness and natural disasters is one in which people grow through facing real challenges.

Hick's own approach to the problem of evil is one that treats evil as something to be tackled and overcome, but with the hope that, ultimately, it will be seen as part of an overall divine plan.

Compensation after death?

The issues concerning immortality, resurrection, reincarnation and the general problems concerning whether survival of any sort is possible or meaningful have been examined briefly in Chapter 4, pp. 103–5.

Notice how the issue of life after death has touched on those of faith, the nature of the universe and the justification of the goodness of God with the suffering of the world. Pascal's wager assumed that there was heaven to gain and hell to avoid, and that the extremes they offered outweighed the consideration of the relative benefits of one's lifestyle on earth. Similarly now, both Augustine and Irenaeus, each in his own way, looks beyond this life for an ultimate justification for suffering. Whether suffering is a just punishment or a means of developing, it only makes sense as the prescription offered by a loving God, if there is some form of compensation beyond death.

The crucial difference between the religious and non-religious evaluation of life, is that – in general – the non-religious approach is that life is of value in itself, not as a preparation for anything beyond this world. The challenge of atheism is the challenge of acceptance of a limited life with an unequally distributed mixture of pleasure and pain.

To say 'Yes' to this life, just as it is, and to be prepared to live this life over and over again, just as it is, is the hallmark of someone radically free from the consolations of religion. Indeed, Nietzsche made such 'Yes-saying' a key feature of his *übermensch* (superman), the higher form to which humankind is challenged to evolve.

Insight

That said, a psychologist might argue that it is exactly the consolations of religion (as opposed to those of philosophy) which explain the continuation of religious belief in the face of rational criticism.

Psychological and sociological explanations of religion

In one of the most quoted passages of all time, Marx said, in his *Contribution to the Critique of Hegel's Philosophy of Right*:

> *Religion is the sign of the oppressed creature, the heart of the heartless world, just as it is the spirit of the spiritless situation. It is the opium of the people.*

> *The abolition of religion as the illusory happiness of the people is required for their real happiness. The demand to give up the illusions about its condition is the demand to give up a condition which needs illusions. The criticism of religion is therefore in embryo the criticism of the vale of woe, the halo of which is religion.*

(as quoted in Paul Helm *Faith and Reason*, OUP, 1999)

In other words, Marx wants people to turn their attention to their present situation and to struggle for real happiness. The assumption he makes is that the sort of happiness associated with life after death is illusory. But at the same time, if such an illusion is believed, the fact of suffering and the longing for a life free from it, is a powerful motivation for continuing to be religious in the face of present adversity.

A parallel explanation for religion is given by sociologists, for example, Emile Durkheim. From the sociological perspective, religion provides a cohesive force within society. If a community is bound together by its religion, then the continuation of that religion does not depend so much on the intellectual acceptance of its articles of belief, but the perceived value it offers society.

Freud's criticism of religion was partly based on the parallels he saw between religious behaviour and obsessional neuroses, like repeated handwashing or tidying routines. In both cases, repeated actions (for example, confessing sins; attending worship) were an attempt to escape from a sense of unworthiness and guilt. But more significant for our argument here are the supposed benefits of religion that he sets out in *The Future of an Illusion* (1927). Just as a child depends on an adult for protection, so he sees religion as offering God to adults as a substitute, heavenly Father – a comfort and protection in the midst of the threatening nature of life and the eventual inevitability of death.

These explanations of religion, mentioned briefly here, but well worth exploring further, are a reminder that the sort of rational arguments examined by the philosophy of religion are far from being the whole story. Religious beliefs may claim to be rational, and may be backed up by rational argument, but religion does not ultimately depend on any of these arguments for its continued existence. As the widespread increase of fundamentalism and literalism in religious circles shows, it is often the rejection of an intellectually sophisticated approach to these issues that appeals.

This is not to suggest that the explanations of religion given by the likes of Marx, Durkheim or Freud necessarily invalidate religious beliefs. Those beliefs (examined rationally) may be true or they may be false. What is clear, however, is that – as a phenomenon – there are many reasons for religion to continue and even to flourish, quite apart from them.

Some general remarks

There are two very different approaches to belief in God, miracles and so on. One (sometimes referred to as 'onto-theology') tends to describe God as a being who exists and interacts with the world, the other ('expressive theology') sees God and religion as a way of exploring and expressing value in this world. The problem – as clearly set out by Simon Blackburn in, for example, *Philosophers Without Gods*, 2007, ed Louise Antony – is that the latter, even if more compatible with secular atheism, is not in line with the sort of impetus that beliefs need to have in order to sustain religion. In other words, if you don't believe that God actually, literally exists, it's difficult to be committed to obeying him.

And underlying the difference between the religious and non-religious viewpoints are also seen in the fundamental way of looking at and valuing the world:

▶ *Is the world fundamentally an imperfect copy of something more real? As we look at the world, do we see it as a half-empty glass, forever lacking fullness and perfection? Both the ontological and cosmological arguments look beyond the partial experience of 'greatness' or movement or causality, to something than which none greater can be conceived, an unmoved mover, or an uncaused cause. The mind is led from a present experience of a half-empty glass to the conception of what a full glass would be like – a perfection which underpins this imperfect world.*

▶ *Or is the world still developing, working towards a perfection that lies in the future? Is the structure of the world (along with everything in it, good and bad) the means by which growth can take place? The argument from design and the moral argument have a contribution to make to this point of view. Darwin's evolution through natural selection is based on the facts of suffering and death which allow only the strongest members of a species to survive and breed. Without suffering and death, were is no evolution. In Marxist theory, the class struggle, with all the suffering that it involves, is the means of bringing about a classless society in the future.*

These are practical, moral and political as well as religious questions. But they raise an enormous philosophical problem: *Everything that we experience is in a process of change.* Birth, death, suffering and evil are all part of that process. How do you understand anything so mobile and ambiguous? How can you say 'yes' to it with conviction? How can you love it? That is the challenge posed by Nietzsche, by modern atheism and humanism, and also by Buddhism, which has always seen life as fragile and subject to change, but has nevertheless proposed insight and compassion as a recipe for overcoming human suffering.

Comment

Where do you find reality?

▶ *Is reality to be found in an ideal realm outside, over and above the flux of life? (Line up behind Plato, Augustine, Aquinas and most traditional theists!)*
▶ *Is reality to be found as an end product to be arrived at through this process of change? (Line up behind Irenaeus, Marx and evolutionary religious thinkers such as Teilhard de Chardin!)*
▶ *Is reality to be found within life itself, including all its limitations and changes? (Line up behind Heraclitus, Spinoza and the Buddha!)*

10 THINGS TO REMEMBER

1 *Foundationalism is the attempt to arrive at statements which are accepted as obviously true.*

2 *Fundamentalism involves a literal acceptance of beliefs and religious texts, often taken out of context.*

3 *Religious language is essentially personal.*

4 *God cannot exist in the sense that ordinary things exist.*

5 *The traditional arguments show what a believer might mean by 'God'.*

6 *There would be no religion without religious experience.*

7 *Religious experience tends to be personal and gives a new perspective in life.*

8 *A miracle is more than a unique event.*

9 *The problem of evil challenges a literal understanding of a loving God.*

10 *The social sciences offer explanations for religion, irrespective of its truth.*

6

Ethics

In this chapter you will learn:
- *about whether or not we are free to act as we wish*
- *the basis of major ethical theories*
- *the relationship between ethics and the values held by society.*

Facts, values and choices

So far we have been exploring questions of knowledge: What can we know for certain? Can we know anything about the nature of reality as a whole? How are our language and our thought related to the experiences that come to us through our senses? These led on to key questions about the nature of science, of the mind and of religion.

But it is a fundamental feature of all sentient life that awareness of its environment enables a creature to act, to find food, to recognize danger, to mate and thereby to survive. Human beings are no different, except that their intellectual ability presents them with a range of choices. So philosophy is also concerned with questions of a very different kind: What should we do? How should we organize society? What is right? How should we understand the idea of justice? On what basis can we choose between different courses of action? These lead to a study of ethics, and of political philosophy.

These more immediately practical aspects of philosophy have a long history. Although the pre-Socratic philosophers of ancient Greece had probed many questions about the nature of reality – questions to which their answers are still interesting in terms of both epistemology and the natural sciences – with Socrates, Plato and Aristotle, the emphasis shifted towards issues of morality. So, for example, Plato's *Republic* is not based on the question 'What is society?' but 'What is justice?', and it is through that question that many other issues about society and how it should be ruled are explored.

Aristotle (in *Nicomachean Ethics*) asked about the 'good' which was the aim of every action, and about what could constitute a 'final good' – something worthwhile for its own sake, rather than for the sake of something higher. He came to the view that the highest good for man was *eudaimonia*, which literally means 'having a good spirit', but perhaps can be translated as 'happiness'. He saw it as the state in which a person was fulfilling his or her potential and natural function. It expressed a form of human excellence or virtue (*arete*). This tied in with his general view that everything had a 'final cause': a goal and a purpose to which it moves. If you understand the final cause of something, you also understand its fundamental essence, which finds its expression in that goal. If a knife had a soul, Aristotle argued, that soul would be 'cutting' – that is what makes it a knife, that is what it is there to do. What then is the essence of humankind? What is it there to do? What is its goal?

Aristotle linked his ethics to his whole understanding of human life. He refused to accept any simple rule which could cover all situations, and he also considered human beings in relationship to the society within which they lived, recognizing the influence this has on human behaviour. Aristotle saw man as both a 'thinking animal' and a 'political animal'. It is therefore not surprising that ethics becomes the study of rational choice in action, and that it should have a social as well as an individual aspect. In this chapter we shall take a brief look at some of the main philosophical approaches to moral issues and in the following chapter we shall examine issues of a social and political nature. Although, for

convenience, morality and politics are separated, it is important
to remember that morality is more than the establishing of a set of
personal values. It is equally possible to examine morality in terms
of the requirements of the state and the place of individuals within
society; in ethics the personal and the social cannot be separated.

'IS' AND 'OUGHT'

Once you start to talk about morality, or about the purpose of
things, you introduce matters of value as well as those of fact.
An important question for philosophy is whether it is possible
to derive values from facts, or whether facts must always remain
'neutral'. In other words:

▶ *Facts say what 'is'.*
▶ *Values say what 'ought' to be.*

Which leads to the question:

> *Can we ever derive an 'ought' from an 'is'?*

If the answer to this question is 'no', then how are we to decide
issues of morality? If no facts can be used to establish morality,
can there be absolute moral rules, or are all moral decisions
relative, dependent upon particular circumstances, feelings or
desires?

Later in this chapter we shall examine two ways in which
philosophers have presented facts that they consider to be relevant
to what people 'ought' to do:

1 *An argument based on design and purpose (following
Aristotle's comments given earlier).*
2 *An argument based on the expected results of an action.*

We shall also examine other features of ethical language:
expressing approval or otherwise, recommending a course of

action, or expressing emotion. But first, if ethics is to make any sense, we must ask if people are, in fact, free to decide what to do. If they are not free, if they have no choice, then praise and blame, approval or disapproval are inappropriate.

> **Insight**
>
> It is illogical to tell someone that they **ought** to do something, unless we believe that it is at least **possible** for them to do it.

Freedom and determinism

If (as Kant argued) space, time and causality are categories used by the human mind to interpret experience, it is inevitable that we shall see everything in the world as causally conditioned – things don't just happen, they must have a cause!

This process of looking for causes, which lies at the heart of the scientific quest, has as its logical goal a totally understood world in which each individual thing and action is explained in terms of all that went before it. In theory, given total knowledge of all that had happened in the past, everything that will happen in the future could be predicted. This reflects what we may call the Newtonian world view, that the universe is like a machine, operating by means of fixed rules.

We saw that this created problems in terms of the relationship between mind and body. What is the human mind? Can it make a difference? If everything is causally conditioned, then even the electrical impulses in my brain are part of a closed mechanical system and my freedom is an illusion. I may feel sure that I have made a free choice, but in fact everything that has happened to me since my birth, and everything that has made the world the way it is since the beginning of time, has contributed to that decision.

In other words

'I just knew you'd say that!' One of the annoying things about people who claim to predict our choices is that we like to think we are free, but are forced to recognize that we may not always be the best judge of that.

One of the fundamental issues of philosophy is freedom and determinism. It is also related to reductionism – the reduction of complex entities (like human beings) to the simpler parts of which they are composed. If we are nothing more than the individual cells that comprise our bodies, and if those cells are determined by physical forces and are predictable, then there seems no room for the whole human being to exercise freedom.

For now, dealing with ethics, one distinction is clear:

▶ *If we are free to make a choice, then we can be responsible for what we do. Praise or blame are appropriate. We can act on the basis of values that we hold.*
▶ *If we are totally conditioned, we have no choice in what we do, and it makes no sense to speak of moral action springing from choices and values, or action being worthy of praise or blame.*

By the same token, there are levels of determinism. It is clear that nobody is totally free:

▶ *We have physical limitations. I cannot make an unaided leap 30 metres into the air, even if I feel I have a vocation to do so. Overweight middle-aged men do not make the best ballet dancers. It's not a matter of choice, merely of physical fact.*
▶ *We may be psychologically predisposed to act in certain ways rather than others. If you are shy and depressed, you are unlikely to be the life and soul of a party. But that is not a matter of choice, merely of present disposition.*

- ▶ *We may be socially restrained. I may choose to do something really outrageous, but know that I will not get away with it.*
- ▶ *We may also be limited by the financial and political structures under which we live. There are many things that I cannot do without money, for example.*

In considering the moral implications of actions, we have to assess the degree of freedom available to the agent.

Examples

Is a soldier who is *ordered* to shoot prisoners or unarmed civilians thereby absolved of moral responsibility? Is he free to choose whether to carry out that act or not? Does the fear of his own death, executed for refusal to obey an order, determine that he must obey?

If a person commits a crime while known to be suffering from a mental illness, or if a psychiatric report indicates that he or she was disturbed at the time, that fact will be taken into account when apportioning blame. But how many people who commit crimes could be described as clear-headed and well balanced? How many have no mitigating circumstances of some sort when family background, education, deprivation and other things are considered?

If we are all obeying orders, even those that have been lodged in our unconscious mind since childhood, or influenced by circumstances, are we ever responsible for our actions? Are paedophilia or kleptomania crimes, or illnesses, or both? Do they require punishment or treatment?

We are all conditioned by many factors, there is no doubt of that. The difference between that and determinism is that determinism leaves no scope for human freedom and choice (we are automata), whereas those who argue against determinism claim that there remains a measure of freedom that is exercised within the prevailing conditions.

But keep in mind that everything we are, everything we believe, and everything we understand about the world is there in the moment when we make a moral choice; not necessarily consciously, but there in the background, exerting an influence.

Not all philosophers have presented the issues of freedom, determinism and moral choice in quite this way. A notable exception in Western thought is Spinoza. He argued that freedom was in fact an illusion, created because we do not know all the causes of our actions. Things that happen to us produce in us either passive or active emotions. The passive emotions, such as hatred, anger or fear, lead a person into bondage, whereas the active ones, those generated by an understanding of our real circumstances, lead to a positive view of life, and an ability to be ourselves. Spinoza held that the more one understood the world, the more the negative emotions would diminish and be replaced by positive ones. One might perhaps say of this that freedom (and the only freedom that Spinoza will accept) is the ability to see life exactly as it is and say 'yes' to it.

Kinds of ethical language

What does it mean to say that something is 'good' or that an action is 'right'? Do these words refer to a hidden quality in that action, something over and above what is actually observed? What sort of evidence can be given for such a description?

I can show you what I mean by 'red' by pointing to a range of red objects, and relying on your ability to identify their common feature. Can I do the same by pointing to a range of actions that I consider to be morally right? Take for example:

▶ *a married couple having sexual intercourse*
▶ *someone helping a blind person across a road*
▶ *paying for goods in a shop (as opposed to stealing them).*

Considering only the *factual description* of each action, what do they have in common? What quality of the actions make them 'moral'? And if moral language is not the same as physical description, what is it and how is it justified?

DESCRIPTIVE ETHICS

This is the most straightforward form of ethical language. It is simply a description of what happens: what moral choices are made and in which particular circumstances. Rather than making a statement about the rights or wrongs of abortion, for example, descriptive ethics simply gives facts and figures about how many abortions take place, how they are carried out, and what legal restraints are placed on that practice. *Descriptive ethics is about 'is' rather than 'ought'.*

NORMATIVE ETHICS

Normative ethics deals with the norms of action, in terms of whether an action is considered good or bad, right or wrong. It expresses values, and makes a moral judgement based on them. It may relate to facts, but it is not wholly defined by facts. It may be justified in a number of ways that we shall examine shortly. *Normative ethics is about 'ought'; it makes judgements.*

META-ETHICS

When philosophy examines the claims made in normative ethics, a number of questions are raised:

- ▶ *What does it mean to say that something is right or wrong?*
- ▶ *Can moral statements be said to be either true or false?*
- ▶ *Do they express more than the preferences of the person who makes them?*
- ▶ *What is the meaning of the terms used in ethical discourse?*

These questions are not themselves moral statements; they do not say that any particular thing is right or wrong. Meta-ethics is a branch of philosophy which does to normative ethical statement what philosophy does to language in general. It examines ethical language to find what it means and how it is used.

Insight

Meta-ethics produces theories about the nature of ethical language, rather than discussing right and wrong. At one time, many professional philosophers thought that was all philosophy should do. Nowadays, however (prompted by the work of Peter Singer and others) philosophers are expected to make a direct contribution to moral debates.

INTUITIONISM

In his book *Principia Ethica* (1903), G. E. Moore argued that the term 'good' could not be defined, and that every attempt to do so ended in reducing goodness to some other quality which was not common to all 'good' things. In other words, goodness could involve kindness, altruism, generosity, a sense of social justice – but it is not actually *defined* by any of these. Moore therefore claimed that:

> **Everyone does in fact understand the question 'Is this good?'**
> **When he thinks of it, his state of mind is different from what it**
> **would be, were he asked 'Is this pleasant, or desired, or approved?'**
> **It has a distinct meaning for him, even though he may not**
> **recognize in what respect it is distinct.**

Principia Ethica, Chapter 1

He likened it to describing the colour yellow. In the end you just have to point to things and say that they are yellow without being able to define the colour. You know what yellow is by intuition. In the same way, you know what goodness is, even though it cannot be defined. This approach is generally referred to as **intuitionism**.

Insight

Moore himself did not use the term 'intuitionism' for his work. He simply wanted to point out that 'good' was known but could not be further defined, whereas intuitionists generally want to go further and say that all moral claims are based on intuition.

NATURALISM AND METAPHYSICAL ETHICS

G. E. Moore had argued that you could not get an 'ought' from an 'is' – that you could not derive morality from the facts of human behaviour. He made an absolute distinction between facts and values. From Plato and Aristotle onwards, however, there have been philosophers who have argued that moral principles and values should be derived from the examination of human beings, their society, and their place within the world as a whole. This task is termed 'naturalism' or 'metaphysical ethics', and it implies that what you 'ought' to do has some close relation to what 'is', in fact, the case about yourself and the world. In other words, that morality should be more than an expression of personal choice, it should be rooted in an overall understanding of the world.

EMOTIVISM

According to this theory, saying that something is good or bad is really just a way of saying that you approve or disapprove of it. In Chapter 3 we saw that, early in the twentieth century, there developed an approach to language known as logical positivism. In this, statements were called meaningless unless they either corresponded to empirical data, or were true by definition. On this basis, moral statements were seen as meaningless.

One response to this challenge was to argue that moral statements were not factual descriptions, but were simply expressing approval or otherwise. They were therefore not true or false by reference to that which they described, but according to whether or not they correctly reflected the emotions or preferences of the speaker. A J Ayer, who popularized logical positivism in the English-speaking world, took this view.

PRESCRIPTIVISM

This is another response to the challenge of logical positivism. It claims that moral language is actually recommending a course of action. If I say that something is good, I am actually saying that I feel it should be done – in other words, I am prescribing it as a course of action.

In other words

▶ If you describe someone's actions or decisions, the truth of what you say is known by checking the facts.
▶ If you say that something is 'right' or 'wrong', there are no straightforward facts to check in order to verify your claim.
▶ Meta-ethics, therefore, looks at these ethical claims and asks what they mean, whether they can be true or false, and, if so, how that truth may be established. If ethics is not about external facts, it may be about intuitions, or emotional responses, or recommendations, or the general structures of life and their implications for individual action.

The theories mentioned here have been developed within the philosophical debate about the nature of language in general and of the status of moral language in particular. But whatever the status of the language they use, the fact is that people continue to make moral claims. It is therefore important to examine the bases upon which such claims may be made.

Three bases for ethics

If moral language is simply expressing an emotion or a preference, then it does not seem to need further justification, it implies no more than the feelings of the moment. If we want to argue for a moral position, however, we need to find a rational basis for ethics. Within the history of Western philosophy there have been three principal bases offered: **natural law, utilitarianism** and the **categorical imperative**. We shall examine each of these in turn.

NATURAL LAW

In Book 1 of *Nicomachean Ethics*, Aristotle says:

> *Every art and every enquiry, and similarly every action and pursuit, is thought to aim at some good; and for this reason the good has rightly been declared to be that at which all things aim.*

p.1094a

Aristotle develops this into the idea of the supreme good for human beings: happiness (*eudaimonia*). If you agree with Aristotle that everything has a final cause or purpose, a 'good' for which it exists, or if you accept with Plato that the 'Forms' (especially the 'Form of the Good') have a permanent reality, independent of our own minds and perceptions, then it should be possible to specify which things are 'good' and which 'bad', which actions are 'right' and which 'wrong' in an independent and objective way.

Natural law is the approach to ethics which claims that something is right if it fulfils its true purpose in life, wrong if it goes against it.

Examples

Sex Natural law, based on the idea of a natural purpose inherent in everything, might seem particularly appropriate for dealing with issues of sex, since it is clear that sex does have a natural purpose that is essential for life. In natural law terms:

▶ *the 'natural' function of sex is the reproduction of the species*
▶ *non-reproductive sexual activity is 'against nature' and therefore wrong (or at least a misuse of the natural function of sex). Masturbation, contraception and homosexuality could all be criticized from this standpoint.*

Abortion and euthanasia It is natural for every creature to seek and preserve its own life. If everything has a natural purpose to fulfil, then abortion and euthanasia can be seen as wrong, since they go against this natural outworking of the processes of life.

▶ *Unless there is something sufficiently wrong for there to be a miscarriage, the newly fertilized embryo will naturally grow into a new, independent human being. The 'final cause' of the embryo (to use Aristotle's term) is the adult human which it will one day become. On a natural law basis, it would therefore be wrong to frustrate that natural process through abortion even if the child is not wanted and its life is likely to be an unhappy one.*

▶ *When the body can no longer sustain the burden of illness, it dies. To anticipate this is to frustrate the natural tendency towards self-preservation. The results of an act of euthanasia may be to lessen a burden of suffering, but it would still be seen as wrong in itself, even if the person making that moral judgement had great sympathy for those involved.*

Notice how this approach to ethics relates to the philosophy of religion. The basis of the natural law approach is that the world is purposeful and that the purpose of any part of it may be understood by human reason. It may be seen as the ethical aspect of the traditional argument from design (see p. 163).

Natural law is not the same as a consideration of what appears as a natural response to a situation – natural in the sense that it reflects the nature that humankind shares with the rest of the animal kingdom. Rather, it is *nature as seen through the eyes of reason*; indeed, for most of those who would use a natural law argument, it is also coloured by religious views, with the world seen as the purposeful creation by God.

A newspaper article on adultery (Anne Applebaum, *The Daily Telegraph*, 29 August 1994, p. 17) was headed, 'We have descended from apes but we don't have to behave like them'. In it the author opposed the fashionable theory that it was 'natural' to commit adultery, arguing that, although people are instinctively 'bad', they are capable of exercising self-restraint. In particular, she opposed the idea that adultery was simply the natural expression of a genetic urge to reproduce in the most favourable way possible, and that men would therefore 'naturally' be attracted to a number of other women. She argued that to say that 'we are all genetic adulterers' sounds similar to the traditional Christian view that 'we are all sinners', but with the fundamental difference that the latter regarded moral codes and practices as existing to control our natural instincts, whereas the former seemed to use those instincts to justify behaviour as well as to explain it.

For reflection

▶ Is it possible for something to be natural but wrong?
▶ Is self-restraint always unnatural?
▶ Is the genetic strengthening of a species (which presumably could be helped by allowing the strongest to breed freely with the most beautiful) itself a final 'good' to be sought?

There are many issues within medical ethics that have a 'natural law' component. For example, a 'naturally' infertile couple may be offered IVF or other treatments to help them to conceive a child, and it is 'natural' that they should want to do so. But what about the nature and purpose of the treatments involved? Should they be approved by natural law, in the sense that they facilitate the 'final purpose' of having the child? Furthermore, may it not be part of a natural mechanism of population limitation that some couples are infertile, and that to introduce an artificial process is therefore against the natural reasons for their infertility?

If such treatment is branded as 'unnatural', what is there to be said about medicine in general? It may be natural to die from an infection, and it is therefore unnatural to be saved by an antibiotic. But, if natural law seeks the fulfilment of each human being, is not the prevention of premature death a decision based on the recognition that an individual might well fulfil his or her potential only by being given a chance to live?

Insight

This illustrates again that Natural Law places its emphasis on 'Law'. It considers a *rational interpretation* of nature and its purposes, not an observation of nature itself, which can all too often be brutal and impersonal.

UTILITARIANISM

Utilitarianism is a moral theory associated particularly with Jeremy Bentham (1748–1832), a philosopher, lawyer and social reformer, involved particularly with the practical issues of prison reform, education and the integrity of public institutions, and further developed by John Stuart Mill (1806–73), a campaigner for individual liberty and for the rights of women. Its roots, however, are found earlier in the basic idea of hedonism.

Hedonism is the term used for a philosophy which makes the achievement of happiness the prime goal in life. Epicurus taught in

Athens at the end of the fourth century BCE. He took an atomistic view of the world (everything is composed of indivisible atoms), regarded the gods as having little influence on life, and generally considered the main purpose of life to be the gaining of pleasure, in the broad sense of well-being. Pain, he held, was of shorter duration than pleasure, and death was nothing but the dissolution of the atoms of which we are made, with no afterlife to fear. He therefore considered that the wise should lead a life free from anxiety, and if morality had any purpose it was to maximize the amount of well-being that life can offer.

To be fair to Epicurus, this crude outline does not do justice to the fact that he distinguished the more intellectual pleasures from the animal ones, and that Epicureans were certainly not 'hedonists' in the popular sense. Nevertheless, Epicurus did establish the maximizing of happiness as the prime purpose of morality.

This was to become the basis of utilitarian theories of ethics: that the right thing to do on any occasion is that which aims to give maximum happiness to all concerned. This may be expressed in the phrase 'the greatest good for the greatest number', and Bentham made the point that everyone should count equally in such an assessment – a radical point of view for him to take at that time. Utilitarianism is therefore a theory *based on the expected results of an action, rather than any inherent sense of right or wrong.*

This is very much a common-sense view of ethics; to do what is right is often associated with doing what will benefit the majority. From a philosophical point of view, however, there are certain problems associated with it:

▶ *You can never be certain what the total effects of an action are going to be. To take a crude example: you may save the life of a drowning child who then grows up to be a mass murderer. In practice, there always has to be a cut-off point beyond which it is not practicable to calculate consequences. Added to this is the fact that we see the result of actions only with hindsight; at the time, we might have expected something quite different. Thus, although utilitarianism seems to offer a straightforward way of assessing moral issues, its assessment must always remain provisional.*

▶ *The definition of what constitutes happiness may not be objective. Other people may not want what you deem to be their happiness or in their best interests. The utilitarian argument appears to make a factual consideration of results the basis of moral choice, but in practice, in selecting the degree or type of happiness to be considered, a person is already making value (and perhaps moral) judgements.*

▶ *How do you judge between pain caused to a single individual and the resulting happiness of many others? Would global benefit actually justify the inflicting of pain on a single innocent person?*

An outrageous example

A perfectly healthy young visitor innocently walks into a hospital in which there are a number of people all waiting for various organ transplants. Might a utilitarian surgeon be tempted?

But more serious examples

In allocating limited healthcare budgets, choices have to be made. Do you spend a large amount of money on an operation which may or may not save the life of a seriously ill child, if the consequence of that choice is that many other people with debilitating (but perhaps not life-threatening) illnesses are unlikely to receive the help they need? How do you assess the relative happiness or benefit of those concerned?

Consider the situation of an unborn child known to be seriously handicapped but capable of survival. Is the potential suffering of both child and parents as a result of the severe handicap such that the child's survival does not add to the total sum of happiness? And who could possibly make such an assessment objectively?

Further difficulties arise in a consideration of the first of the above examples, in that experimental surgical procedures carried out today may benefit many more patients in the future.

Insight

The argument for fundamental research in the sciences is often justified on this utilitarian basis – that without it, the long-term development of new technology will be stifled, with the corresponding loss of its future benefits.

Forms of utilitarianism

So far we have considered only *act utilitarianism*. This makes moral judgements on the basis of the likely consequences of particular acts. There is also *rule utilitarianism*, which considers the overall benefit that will be gained by society if a particular rule is accepted. In other words, breaking a rule may benefit the individual concerned, but allowing that rule to be broken may itself have harmful consequences for society as a whole. This was a form of utilitarianism put forward by Mill. There are two forms of rule utilitarianism: strong and weak. A strong rule utilitarian will argue that it is never right to break a rule if that rule is to the benefit of society as a whole. A weak rule utilitarian will argue that there may be special cases in which breaking the rule is allowed, although the overall benefit to society of not doing so should also be taken into consideration. *Preference utilitarianism* is based on taking the preferences of all those who are involved into account. (In other words, the basis on which the 'good' is to be assessed in a particular situation is not impersonal, but takes into account the views and wishes of all concerned.)

Without doubt, utilitarianism is the most popular ethical theory today – and one that, to many people, is taken as common sense. It can be used to present radical moral challenges, as for example in the many books by Peter Singer (b. 1946), who argues that you should give equal consideration to others as to yourself. Thus, if you are able to prevent something bad from happening to another person, without thereby sacrificing anything morally significant to yourself, you should always do so. This has huge implications for tackling the issue of world poverty. He asks how one can morally justify retaining wealth in a situation where one is aware of the benefits it can offer others. The problem, of course, is that it seems 'natural' to care for yourself and your family and friends more than those who live at a distance and are not known personally; but it is difficult to give a rational justification for the resulting disparity in wealth and chances in life.

Insight

This touches on a huge issue – is reason 'natural'? Should a philosopher, motivated by reason, behave in ways that are noticeably different from people who are primarily motivated by their hormones and appetites? Plato clearly thought so – since he argued that only philosophers should rule. Singer implies it, in presenting a clear challenge to the radical selfishness that inhibits people from wholeheartedly doing what is in the common good.

Both utilitarianism and natural law appear to give rational and objective bases for deciding between right and wrong. Both of them, however, have presuppositions which are not accounted for by the theory itself. One depends on the idea of a rational final cause, the other on the acceptance of well-being of all as the highest good.

THE CATEGORICAL IMPERATIVE

We have already looked at the work of the eighteenth-century German philosopher Kant in connection with the radical distinction he made between things as we perceive them and things as they are in themselves, and the categories of space, time and causality by which we interpret our experience. But Kant also made an important contribution in the field of ethics. He sought to formulate a general and universally applicable principle by which the pure practical reason could distinguish right from wrong.

He started with the fact that people have a sense of moral obligation – what he calls the **categorical imperative**. In other words, we all know that there are things we 'should' do, irrespective of the consequences. He contrasted this with a 'hypothetical' imperative, which says what you need to do in order to achieve some chosen result. Thus:

▶ *You should work hard (categorical imperative).*
▶ *You should work hard if you want to succeed in this business (hypothetical imperative).*

Insight

Of course, you might want to argue that all categorical imperatives are really hypothetical imperatives in disguise – prompted by the unconscious programming of your childhood and social pressure.

Kant's aim was to express this experience of the categorical imperative in the form of universal principles of morality. These principles are generally referred to as the three forms of Kant's categorical imperative. He expressed them using various forms of words, but they amount to this:

▶ *Act only on that maxim (or principle) which you can – at the same time – will that it should become a universal law.*
▶ *Act in such a way as to treat people as ends and never as means.*
▶ *Act as though you were legislating for a kingdom of ends.*

The first of these expresses the idea that, whatever one wishes to do, one should be prepared for everyone else to act upon that same principle. If you are not prepared for the maxim of your action to become a universal rule, then you should not do it in your individual circumstances.

Here you have the most general of all principles, and one which, on the surface, has a long pedigree. It follows from the golden rule – to do to others only that which you would wish them to do to you.

One problem with this, however, is that there may be circumstances in which a person may want to kill or lie, without wishing for killing or lying to become universal. Suppose, for example, that the life of an innocent person is being threatened, and the only way of saving him or her is by lying, then a person would wish to do so. In this case, following Kant's argument, one would need to argue that you could wish that anyone in an *identical* situation should be free to lie, without thereby willing that anyone in *any* situation should be free to do so – and here we are back to the most general of all moral problems, how you relate a particular action and set of circumstances to the general moral principle.

The second form of the categorical imperative follows from the first. If you want to express your own moral autonomy, you should treat all others on the basis that they would want the same. So you should not treat them as 'means' to your own end, but as 'ends' in themselves. And the third form suggests that you should make your moral judgements as though you had responsibility for legislating in a kingdom in which everyone was an 'end', respected as an autonomous moral being.

An example

An article entitled 'Kant on Welfare' (Canadian Journal of Philosophy, June 1999), by Mark LeBar of the University of Ohio, illustrates the problem of applying Kant's universal principle that people should be treated as ends rather than means. It opens:

> *Contemporary debate over public welfare policy is often cast in Kantian terms. It is argued, for example, that respect for the dignity of the poor requires public aid, or that respect for their autonomy forbids it.*

This is a perfect example of where a general principle is not enough to establish whether the one or the other approach is morally right. We know what we might want in theory, what we do not know is the practical steps that are needed to achieve it; but it is in facing those practical steps that we are confronted with moral dilemmas.

Natural law, the assessment of results, and the sense of moral obligation: these three (sometimes singly, sometimes mixed together) form the basis of ethical argument. Natural law and a sense of moral obligation usually lead to the framing of general moral principles: that this or that sort of action is right or wrong. It is quite another matter whether it is fair to apply any such general rule to each and every situation. By the same token, the utilitarian assessment of results, although apparently more immediately practical, is always open to the ambiguity of fate, for we never really know the long-term consequences of what we do.

Insight

So no one basis for ethics is without its problems; sometimes one may seem more useful, sometimes another. Taken together, however, they do provide a broad range of rational strategies for dealing with moral dilemmas.

Absolute or relative morality?

If moral rules are absolute, then a particular action may be considered wrong no matter what the circumstances. So, for example, theft may be considered to be wrong. But what is theft? In one sense, the definition is straightforward: theft is the action of taking what belongs to another without that person's consent. The problem is that 'theft' is a term that may be used to interpret individual situations. Can we always be sure that it is the right term? If not, then is it right to treat an action as morally equal to 'theft', if that is not the way one or more of the people concerned see the matter.

One example of this dilemma might be 'mercy killing', where someone who is seriously ill and facing the prospect of a painful or lingering death is helped to die by a relative or close friend. If you take a view that there are moral absolutes, you may say: 'Murder is always wrong.' The next question then becomes: 'Is mercy killing the same thing as murder?' In other words, you start with absolute moral principles and then assess each particular situation in terms of which of these moral principles are involved (a process that is generally termed **casuistry**).

If you do not think that there are moral absolutes, you are more likely to start with particular situations and assess the intentions and consequences involved. In making such an assessment you bring to bear your general views about life and of the implications that various actions have on society as a whole.

In 1966, Joseph Fletcher published a book entitled *Situation Ethics*, which reflected a reaction against the perceived narrowness of traditional Christian morality at a time of rapid social change. Rather than simply obeying rules, he argued that one should always do what love required in each and every situation, and claimed that his view represented a fundamental feature of the Christian approach to life, as seen in the emphasis on love in *I Corinthians*, the rejection of Jewish legalism, or St Augustine's view that, if you love, what you want to do will be what is right.

By following the law of love and the demands of each situation, this approach suggested that it would sometimes be right to set aside conventional moral rule or go against the expectations of society. Although critics from a traditional position tended to accuse **situation ethics** of leading to moral anarchy, it was a genuine attempt to combine an overall moral principle (love) with a recognition of the uniqueness of every situation.

An example

To illustrate the complexities of applying general rules to particular situations, let us take one actual example of what is generally known as 'date rape'. This is the term used when a charge of rape is made against a person known to the 'victim' (itself a loaded term, pre-judging the outcome of the enquiry) and carried out in the course of a date. Date rape is a good example of the ambiguities that arise in legal and moral debates, since any straightforward description of the situation (sexual intercourse against the will of one partner or, in the particular case we shall be examining, attempted intercourse) is made more complicated by the circumstances in which it takes place, namely that the two people involved have chosen to be together socially.

A solicitor took a colleague to a ball at a London hotel. Each had assumptions about the nature of the relationship between them that was established by his inviting her to the ball and her accepting that invitation. She made a complaint against him, and he was charged with attempted rape. According to a newspaper report, he committed the offence after a night of dancing reels and drinking whisky and champagne with his 'victim', known throughout the trial as Miss X. She invited him to share a room with her at a friend's flat, undressed in front of him, and fell asleep. She alleged that she awoke to find him on top of her, wearing only his frilly cuffs and a green condom.

A newspaper report presented the argument that Miss X, by undressing down to her knickers in full view of a man with whom she had spent the evening, was behaving foolishly and should therefore accept some responsibility for what followed.

At the trial, the solicitor was found guilty of attempted rape and sentenced to three years in prison, later reduced to two years on appeal. He was released after serving half this sentence, on grounds of good conduct, but (at the time of his release) it was anticipated that he would face a disciplinary hearing before the Solicitors' Complaints Bureau, with a good chance that he would be prevented from continuing his legal career.

There are various matters that need be taken into consideration:

Rape and attempted rape are serious matters, involving violence (physical and/or emotional) towards the victim. That is the general principle; the question here is whether this particular situation should be classified as rape.

▶ *If one person invites another to share a room, is that invitation to be taken as at least implying that the idea of having some sort of sexual relationship is not out of the question (i.e. the invitation to share a room might not be a direct invitation to have sex, but might it not suggest that the matter is at least a possibility?).*

▶ *Does an act of sexual intercourse between two people who have voluntarily shared some time together (i.e. on a 'date') require a specific act of verbal consent?*

▶ *If no specific verbal or written consent is given (i.e. there is no exchange of contracts before clothes are removed – even between solicitors!) does a misinterpretation of the situation by one party constitute rape or attempted rape?*

▶ *Consider another possibility. If a woman were to invite a man back to her room after such an evening, hoping for sex (and under the impression that he was willing), but the man – perhaps because of an excess of whisky – were to fall asleep on the sofa, could she take a civil action against him for breach of implied promise?*

▶ *In such circumstances, is the action 'rape' or simply the result of misunderstanding?*

▶ *Can the act of undressing before another person be considered 'contributory negligence' if a rape or attempted rape ensues?*

Contrariwise, a person bringing the charge of date rape could argue:

▶ *Rape, violence and other forms of abuse often take place between people who know one another. The fact of their previous relationship does not lessen the seriousness of the action that takes place or is threatened.*

▶ *There can be no objective proof of misunderstanding. Claiming that you misunderstood something may be a later rationale of the situation, or an excuse.*

Becoming drunk may render a person incapable of behaving rationally or following previously accepted moral principles. That may *explain* subsequent behaviour, but it does not *excuse it*. Two drunken people together may act foolishly, and may regret their behaviour once sober, but that should not, in itself, mean that legal and moral considerations are suspended while they are under the influence. What is more, giving alcohol or drugs in order to render a person incapable of rational thought or behaviour, with the intention of taking advantage of that fact, is itself an act of abuse against that person.

The problem for ethics is that a unique situation may be understood in many different ways. The words chosen (attempted rape; victim) interpret, rather than describe, the event. Even if it is agreed that rape is *always* morally wrong, there remains the problem of deciding *exactly when that term should be used*. Hence there may need to be flexibility, even within a framework of absolute moral values.

That said, allowing each event to determine its own rules is likely to lead to moral and social chaos. As with so many issues in philosophy, the problem here is to know how the particular is related to the universal.

VALUES AND SOCIETY

There is a broader sense in which we need to be aware of relativity in ethics. Each society has its own particular way of life, along with the values and principles that are expressed in it. What might be considered right in one society may be thought wrong in another. A set of moral rules may be drawn up that are valid for a particular society, but cannot be applied universally.

However, if we live in a multicultural and complex society, we have to face the relativity of moral judgements. To this may be added the general sense in a postmodernist era (see p. 257) that everything depends upon taking, using and mixing the cultural, linguistic and mental ideas that we find around us. In such a situation, it is very difficult to try to impose uniform moral principles. Apart from anything else, the principles may tend to be rejected on the grounds of their origin – in the Catholic Church, in the case of natural law, or in the words of a long-dead, male philosopher, in the case of Kant.

Of the theories we have examined so far, preference utilitarianism gets round this problem most straightforwardly, since individual preferences (and therefore the cultural and social factors that give rise to them) are taken into the utilitarian assessment.

Kantian ethics has the greatest problem with relativism. On the one hand, it wants to establish universal moral principles (which relativism will not allow) and on the other it wants to treat each individual as an autonomous moral agent (of which relativism approves).

> ## Insight
> Kant may perhaps be forgiven for not appreciating the scale of the relativist challenge in a multicultural society, since he spent his whole life in his native Köningsberg.

But the real problem for many ethical thinkers today is with a full-blown relativism which simply refuses to accept any general moral norms. In other words, it becomes increasingly difficult to make any moral judgements that may not be challenged on the basis of the gender, race, religion or social position of the person making that judgement. Sensitivity to social norms or particular circumstances has always been a key feature of ethics – and even the much maligned process of 'casuistry' attempted to apply moral principles to particular situations rather than impose them. But at some point, if moral discussions are to be effective, there needs to be a shared set of values, and that implies that there must be a limit to relativism.

THE VALUES YOU CHOOSE

Is morality something discovered, or something created? Some approaches – natural law for example – clearly see morality as linked to objective facts about the world, moulding human morality to fit an overall sense of purpose. There is another approach, however, which suggests that we are free to choose the basis for our morality.

This approach is illustrated by Nietzsche, the title of one of whose books is *Beyond Good and Evil*. For Nietzsche, humankind has a responsibility to develop towards something higher, to say 'Yes!' to life and affirm the future. He saw both Christianity and democracy as fundamentally a morality for slaves, attempting to protect the weak at the expense of the strong, and thereby weakening the species. Rather, he looks to a master morality, deliberately choosing the *übermensch*, or higher man, as the meaning of the Earth.

Equally, existentialism (which we shall look at briefly in Chapter 8), in emphasizing person authenticity, tends to see morality in terms of the affirmation of the self. I shape my life by the choices I make, and take responsibility for that shaping. But choices have ethical implications; so existentialism gives a particularly self-referential approach to morality.

Virtue ethics

Rather than looking at actions, and asking if they are right or wrong, one could start by asking the basic question 'What does it mean to be a "good" person?', and develop this to explore the qualities and virtues that make up the 'good' life. This approach had been taken first by Aristotle who linked the displaying of certain qualities with the final end or purpose of life.

As it developed in the 1950s, this approach appealed to feminist thinkers, who considered the traditional ethical arguments to have been influenced by particularly male ways of approaching life, based on rights and duties, whereas they sought a more 'feminine' approach and a recognition of the value of relationships and intimacy.

Virtue ethics was also seen as '*naturalistic*', in that it moved away from the idea of simply obeying rules, to an appreciation of how one might express one's own fundamental nature, and thus fulfil one's potential as a human being.

Virtue ethics raises some basic questions:

- *Do we have a fixed* **essence**? *Are there particular masculine or feminine qualities that give rise to virtues appropriate to each sex? Or is our nature the product of our surroundings and upbringing?*
- *If our nature has been shaped by factors over which we have no control (e.g. the culture into which we have been born, traumatic experiences in childhood)* **are we responsible for our actions?**
- *How should we relate the expression of an individual's virtues to the actual needs of society?*
- *How are you able to decide between different ways of expressing the same virtue? For example, a sense of love and compassion might lead one person to help someone who is seriously ill to die, yet another might find that love and compassion lead them to struggle to keep that same person alive. In some way, you need to fall back on other ethical theories if you want to assess the actions that spring from particular virtues.*

Comment

Notice that beneath some of these 'virtue ethics' approaches lie the basic questions raised by Aristotle about the end or purpose of human life. Whereas 'natural law' generally examines an action in terms of its 'final cause', virtue ethics examines human qualities in terms of their overall place within human life, and the appropriate ways in which they may be expressed.

The social contract

Ethics may be based on social contract. In other words, morality may follow agreements to abide by certain rules, made between people to limit what they are able to do, in order to benefit both themselves and society as a whole. Most would accept that there needs to be some compromise between the freedom of the individual and the overall good of society and its need for security.

Social contract theories apportion *responsibilities* to individuals and to the mechanisms of government by which society is organized. In other words, they set out what can reasonably be expected of people in terms of their relationship with others. They also set out the *rights* to which individuals are entitled. Many areas of applied ethics have focused on rights and responsibilities, especially in the area of professional conduct. For example, they might ask what responsibility a doctor has to his patients, to the society within which he or she practises, and to the development of medicine – and from this a code of professional conduct can be drawn up. Equally, it can ask what basic expectations a person should have in terms of the way in which he or she should be treated by other people or by the state. This has led to various declarations of human rights, which provide a touchstone for whether a society is behaving justly.

Comment

Discussion of rights and responsibilities tends to reflect both absolutist views – as, for example, in claiming that people should enjoy basic human rights, irrespective of who they are – and also utilitarian ones, in that the benefits that might come from agreements about people's social responsibilities are often assessed in terms of the overall happiness of society.

Although rights and responsibilities are key features of ethical debate, the actual agreements which form the basis of social contract ethics will be examined in the next chapter, which is concerned with political philosophy, since they follow from questions about justice and the right ordering of society.

Applied ethics

Throughout history, philosophers have sought to apply their ideas, and this has been most obvious in the field of ethics. Applied ethics started to come to the fore again during the last three decades of the twentieth century, after a number of years during which philosophers had been rather preoccupied by linguistic questions about the meaning and nature of ethical statements.

There is no scope in an introductory text of this sort to do more than point to some of the major areas within which ethics is applied today, but those interested in following up this aspect of ethics will find that there are a huge number of books covering the different professions and issues.

Professional ethics has been concerned principally with standards of conduct expected of members of the professions and also with drawing up guidelines for those situations where there are difficult moral choices to be made. The medical, nursing and legal professions most obviously provide a whole range of moral dilemmas that need to be examined.

Sometimes advances in technology raise issues that require ethical examination. The rise of information technology, for example, raises issues about privacy, identity theft, and the limits to what can be done with stored information. Should the state be responsible for, and have control of, whatever data it manages to gather on its citizens? Should I have a right to see what information is held about me? Of course, issues of privacy have been around for a long time, but they are brought into sharper focus by the ability to store and retrieve data in digital form. Equally, genetic manipulation of the food we eat is an old issue presented in a very new form. These are matters that affect everyone, and are therefore not limited to those who work in the relevant industry.

Business ethics is an important and growing area of interest, with the conflict between those who favour a market-led approach and those who want more political and social control. Equally, media ethics is relevant to everyone, since assumptions are made about the veracity of news items, the morality of public humiliation or deception, and whether the media should have social and political responsibilities.

A huge and increasingly important set of applied ethical issues concern the environment. The debates about global warming highlight a clash of interest between the potential harm done to the global environment and the economic benefits of increasing industrialization. It spans the globe, and therefore touches on the broader economic and social issues about sustainable development and the obligations of richer nations to help poorer ones. And that, of course, touches on the absolutely crucial issue of the existence of abject poverty in a world of plenty, an issue highlighted starkly by Peter Singer, along with that of our treatment of other species.

Insight

You will find that most arguments in this area are fundamentally utilitarian, with a clash of interest between the short-term economic benefits to the relative few and the potential long-term benefits to all.

And there is, of course, the huge issue of the morality of warfare, raised again in recent years, particularly by debates over the justice of launching the second Iraq war and over the aims, human cost, and likely outcome of the war in Afghanistan. Traditionally, this application of ethics has been divided into issues over when it is right to go to war, and how wars should be fought, once they have started. Hence morality examines both the right of a nation to defend itself against a real or perceived threat, and the types of weapons that are used in battle.

Note

Ethics is a huge subject, both in terms of the range of ethical theories and the way in which these may be applied to moral and social issues. It has provided the impetus for much work in

(Contd)

philosophy as a whole, and is the single largest area of study within departments of philosophy (judging by the number of papers published). It is particularly valuable as an area of philosophical study, since the benefits of clear thinking, analysis and the clarification of concepts and presuppositions can be seen to have immediate relevance to practical areas of life.

Faced with the dilemma of whether or not to turn off the life-support machine of someone in a deep coma and unable to recover, one starts to ask not just about the ethical status of euthanasia, but also what it means to be a human being, what constitutes human life, and therefore whether the person whose body is being maintained by a machine can be said to be living in any meaningful way.

For further treatment of some of these issues see *Understand Ethics* in this series. Readers wanting to examine the ethical issues in particular professions should move on to the very extensive literature now available in this area.

10 THINGS TO REMEMBER

1 *You cannot derive an 'ought' from an 'is'.*

2 *Moral responsibility implies freedom of action.*

3 *Descriptive ethics simply says what happens.*

4 *Normative ethics argues for what should happen.*

5 *Emotivism and prescriptivism attempt to avoid the positivist claim that ethics is meaningless.*

6 *Natural law is concerned with a rational interpretation of nature, not a description of nature.*

7 *Utilitarianism argues in favour of the greatest benefit for the greatest number.*

8 *Kant attempted to frame universal moral principles based on pure practical reason.*

9 *Ethical values may be relative to social norms and may be created rather than discovered.*

10 *The practical application of ethical principles is the most popular area of philosophy today.*

7

Political philosophy

In this chapter you will learn:
- *about the social contract and other political theories*
- *about how society changes and progresses*
- *about key issues of justice, fairness and human rights.*

From time to time, politicians speak of 'getting back to basics', or of the fundamental principles of democracy, or socialism, or human rights, or international law. They seek to explain and justify particular legislation, or the decision to take some action in terms of the good of society as a whole, or concepts of justice.

But what are the 'basics' to which politicians might choose to return?

▶ *Are they the bases upon which a political system is established? If so, what are they?*
▶ *Does it mean 'back to basic values'? Does that imply, for example, conventional 'family values'? Or might they be the values of capitalism, or socialism? Or might it refer to a return to the conventional attitudes of some ideal, past age?*
▶ *But what are the basic human needs? Does everyone need or expect the same sort of things from a government?*

- *More generally, what is the 'basis' of civilized life?*
- *What basic values, if any, can be agreed on? Is a basis something you start from and then develop, or is it something fixed and unchanging to which you need to return from time to time?*

Starting from the phrase 'back to basics', we enter into some of the issues with which political philosophy is concerned. Set out in more abstract terms these concerns are:

- *the concepts of freedom, justice, liberty and equality*
- *the role of the state*
- *the relationship between the state and the individual*
- *the nature of authority*
- *the status of law*
- *the role of power*
- *human rights.*

Only individuals?

Does the state exist? Is there any such thing as society? If I were suddenly to declare that the USA did not exist, I would be thought insane, but is it that obvious? There are two ways of looking at individuals and society:

1 *Society, or the nation, is a reality over and above its individual citizens. It is 'real' in the sense that it can exert its power over them, forcing them to take part in a war, claiming taxes from them, imposing laws on them. Patriotism depends on the idea that the nation is real, worth fighting for.*
2 *There is no such thing as society. There are just individuals who decide on rules and regulations for their mutual benefit and who band together to do things that are beyond the abilities of any one person or family. In this case, Great Britain or the USA are just names: they have no reality other than the millions of people who happen to live in those parts*

of the world, and the various institutions by which they organize their lives.

If you tend towards the first of these, you might take a further step and claim that individuals can only exist as part of larger social groups. You could argue, for example:

▶ *You are part of a family and circle of friends: you are a mother, father, child or friend by virtue of your relationships. Without other people you would be none of these things.*
▶ *You speak a language that is not of your own devising. You share in a common store of words and thoughts. Without society, there would be no language. You have 'rights' as an individual only because they are given to you by society.*

Therefore, although you would continue to be a human being, you would not really be an 'individual', with a name, rights, a language and a stock of inherited ideas, without society.

In other words

▶ *Confronted by a cat, a mouse cannot argue its case for the right to life, liberty and happiness.*
▶ *Individual rights or social obligations are not discovered in nature, they are devised by society.*
▶ *Without society there would be no rights, no obligations, no laws, no morality.*

The idea of the individual or citizen is closely linked to that of society or the state. Each is defined with reference to the other. A central issue for the philosophy of politics is to find an acceptable balance between these two things. Individualism; democracy; totalitarianism; socialism; cultural imperialism; regionalism; internationalism: these are all about the balance between individuals or groups and the larger social wholes of which they are a part.

Insight

Margaret Thatcher, at the Conservative Party Conference in 1987, famously declared 'And, you know, there's no such thing as society. There are individual men and women and there are families. And no government can do anything except through people, and people must look after themselves first.' Such a view minimizes the role of government and puts individuals centre-stage.

The social contract

Self-preservation is a fundamental human need. Born in 1588, Thomas Hobbes knew first hand the traumas of civil war in England and used such a lawless and dangerous state as the starting point for his political theory. In Chapter 13 of *Leviathan*, published in 1651, he considers what life is like when a person can rely only on his own strength for protection:

In such condition, there is no place for industry, because the fruit thereof is uncertain; and consequently no culture of the earth; no navigation, nor use of the commodities that may be imported by sea; no commodious building, no instruments of moving or removing such things as require much force; no knowledge of the face of the earth; no account of time; no arts; no letters; no society; and, which is worst of all, continual fear and danger of violent death; and the life of man solitary, poor, nasty, brutish, and short.

Hobbes considered that the need for self-preservation was so basic to human life, that (using a 'natural law' form of argument) reason could show that the basis for political science was the preservation of life. He also showed, in the passage just quoted, that society depends upon personal security, and that without it civilization is impossible.

In this situation, Hobbes argued that people would band together for their mutual protection, and would set up a ruler who would maintain order. The value of the state is seen in its ability to protect and benefit the individuals of which it is comprised. His political theory, the start of what is called the 'social contract' tradition, springs from this need for self-preservation. Hobbes believed, however, that the ruler so appointed should be given absolute power, and that only by doing so could the security of the state be maintained.

John Locke (1632–1704) argued from a similar starting point. He saw the laws imposed by a ruler on individuals as based on the need for the preservation of life and private property within the state, and defence from foreign threats. But he went beyond Hobbes, arguing that the people who entered into their social contract should have the right, if the rulers did not benefit them, to replace them with others. In other words, he argued for a representative democracy, with rulers accountable to those who have put them in power. Thus we have a constitutional government, where rulers have power, but only to the extent that they are given it by the people, and within principles that are set out within a constitution.

Such political systems are based on a social contract; on the agreement between people that they shall act together for their mutual benefit. The problem arises over exactly what is to the benefit of society, and who is to decide it. To what extent can an individual, on the basis of a social contract, act on behalf of all? Do all have to agree before some action is taken? On what basis is there to be arbitration between conflicting interests. Locke is clear that decisions must reflect the wishes of a majority, and any minority must accept that judgement:

> *Every man, by consenting with others to make one body politic under one government, puts himself under an obligation to every one of that society to submit to the determination of the majority, and to be concluded by it; or else this original compact, whereby he with others incorporates into one society, would signify nothing, and be no compact if he be left free and under no other ties than he was in before in the state of Nature.*
>
> The Second Treatise of Government, Chapter 13, section 97

Thus a government can act as long as it has the consent of a majority. But what if a government seeks to act in a way which the rulers consider to be in the interests of the people, even if that is not what people as individuals actually want?

The general will

Jean-Jacques Rousseau (1712–78), was a Swiss philosopher who, in spite of having little formal education and a hard and colourful personal life, produced ideas about democracy that were to be hugely influential, particularly at the time of the French Revolution.

Rousseau, recognizing that all existing states were imperfect, sought to start from first principles and establish the basis of a legitimate political system. Like Hobbes and Locke, he looked back to man in a state of nature but, unlike them, he thought that in such a natural state people's needs would be few and relatively easily satisfied, and would be unlikely to lead to conflict.

By contrast, once society becomes established, people enclose property and deprive others of the use of it. The basic requirements of food and shelter become commodities which people have to get through barter, and many are therefore reduced to misery. With private property, inequality increases and leads to civil strife. Thus, where Hobbes and Locke saw private property as a natural right to be defended, Rousseau saw it as something artificially imposed by society. He saw society as tending to corrupt natural man rather than improve him.

Insight

For Rousseau, natural human feelings and instincts are fundamentally good; it is the government imposed by reason that threatens humankind by offering temptations and highlighting inequalities.

Rousseau presents a form of social contract, but one that differs significantly from that set out by Hobbes or Locke. A central issue for Rousseau is how an individual can retain his or her freedom, while at the same time accepting the terms of a social contract, and the requirement that an individual is bound by the wishes of society as a whole. He does this through the idea of the 'general will'. He argues that an individual must give himself or herself totally, including all rights, to the whole community. The general will is sovereign, and individuals find their own freedom by conforming to it.

For Rousseau, natural freedom is, in fact, a slavery to individual passions. By contrast, to set aside one's individual, personal will, and to accept the general will, is to discover one's higher aspirations and moral freedom. There will be occasions when individuals will oppose the general will, but on those occasions the individual concerned should be forced to accept it, for the good of all.

In any political system, someone has to decide how general laws should be applied to individual situations. Rousseau held that there should be a legislator, someone who would know instinctively what the general will was and be able to apply it.

In general, one might say that, whereas for Hobbes and Locke, individuals are freely able to decide what is in their own best interests (although sometimes required to set these interests aside for the benefit of the majority), for Rousseau, individuals are not able to decide what is best, and therefore are required to accept what is deemed to be best by the general will – in other words, by the state.

The implications of this aspect of Rousseau's thinking are
enormous. A state can carry out the most drastic action
(decapitating the aristocracy, eliminating whole classes of people
in state purges) on the basis of carrying out the 'general will'. The
problem lies in the inability to challenge the 'general will' and
therefore the possibility that what is being done is not in fact
the will of the people. In the twentieth century, the examples of
Stalin's Russia, China under Mao and Cambodia under Pol Pot all
illustrate the power of the state to claim to act for the benefit of
all, while actually perpetrating state terror.

Marx and materialism

Karl Marx (1818–83) has been an enormously influential thinker.
Indeed, one cannot start to describe the history of the twentieth
century without reference to Marxism and the communist regimes
that sprang from it. Born in Germany, he moved to Paris when
the newspaper he was editing was forced to close. Expelled from
both Paris and then Brussels, he finally settled in London. His most
important book, *Das Kapital* (1867), predicts that capitalism has
within it the seeds of its own destruction and will give way
to socialism.

Marx argued that religion, morality, political ideas and social
structures were fundamentally rooted in economics, particularly
the production and distribution of goods. People have basic needs
which must be fulfilled in order for them to live, and society
becomes more and more sophisticated in order to produce the
goods and services to meet those needs. He therefore interpreted
history in economic terms, as shaped by the struggle between
different social classes. The bourgeoisie confronts the proletariat;

employers facing employees as once landowners faced their peasants. Individual actions are judged by the way in which they contribute to the class struggle, and the actions of a class as a whole is seen in a broader context of the movement of society.

In terms of the history of philosophy, Marx was influenced by Hegel (1770–1831) who saw the lives of individuals as bound up with the tide of history, which itself was unfolding by a rational process. Like Hegel, Marx saw reality as working itself out through a process of change. Hegel had introduced the idea of a 'dialectic': first you have a thesis, then in response to this you have the opposite (an antithesis), and bringing these two together you get a synthesis. But for Hegel, this process was non-material, leading to a harmonious awareness of the Geist, or spirit of the age, in which everyone freely accepts the interest of the whole of society.

For Marx, by contrast, the process of dialectic is material. It is the economic conditions under which the classes live and work that produce the urge to change, as a result of which the existing economic system is overthrown through a revolution and a new system is set up, but that, in turn, leads to further class confrontation, and so on. Marx looked towards the achievement of a classless society, where there would be no more confrontation, but where working people would own the means of production and distribution. This classless society would therefore be characterized by economic justice, in which each benefited from his or her own labour.

This was linked to his view of the fulfilment of the human individual. Marx argued that, in a capitalist system, an individual who works for a wage, producing something from which someone else is going to make a profit, becomes alienated from that working situation. He or she cannot exercise true creativity or humanity, but becomes an impersonal 'thing', a machine whose sole purpose in life is production, a means of making 'capital'. He saw this process leading to more and more wealth being concentrated in the hands of a small number of 'bourgeoisie', with the working proletariat sinking into poverty. This, he believed, would eventually lead to the overthrow of the capitalist system by the workers acting together. He believed that, with the advent of the classless society, each individual would be able to develop to his or her full potential.

Marx has things to say about the nature of history, of work, of the self, of political institutions and of social classes, but he is also a prime example of the way in which a philosopher can influence the course of history. It is difficult to study Marx without being aware of the global impact of Marxist ideology in the twentieth century. The decline of communism in the last decades of the twentieth century, and capitalism's failure to self-destruct in the way he predicted, will obviously be taken into account by anyone who studies his political philosophy. Contrariwise, it is difficult to overestimate the general impact of his thinking, particularly, perhaps, in the view that politics is based on economics.

Insight

Although Marx's main work was *Das Kapital* (1867), it may be easier to approach him first through his earlier works, particularly *The German Ideology* (1846) and *The Communist Manifesto* (1848).

Notice that Marx (following Rousseau and, indeed, Hegel) saw the individual as subsuming his or her interests for the benefit of the wider group. The individual acts as a representative of his or her class or nation, and those actions are judged by whatever is deemed to be right by that larger social group. This is in contrast to the tradition which stems from Hobbes and Locke, where the emphasis is on the individual. We shall see in the next section that this divide is still found in political philosophy, as reflected in the differing views of justice taken by two modern philosophers, Rawls and Nozick.

Comment

Mikhail Gorbachev, leader of the Soviet Union from 1985–1991, writing in 2009 to mark the twentieth anniversary of the fall of the Berlin Wall, commented, 'The real achievement we can celebrate is the fact that the twentieth century marked the end of totalitarian ideologies, in particular those that were based on utopian beliefs.' (*The Guardian*, 31 October 2009, page 35). Looking back on the terrible suffering that such ideologies caused throughout the twentieth century, one is reminded of just how important and relevant political philosophy can be – get it wrong and swathes of humankind bear the burden.

Justice

The idea of justice is fundamental to political philosophy. If people are to band together for mutual protection, if they are to enter into social contracts, if they are to set their own interests aside, they need to be persuaded that the society within which they live is based on principles that are just. But what constitutes political justice?

We shall look at ideas of justice presented by three philosophers, one ancient and two modern.

PLATO

The question 'What is justice?' dominates one of the greatest works of philosophy, Plato's *Republic*. In this book (presented as a dialogue between Socrates and the representatives of contemporary schools of thought), various answers are proposed and rejected, as, for example, the popular but rather cynical view that justice is whatever is in the interest of the stronger! Plato recognizes that human nature can be deeply selfish, and that – given the opportunity to act with absolute impunity – people will generally seek their own benefit rather than that of others, or of society as a whole, and also explores the idea (later to be developed by the 'social contract' theory) that people need to be restrained for the good of all. But what is the value of justice in itself?

Socrates considers the various classes of people that make up the
city, and argues that each class offers particular virtues, but that
justice is found in the fact that each class performs its own task.
In the same way, the individual soul is divided into three parts –
mind, spirit and appetite – and that justice for the individual
consists in the balance, with each part performing its own task
for the benefit of that individual.

Justice is seen in the harmony and proper functioning of each
part of society, and Plato wanted the rulers of his *Republic* to be
philosophers, seeking only the truth rather than their own self-
interest. This, he argued, would be necessary if justice was to be
established for all rather than in the interests of a particular section
of the population.

Every philosophy needs to be seen against the background of
its particular time and society, and Plato is no exception. His
concept of a state ruled by philosophers, seeking a balance between
elements in society and in the self, with priority given to the
intellectual faculty, is not easily translatable into a modern political
context. What is clear, however, is that justice (for Plato) is seen
neither in equality (he never envisaged a society of equals) nor in
sectional interest (he rejected the idea that it was the interest of the
stronger), but in a balance in which different people and classes,
each doing what is appropriate for them, work together for the
common good.

RAWLS (JUSTICE AS FAIRNESS)

In *A Theory of Justice* (1972) John Rawls considers (as a thought
experiment) a situation in which a group of people come together

to decide the principles upon which their political association should operate. In other words, they set about forming a social contract. But he adds one further important criterion: that they should forget everything about themselves as individuals. They do not know if they are poor or wealthy, men or women. They do not know their race or their position within society. They come together simply as individuals, nothing more. He therefore seeks by this means to establish principles that:

> *free and rational persons concerned to further their own interests would accept in an initial position of equality as defining the fundamental terms of their association.*
>
> p. 11

In other words, they are concerned to benefit themselves, but do not know who they are. By this means, Rawls hopes to achieve justice, for people will seek to legislate in a way that will benefit themselves, whoever they eventually turn out to be.

Rawls argues that such a group would require two principles:

1 **Liberty:** *Each person should have equal rights to as extensive a set of basic liberties as possible, as long as that does not prevent others from having a similar set of fundamental liberties.*
2 **Distribution of resources:** *Given that there are social inequalities, Rawls argues that the distribution of resources should be such that the least advantaged in society receive the greatest benefit.*

This is justice based on 'fairness'. Rawls argues that it is fair to grant everyone equal freedom and opportunity, and that, if there is to be inequality at all, it should only be allowed on the grounds that it benefits those who have the least advantages in life. The task of society (in addition to the basic protection of individuals who have come together to form it) is, according to Rawls, that it should organize the fair sharing out of both material and social benefits.

Not all philosophers would agree with Rawls' attempt to reduce inequalities. In the nineteenth century, Nietzsche's view was that the strong should not be restrained because of the needs of the weak. His views were that democracy and Christianity had a negative effect, weakening the human species by seeking special advantage for those who are weak or poor and handicapped in some way. By contrast, he looked towards an *übermensch* – an 'over-man' or 'beyond-man' – expressing the idea of striving to be something more. For Nietzsche, man is something that has to be overcome: a starting point from which we move forward and upward.

Insight

Natural selection suggests that competition, rather than fairness and consideration for others, is the basis of evolutionary advance. Applied to human society this evolutionary perspective has a sad history, from Spencer's 'survival of the fittest' to Eugenics, ideas of *racial* superiority, ethnic cleansing, and – under the Nazis for example – to genocide.

But there is a more general criticism of his approach. A little earlier in this chapter we looked at the basic division between those who would give priority to the individual (and for whom the state should have a minimal role), who may go so far as to argue that the state does not exist, and those who give priority to the state, so that it is only in the context of society that individuals come to their full potential. Let us examine Rawls' theory from this perspective.

By making the people who come together to establish the principles of society forget who they are, they also relinquish all that they might naturally have gained and achieved. The successful person is made to forget all that he or she has gained by hard work, and to opt for an equal share of the pooled resources for fear of finding out that he or she was, in fact, the poorest.

In theory this might establish a society where all are offered fair shares. But could it work like that in the real world? It could be argued that there never was, and never will be, an 'original position' from which to devise the rules of a society. All actual legal systems, and all ideas of justice, are framed within, and grow out of, an historical context.

Another criticism of this approach is made by Ronald Dworkin. He argues that, before you can ask 'What is justice?' you need to ask the prior question 'What kind of life should men and women lead? What counts as excellence in a human being?' He argues that the liberal position, as given by Rawls, does not take this into consideration. Rawls' treatment of individuals does not depend on *anything about them as individuals*.

For reflection

If every inequality is allowed only on the basis that it benefits the least well off (Rawls' view), there is little chance that excellence will be developed, since every facility offered for the development of excellence is likely to increase rather than decrease the gap between the most able and the least able. How can such a theory avoid bland mediocrity?

NOZICK (JUSTICE AS ENTITLEMENT)

If the purpose of society is to protect the life, liberty and property of individuals, then each person should be enabled to retain those things which are rightly theirs. A society which, in the name of establishing equality, redistributes that wealth is in fact depriving an individual of the very protection which led to the formation of society in the first place.

This approach to the question of justice is taken by Robert Nozick. In *Anarchy, State and Utopia* (1974), he argued that it is wrong for the state to take taxes from individuals or force them to contribute to a health service that benefits others. It infringes their liberty to gain wealth and retain it. For Nozick, it is perfectly right to give what you have to another person if you so choose, but not to demand that another person give to you. On this social theory, voluntary contributions are welcomed, but enforced taxes are not. He argues that justice is a matter of the entitlement of individuals to retain their 'holdings' – wealth that they have gained legitimately.

An important feature of Nozick's case is that, at any one time, the actual wealth that a person owns is related to history: that of the individual (through having worked for years, for example) or that of his or her family (through inheritance). In practice, however, it is not always easy to establish that all wealth has been gained legitimately. Land which has been in a family for generations may originally have been gained by the most dubious of means.

Nozick also argues, against those that seek equality, that even if people were made equal, they would immediately start trading, and would quickly establish new inequalities.

In other words

▶ *Private property is theft! (This implies that all property should belong to the state, or ultimately to the global community.) Justice demands redistribution on the basis of need.*

Or

▶ *Redistribution is theft! (This implies that each individual has the right to that which is lawfully gained.) Justice demands that each should develop to his or her potential, unhampered by false notions of equality.*

In the name of liberty, it is tempting to suggest that politics should be morally neutral. In other words, there should be equal scope and equal respect for all views, values and beliefs, and that politicians should keep out of issues of personal choice and morality. The danger with this is that politics may become a mechanism for ensuring that everyone is happy, but does not address the moral questions about what should constitute the good life. But where fundamental values differ, agreement on political ends is very difficult to establish. Politics should therefore remain open to moral discussion and debate. This is argued strongly by, for example, Michael Sandel, who teaches a course on 'Justice' at Harvard, and who is concerned that politics should not lose sight of the fundamental questions about what it means to lead a good life. His argument that political argument today is morally impoverished is set out in his recent book *Justice: What's the Right Thing to Do?*, Allen Lane, 2009.

Freedom and law

Freedom in this context means something rather different from the 'freedom/determinism' debate outlined earlier. In that case, the determinist argument was that everything depends on prior causes and may (in theory) be predicted scientifically. Hence we are never free to choose what we do, even if our lack of understanding of the determining causes means that we retain the illusion of freedom.

Here, the debate is about the degree of freedom that the individual has a right to exercise within society, given the impact that such freedom may have upon the freedom of others: freedom to act within certain parameters set out by the law. Once a person acts outside those parameters, society, through the police and the courts, can step in and impose a penalty on the 'outlaw'.

Taking a utilitarian view of morality (see Chapter 6), J. S. Mill argued that in the case of some private matter, where an action and its consequences affect only the individual concerned, there should be absolute freedom. The law should step in to restrain that freedom only when the consequences of an action affects other people. This is the common-sense basis for much legislation.

An example

If smoking cigarettes were a private activity, with consequences, however harmful, suffered only by the person who chose to smoke, there would be no need to legislate against it. The law may step in to prohibit smoking in public places if:

▶ *it constitutes a fire hazard* or
▶ *non-smokers want to be free to breathe air that is not filled with smoke.*

Legislation can be justified on a simple utilitarian basis. The law protects other people from the effects of an individual's action.

But should society as a whole, through its medical services, be required to pay the price for an individual's decision to smoke, take drugs, or practise a dangerous sport? Here the law has to balance a utilitarian moral position with the preservation of individual human rights.

The idea of individual liberty has been of fundamental importance in modern political thinking, responding perhaps to the experience of horrific excesses of twentieth-century totalitarian systems in Nazi Germany, the Soviet Union and elsewhere. Karl Popper's book *The Open Society and its Enemies*, published in the 1940s, made the issue of freedom central. In the 1960s, much political debate centred on how to maintain social order and yet allow maximum freedom. Rawls' theory of justice may be seen as an attempt to justify liberal views of society, and in which the redistribution of wealth is a logical choice of free individuals. Rawls took the view that, provided all the essentials of life were met (a presupposition of his theory), people would choose freedom rather than, for example, the chance of getting more wealth. This view has been challenged by Ronald Dworkin and others, who think that some people would rather gamble that they would win, rather than play it safe and follow the liberal and egalitarian views of Rawls.

HUMAN RIGHTS

In an ideal society, the law would always be framed on the basis of the agreement between free individuals, and every person would be equally free to enjoy basic human rights. There is, however, a difference between having a set of rights and being free to exercise those rights. In general, even though rights are given irrespective of age and capacities, it is sometimes necessary for the exercise of those rights to be curtailed:

▶ **On grounds of age.** *Children have rights, and are protected by the law from exploitation by others, but cannot, for example, buy cigarettes or alcohol, drive a car or fly a plane. These limits are imposed because below the relevant age the child is considered unable to take a responsible decision and parents, or society, therefore impose a restriction on the child's freedom.*

▶ **On grounds of insanity.** *Those who are insane and are liable to be a danger to themselves or to others are also restrained.*

▶ **On grounds of lack of skill.** *Flying a plane or driving a car (other than on private property) without a licence is illegal. This can be justified on utilitarian grounds, since others in the air or on the roads could be in danger. Equally, to pose as a surgeon and perform operations without the appropriate qualification is illegal. Without the public acknowledgement that a person has the required skills, many such tasks would endanger the lives or well-being of others.*

Rights are also taken from those who break the law, for example:

- *through prison sentences*
- *through legal injunctions to stop actions being carried out or to prevent one person from approaching another, or visiting a particular place. This may be taken retrospectively, if a person has already broken a law, or proactively, for example, to stop publication of a potentially damaging story in a newspaper.*

In all these cases, a person retains his or her fundamental rights, but cannot exercise them, on the basis that to do so would be against the interests of society as a whole. This approach is based on the idea of social contract, where the laws of society are made by mutual agreement, and the loss of certain freedoms are exchanged for the gain of a measure of social protection. It may also therefore be justified on utilitarian grounds.

But Dworkin argues that a 'right' is something that an individual can exercise even if it goes against the general welfare. After all, there is no point in my claiming a right to do something, if nobody would ever want to challenge it. A right is something that I can claim in difficult circumstances.

This means that (at least in the immediate context) rights cannot be justified on utilitarian grounds. They do not necessarily offer the greatest good to the greatest number. Rights are claimed by minorities. Rights are established by social contract (for example, within the US Constitution or the United Nations) and represent a basic standard of treatment that an individual can expect to receive by virtue of the social and legal system within which those rights are set down.

In other words

- *Individual freedom needs to be balanced against the needs of society as a whole. The morality of exercising individual freedom may be assessed on utilitarian grounds.*

> ▶ Human rights represent the basic freedoms and opportunities that an individual can expect to receive from society. They may sometimes be withheld if their exercise would pose a threat to the individual or society as a whole.
> ▶ The exercise of human rights cannot always be justified on utilitarian grounds. It is important for an individual to be able to claim a right, even if it is not to the benefit of the majority.

Feminism

It may not have escaped the notice of many readers that almost all the philosophers mentioned so far in this book are male. The agenda, both philosophically and politically, appears to have been set by men, and the rational and legal approaches to many issues seem particularly appropriate to a male intellectual environment, but may be thought to ignore the distinctive contribution of women.

Feminism, therefore, introduces the issue of gender into the concepts of justice, fairness and rights, pointing out those areas where men have sought to exclude or marginalize women. A key work in the campaign on behalf of women was Mary Wollstonecraft's *A Vindication of the Rights of Women* (1792), where she argued for equality on the grounds of intellect. This did not imply that there should be no distinction between men and women, however, and she was quite happy to see women and men play very different roles within society. In fact, she saw women as primarily contributing from within the home.

In the nineteenth century, the key issue for the feminist perspective on British political life was the campaign for women to receive the vote. This was not an issue presented only by women, for it received the support of J. S. Mill, the utilitarian philosopher.

Feminism has generally sought to present an historical critique of the social injustices suffered by women, suggesting that gender bias is not simply a matter of individual prejudice, but is inherent in social and political institutions. On a broader front it has also opened up discussion on the relationship between the sexes, the distinctive role of women, and the ethical implications of gender. Notable here is the contribution of Simone De Beauvoir (1908–86), the existentialist philosopher. Her book *The Second Sex* (1949) opened up a serious consideration of the myths and roles that women were expected to play within society, as mothers, wives, lovers and so on, and of their place in society. Perhaps her most famous quote 'One is not born, but rather becomes a woman' suggested that the roles of womanhood were imposed upon women (by a male-dominated society), rather than being essential to her nature.

Insight

De Beauvoir's key complaint is that, in a society shaped by men, women are seen as 'relative beings', existing only in relationship to men. The male philosopher Immanuel Kant would no doubt agree with her, since he argued that everyone should be treated as an end rather than a means, autonomous and independent.

Some conclusions

The problem with political philosophy (and perhaps with all philosophy) is that it works with abstract and generalized concepts, and seldom does justice to the actual situation within which people find themselves. The world is complex. Wealth in one place is gained at the price of poverty in another. A 'free' market will lead some to success, others to failure. Laws that benefit those who want to retain their wealth are seen by those who are the least privileged as an excuse for continued greed.

What we see in the philosophy of politics is an examination of the principles upon which legal and political systems are founded. Human rights, justice, fairness, social contract, democracy – these are all terms that can be examined by the philosopher in order to clarify exactly what they imply. But such ideas arise as a result of more general concepts about human life, its meaning and its value. Political philosophy is therefore the practical application of a fundamental understanding of the value, meaning and purpose of human life.

Once you get beyond Hobbes' view that society is constructed for mutual protection, once you say that it is right to organize society in a particular way, not just that it is necessary for survival to do so, then you imply ideas of justice, of freedom, of equality, of the valuation of human life, and of the place of human life within an understanding of the world as a whole.

A general point

If we divide philosophy up into sections, each dealing with a limited number of issues, it is sometimes possible to forget the more fundamental questions as we concentrate on particular issues of politics or the law. But philosophy grows and develops as an organic whole:

▶ *How you organize society depends on your basic view of ethics.*
▶ *Ethics in turn depends on your view of the self and of what it means to be an individual human being.*
▶ *'The self' has implications for the more general questions about the meaning and value of life that are explored in the philosophy of religion.*
▶ *Religious issues arise out of the fundamental questions about life – questions such as 'What can I know for certain?', 'Why is there anything rather than nothing?', 'What is life for?', 'What should I do?' – which are the starting point for all philosophy.*

10 THINGS TO REMEMBER

1 *You have to decide which takes priority, the individual or society as a whole.*

2 *Hobbes saw the Social Contract as a basis for mutual security.*

3 *Locke established the principles of representative democracy.*

4 *Rousseau thought that the 'general will' could be imposed.*

5 *Marx saw political change in terms of dialectical materialism.*

6 *Plato saw justice in terms of each part of society taking its appropriate role.*

7 *Rawls sees justice in terms of fairness.*

8 *Nozick argues that one should retain wealth that has been legitimately gained.*

9 *Mill argued for maximum freedom compatible with the freedom of others.*

10 *Feminists reject the imposition of roles upon women by a male-dominated society.*

8

....

Continental philosophy

In this chapter you will learn:
- **the basic difference between analytic and Continental philosophy**
- **key features of existentialist philosophy**
- **some philosophical aspects of the structuralist and postmodernist movements.**

Within Western philosophy there has been a broad division, relating both to the way of doing philosophy and the sort of subjects covered. Most philosophers may be described as belonging either to the 'Analytic' or the 'Continental' tradition of philosophy.

▶ *Analytic philosophy is a tradition that has flourished particularly in the USA and Britain. It is especially concerned with the meaning of statements and the way in which their truth can be verified, and with using philosophy as an analytic tool to examine and show the presuppositions of our language and thought. Well-known philosophers in this school today would include Quine, Putnam, Searle, Rawls, Hampshire and Strawson. It also includes many philosophers already mentioned, including Russell, Ryle and Ayer. The twentieth-century philosophy described so far in this book has come from this tradition.*

▶ *Continental philosophy is a term which may be used to describe a range of philosophers from mainland Europe whose work is generally considered separately in courses on philosophy, although they do have relevance to the basic issues considered already. They include Husserl (1858–1938), whose phenomenology has influenced many other Continental philosophers, Heidegger and Sartre (existentialism) and, more recently, Lacan, Derrida and others. It is in this 'Continental' school that we meet the terms* **structuralism**, **postmodernism** *and* **hermeneutics** *(the study of interpretation: a term originally used of the study of scriptures, but now used more generally of the way in which any text is examined).*

Insight

Continental philosophy often reflects an intellectual approach to the creative arts in general, rather than the more narrowly defined tasks of the Analytic school. Sartre, for example, explored his ideas through novels, short stories and plays. Foucault was interested in the history and 'archaeology' of ideas and how they are shaped by society.

While there is no space in this book to give an adequate account of the thinkers of the Continental tradition, a brief outline of some of the main themes may serve to set it within the context of philosophy as a whole. This is important, because today there is far more mingling of the concerns of the two schools than would have been the case in the mid-twentieth century. Also, although the approach and content of philosophy as taught in universities in the UK and USA is still very much influenced by the broadly Analytic tradition, the philosophers of the Continental tradition are now more widely studied – with some, like Sartre and Heidegger, being hugely popular. It is also important to recognize that the Continental approach to philosophy, as it developed in the twentieth century, looked back and responded to the work of Nietzsche, Hegel, Kant, Rousseau and other great thinkers, back to Descartes – thinkers that have always been there in the core of philosophical study.

Phenomenology

Edmund Husserl (1859–1938), the founder of **phenomenology**, was a Jewish-German philosopher, who taught at the University of Freiburg. Like Descartes, he wanted to find the basis of knowledge, making philosophy a 'rigorous science' that was founded on necessary truths independent of all presuppositions. His most important work was *Logical Investigations* (published in two volumes in 1900 and 1901). In this he declared that, for certainty, we had to start with our own conscious awareness. What is it that we actually experience? Husserl suggested that every mental act is directed towards an 'intentional object': what the mind is thinking about, whether or not that object actually exists.

Examples

▶ *I want to eat a cake. I need a physical cake if I am going to eat; but thinking about a cake requires only an 'intentional object' – indeed, I am especially likely to think about a cake when there is no actual cake to be had!*

▶ *If I reflect on feeling depressed, depression is an 'intentional object' of my thought, although there is no external object corresponding to it. Someone may say 'depression is nothing, it doesn't exist'; but for me, at that moment, it is real.*

Husserl takes the subject matter of philosophy to be these 'objects of consciousness': whatever it is that we experience, quite apart from any questions about whether or not it exists in an objective, external world. Phenomenology also seeks to strip individual objects of all that makes them particular, seeking the pure essence – what they share with other objects of the same sort. These fundamental 'essences', he argues, are known by intuition. As soon as we think about something, it takes on meaning for us because of the various essences by which we understand it. I have a consciousness of 'tree' as a pure essence, and as soon as I see (or think about) an actual tree, that essence is there to give it meaning for me.

Examples

A child is shown a number of red objects. The mother says 'That's red.' The child automatically sorts out the common denominator of the experience, and quickly grasps the pure essence 'red'. When subsequently presented with objects of the same colour, the essence 'red' is already there, and becomes one of a number of essences by
(Contd)

which any new object is understood. More sophisticated, the artist will play with unusual shades of red, testing out the 'horizon', the limits of the essence 'red'. Is it red, or is it really magenta? Add a touch more blue to the paint: now how do we see it?

Husserl argued that consciousness required three things:

1 *a self (what he called the 'transcendental ego')*
2 *a mental act*
3 *an object of that mental act.*

Objects become objects of consciousness only when they have been given meaning and significance. An object is only understood (only really 'seen') once the mind has gone to work on it and given it meaning in terms of its pure essences. Everything is therefore dependent on the 'transcendental ego' for its meaning and significance. Once we encounter the world, we start to give it meaning, we start to interpret it in terms of pure essences; in other words, we start to deal with it in terms of its 'objects of consciousness'.

One reason why Husserl has been so important for Continental philosophy is that he allowed questions of meaning and value, and the whole range of emotions and other experiences, to become a valid subject matter of philosophy.

Insight

Continental philosophy was thus set free to explore many aspects of life that were beyond the concerns of philosophers of the Analytic tradition, who remained primarily concerned with language. They were able to ask not just 'What does this *mean*?' but 'What does this mean *for me*?'

Existentialism

Existentialism is the name given to the branch of philosophy which is concerned with the meaning of human existence – its aims, its significance and overall purpose – and the freedom and creative response to life made by individuals.

Notice how this follows on from phenomenology. If philosophy is free to deal with consciousness and the actions which spring from it, it can explore human self-awareness and self-doubt, and the actions and events that give meaning to life. Two important philosophers for the development of existentialism are Heidegger (1889–1976), a German philosopher controversially associated with the Nazi party, whose *Being and Time* (1927) is a key work of existentialist philosophy, and Sartre (1905–80), the French philosopher, novelist and playwright. His most important work of philosophy is *Being and Nothingness* (1943). Probably his best-known quote is from the end of his play *No Exit* (1945): 'Hell is other people.'

A central feature of existentialism is that it is concerned with the way in which human beings relate to the world. Much philosophy examines external objects and the minds that comprehend them as though the two were separable; the mind just observing the world in a detached way. Existentialism, by contrast, starts from the basis of the self as involved, as engaged with the world. We seek to understand things because we have to deal with them, live among them, find the meaning and significance of our own life among them.

An example

You pick up a hammer and start hammering a nail. You do not first think about the hammer and then decide how to use it; you use it automatically. Your mind is engaged with the activity of hammering. Heidegger sees this as a ready-to-hand way of dealing with things: not as an observer, but as an engaged individual.

Husserl had attempted, by bracketing out any particular features and trying to see only the pure essences of a phenomenon, to get a generally acceptable view of things. Existentialism moved away from that position by emphasizing that there is always an element of personal engagement, a particular point of view. This raises the general philosophical question about whether every view is a view from a particular perspective, carrying with it the values and understanding of the person who has it. The alternative (often sought by science, and by empirical philosophy) is a 'view from nowhere': a view that does not take a personal viewpoint into account. But is that possible?

For Heidegger, we are 'thrown' into the world, and our main experience of *Dasein* ('being there') is 'concern', in the sense that some of the objects we encounter in the world are going to be more important for us than others, and so we become involved with them. Heidegger also argued that we are what we take ourselves to be, we do not have a fixed human nature. You live in an authentic way if you take each situation as it comes and show your true nature through what you do.

Insight

The sad alternative is to try to escape from the anxiety of being true to yourself by conforming to what others expect of you, taking on masks that fit your social roles. Part of the attraction of existentialism was that it encouraged people to dare to throw off such social masks and to take charge of their lives.

For Sartre, particular things take on importance and refuse to be categorized. There is also the sense that a person is radically free. Just as individual things are not totally defined by their essences, so a person need not be defined by his or her duties and responsibilities. Such freedom can be threatening; it produces disorientation and (as in his novel of that title) nausea.

For reflection

Have another look at Chapter 4. We are defined by many things, and by the various roles that we take on. But can we ever be fully defined in this way? Is there a self that refuses to be categorized; that insists on the freedom to be unique?

Sartre described three kinds of being:

1 **Being-in-itself.** *This is the being of non-human objects, things just exist as they are.*
2 **Being-for-itself.** *At the level of consciousness or self-awareness, a being is aware of the world around it, of other things that are not itself. If we are self-aware, we cannot be reduced to a thing-in-itself, e.g. I may work as a postman, but I am not fully described as 'postman' (as a thing-in-itself) because, as a human being, I am always more than any such description. If people treat me simply as 'postman' they dehumanize me, they take from me the distinctive thing that makes me a person.*
3 **Being-for-others.** *As human beings, we form relationships and express our human nature through them. Relating to others, and aware of our own freedom, we are able to live in an 'authentic' way: we are being fully ourselves.*

In other words

▶ *Phenomenology allows human experiences and responses to become a valid object of philosophical study.*
▶ *Existentialism explores the way in which people relate to the world, including issues of value, meaning and purpose; it is about engagement, not detached observation.*
▶ *If I act out a role, I am not engaged with the whole of myself. To be authentic, I act in a way which reflects my self-awareness, and the awareness of my own freedom. this is who I am; this is what I choose to do; this is the real me.*

Insight

Existentialism gave philosophical underpinnings to a view of life that rejected social conformity, promoting self-expression and freedom. Taken up by literature and art, it became a cultural phenomenon, centred on the smoke-filled cafes of Paris in the 1940s and 1950s.

Existentialism can be summed up in Sartre's claim that 'existence precedes essence'. In other words, I do not have a fixed essence and then try to live it out in the world; rather, I give meaning to my life in the course of living it. By my present choices, I can shape my future, taking responsibility for what I become.

Structuralism

The main theme of **structuralism** is that you can only understand something once you relate it to the wider structures within which it operates. Things are defined primarily in terms of their relationships with others. Structuralist approaches were developed in the philosophy of language and in anthropology, but spread into many different cultural areas.

Examples

▶ *To understand a word, consider its meaning in terms of other words and the language as a whole.*

▶ *To understand a political statement, look at the politician, how he or she is to stay in power, what the media expect, what effect he or she needs to make with this statement.*

▶ *A 'soundbite' or a newspaper headline can only really be understood in terms of the significance of the paper or the broadcast within which it is set.*

In Husserl's phenomenology there was an independent self that existed prior to the encounter with the phenomena: the 'transcendental ego'. Existentialism focused on that self, especially in its freedom and choices in its engagement with the world. Structuralism (and particularly its later development, known as post-structuralism) is a reaction against the importance given to this 'self' – structures and relationships now take priority.

Jacques Lacan (1900–80) argued that we do not first become fully formed individuals and then start to express our individuality through language, but we become individuals (we develop our personalities, if you like) through the use of language. And that language, with its ideas and its grammar, predates us. We don't make it up as we go along; we inherit it.

Lacan was primarily a psychoanalyst, and it is interesting to reflect that in psychoanalysis it is through a free flow of ideas that thoughts and feelings buried in the unconscious may appear. The flow of language is not controlled by the ego. Indeed, it is in order to heal and change the ego that the analysis is taking place. The subject emerges through language. For Lacan, it would seem that if there is no speech, then there is no subject, but he goes further; there are no metaphysical entities at all. God, for example, is a function of the 'Other' in language, not something that exists outside language.

Two features of a structuralist/post-structuralist approach:

1 *There is no transcendent self that has some pure idea which it wants to convey, and which is later, imperfectly translated into a medium of communication – spoken, written or visual. Rather, the meaning is just exactly what is spoken or written. It is to be understood in terms of the structures of communication, not with reference to some outside author. A story does not have a meaning; a story is its meaning.*
2 *To understand a piece of writing, one should carry out a process of **deconstruction**, laying bare the presuppositions of the text, and comparing what an author claims to be saying with the actual form of language used and the sometimes contradictory claims that such a written form implies. Deconstruction has been developed particularly by Jacques Derrida (1930–2004), an influential figure in this movement. Deconstruction is the attempt to deal with the end of metaphysics. For Derrida, there is no external or fixed meaning to a text, nor is there a subject who exists prior to language and prior to particular experiences. You cannot get outside or beyond the structure.*

Derrida is concerned with 'actuality', with being in touch with present events. But the information we receive through the media is never neutral, but is the product of the structures by which the media operate. This has practical consequences:

> *Hegel was right to tell the philosophers of his time to read the newspapers. Today the same duty requires us to find out how news is made, and by whom: the daily papers, the weeklies, and the TV news as well. We need to insist on looking at them from the other end: that of the press agencies as well as that of the tele-prompter. And we should never forget what this entails: whenever a journalist or a politician appears to be speaking to us directly, in our homes, and looking us straight in the eye, he or she is actually reading, from a screen, at the dictation of a 'prompter', and reading a text which was produced elsewhere, on a different occasion, possibly by other people, or by a whole network of nameless writers and editors.*

> From 'The deconstruction of actuality', an interview with
> Derrida published in *Radical Philosophy*, Autumn 1994

But Derrida warns against 'neo-idealism': the idea that nothing really happens, that all is an illusion just because it is set within a structure by the media. Rather, he wants to emphasize that deconstruction is about getting down to an event, to a 'singularity', to what is irreducible and particular in an individual happening.

In other words

- ▶ *To understand anything, look at its relationships and the structure within which it is set.*
- ▶ *There is no subject that exists prior to language. I may think of something before I write it down, but even that act of thinking borrows from a whole tradition of language and thought.*
- ▶ *News comes to us through the media; it is the product of a process by which information is sorted and expressed in particular ways, often for a particular purpose. Real events are unique, reports of them put them into categories and start to colour our interpretation of them.*

Insight

Structuralism makes explicit what any critical reader or viewer knows – that we need to see through what is said and ask *why* is it said and *in whose interest* it is published or broadcast. Communication cannot be innocent of the complex web of political, financial, cultural and personal influences within which it is set.

Postmodernism

Postmodernism is a rather vague term for a number of approaches to philosophy, literature and the arts, which have in common a rejection of an earlier 'modernist' view. The 'modern' view, against which postmodernism reacts, is one that sees the image as the production of the unique human subject. Existentialism in particular is focused on the self, its freedom, and the choices by which it creates itself and its world. Structuralism disputed this 'modern' belief in the primacy of the humanist imagination as a creative source of meaning.

Postmodernism is a term used beyond the writings of Derrida, Lyotard and others who work in the fields of philosophy and literary criticism, for it can apply to all the arts. Indeed, the ideas were explored in architecture before transferring to philosophy. Previously, an image could be taken to refer to something external, in the 'real' world or in human consciousness. In postmodernism, an image reflects only other images, it has no fixed reference. There is therefore no 'authentic' image – authentic in the sense that an existentialist would use that term.

A message is, for postmodernism, no longer a message sent from a creative author to a receptive reader. Rather, it is bound up with a mass of reduplication. We shuffle and arrange images, but do not have any creative control over them. In a work of art, a novel or a film, a postmodernist approach undermines the modernist belief in the image as the production of an individual consciousness.

A postmodern image displays its own artificial nature. It clearly represents – but without depth. So, for example, in the art world, one might contrast Picasso (who, as a 'modernist' strove for a unique view and form of communication) with Warhol's use of mass-produced public images. An interesting discussion of this is found in R. Kearney's 'The crisis of the postmodernist image' in *Contemporary French Philosophy*, A. Phillips Griffiths (ed.), Cambridge 1987.

For reflection

Modernism: The dilemma and existential agony of the blank sheet of paper, a set of paints and brushes, and the desire to express oneself through a unique image.

Postmodernism: The word-processing package comes to the rescue, for it contains a great variety of pieces of 'clip art' which can instantly be printed out and arranged on the paper.

Postmodernism is encouraged by the developments in technology, particularly mass communication and the ability to reproduce images. The individual subject is no longer considered to be the creator of his or her images. What we appear to create is what is already there around us. We produce consumer items. It is not so much philosophy that is postmodern, but the whole of society. There are many images to be shuffled, but there is no metaphysical insight to be had, and no transcendental reality to represent.

Insight

For postmodernism, you cannot get behind the images, symbols and reproduced goods of a technological age in order to discern individuality, purpose or meaning. It is a view devoid of what was traditionally known as 'metaphysics'.

This is also reflected in the postmodernist view, explored by Jean-Francois Lyotard, that statements about the overall purpose of life or society (for example, society exists for the benefit of its members), sometimes called 'meta-narratives', are losing their credibility. It is no longer realistic to make general statements of a metaphysical nature about life, since they do not reflect the fragmented nature of modern society.

A final example

I am the author of this book: I address you, the reader, directly in order to illustrate some of the issues connected with structuralism and the postmodern outlook.

What do you think of me as an author? You could say: 'He's just stuck together bits of information that others have given him.' That is true. You could go on to say: 'There is absolutely nothing original in it!' This is a more serious charge, but made complicated because there is a certain originality in the way that the ideas of others are selected, analyzed, arranged and presented.

But suppose I claim to have said something original. Can that claim be justified?

▶ *What of the words I use? Their meanings are already given by the society that uses this language (if they weren't, you would not understand them). They do not originate in my mind.*
▶ *What of the climate of opinion within which I write? Does that not shape my views? Am I responsible for it, or shaped by it?*
▶ *And what of comments for which I claim originality? If you knew everything that I had read, everyone who I had spoken to, could you not predict my views? Could you not analyze my views, show influences, categorize the style, place my views within a particular tradition. A literary critic often shows that what seems to be a unique expression of a thinking self is in fact an intellectual patchwork of influences.*
▶ *This book is being written to fit a certain number of printed pages of a particular size, and in a particular style. Its chapters reflect the range of philosophy taught in some university departments; suggestions*

(Contd)

about content have been made by professional readers; various things have been asked for by editors. What is said is determined by the constraints of space, purpose and market.

▶ *Thus the author of this book can vanish!*

Personal note

I may keep within the overall structure of language, but I feel that, from time to time, I am entitled to peer round the side of the structure and address you, the reader, directly. It is this that structuralism denies, and indeed, the idea of an author making a personal appeal to a reader is just another literary device. I disappear again!

10 THINGS TO REMEMBER

1 *In twentieth-century philosophy there are both Analytic and Continental traditions.*

2 *For phenomenology, knowledge starts with our own conscious awareness.*

3 *Every mental act is directed towards an 'intentional object'.*

4 *Existentialism is concerned with the meaning of human life and how people relate to their world.*

5 *We are 'thrown' into the world and always have a particular perspective on it.*

6 *We can either accept social masks, or choose to live in an authentic way.*

7 *For existentialism, existence precedes essence.*

8 *We need to be aware of the structures within which information is communicated.*

9 *We always 'borrow' our ideas from a tradition of language and society.*

10 *Postmodernism rejects metaphysical statements about the nature of life.*

9

Some other branches of philosophy

In this chapter you will learn:
- *about some issues concerning the philosophy of art*
- *how we interpret the events of the past as 'history'*
- *what some philosophers have had to say about education.*

This book has, of necessity, been selective. In examining some of the major issues in philosophy, it has not been able to show the full breadth of philosophy as it is practised today. Neither has it been possible to include all the major philosophers of the past. Some, for example Hegel, Nietzsche or Frege, have been very influential, but there has been no room to include them, and they certainly deserve more than a brief mention if their thought is to be taken at all seriously. To understand the work of these great individual thinkers is it probably best to look first at general histories of philosophy, in order to set their work in context, and then turn to books on each individual thinker.

This chapter simply attempts to fill a few of the gaps by offering a sketch of three other areas of philosophy, to illustrate the range of interests found in philosophy today and the way in which philosophy is applied to other areas of human experience.

Aesthetics

Most areas of philosophy spring from a simple but fundamental question: epistemology is the attempt to answer 'What can we know?'; political philosophy answers 'What is justice?'. Aesthetics addresses the questions 'What is beauty?' and 'What is art?'

You can trace these questions through the whole history of philosophy, from Greek ideas of art, through mediaeval and Reformation debates about religious images (whether they pointed beyond themselves, or were in danger of being themselves worshipped in an idolatrous way), through Hume's attempt to get a norm of taste and Kant's analysis of the aesthetic experience, to Marxist critiques of art in terms of its social and political function, and on to existentialist and postmodernist views of art.

However, it is far from straightforward to say exactly what makes something 'art'. One could define art as in some way a 'picturing' of reality; but then one would need to leave out music or architecture, which are arts, but which create something that has no direct external point of reference in the natural world. (Both may, of course, suggest or hint at things in the natural world, but that is another matter.) Another approach is to start from the artist, rather than from the work of art. Hence art is the product of a certain kind of human activity, related to the expression of emotion, or the enhancement of perception.

Think of the range of artistic activities that go to produce an opera, for example. There is the designing and painting of sets, the production of costumes, the libretto, the music and the quality of voices that perform it. A single aesthetic experience results from the very special combination of a whole range of 'arts'. Here, as with the appreciation of a 'person', more is understood by synthesis (seeing how everything works together) rather than by analysis (isolating and trying to define each component separately).

The same could be said of literature. Individual words in a work of fiction may well have a straightforward, literal meaning, and the individual events they describe might well be factual (indeed, this leads on to the debate about how much fact can rightly be incorporated into a work of fiction), yet the overall effect – the synthesis – is to create something which reflects, but does not copy real life.

Modern discussions of how to define art may consider its function; in other words, something is art if it is treated as art, or if it works as art for us, even if the medium is entirely new. Alternatively, it is possible to argue that art is defined by the procedures that *lead* to its production and use; does this particular thing or event follow an established tradition (or writing, drawing, composing and so on) and is it accepted as such within the community of those engaged in the arts?

Insight

In this view, art need not have a distinctive form or come within established categories; art is either what works as art, or what the artworld is prepared to accept as art – even if it is quite unlike anything that has been produced before.

Aesthetics links with other areas of philosophy. For example, writing in the USA in the 1950s both the theologian Paul Tillich and philosopher Susanne Langer spoke of art as symbol, as pointing beyond itself to some other transcendent reality. This links aesthetics with the philosophy of religion. Indeed, Tillich held that all religious ideas and images were symbols, pointing to 'being-itself', and that religious truths could not be conveyed other than by symbols. A work of art could therefore be seen as in some sense 'religious', however secular its context, since it pointed to that which was beyond ordinary experience.

How you see the function of art depends in part on how you understand experience and reality. Plato, for example, saw individual things as poor copies of timeless realities (his 'forms'), and therefore criticized art for taking this a stage further, producing copies of copies. Art therefore, for Plato, is presenting something 'unreal' and therefore further from the truth, whereas for Tillich and Langar it is a necessary way of encountering transcendent reality, and therefore supremely 'real'.

The work of the artist also links with the nature of the self, the nature of language and the nature of perception. A novelist, for example, may use language in a rich and subtle way in order to convey a whole range of emotions and intuitions; and not just to convey them, but to evoke them in the reader. A work of fiction thus invites an emotional and imaginative response. No two readers 'picture' the events described in the novel in exactly the same way.

Insight

Contrast this with the ideal analytic philosophy, which presents an argument with as much clarity as possible, or logical positivism, which insisted that a statement could only have meaning if backed up by evidence. That approach seeks language that is clean, precise and straightforward; while a novel or poem may be rich in meaning, evocative, symbolic and often deliberately ambiguous.

The richness of art has produced a variety of responses from philosophers. Plato feared that art in general, and dramatic poetry in particular, had the power to corrupt people by stirring up their emotions. Nietzsche, by contrast, welcomed this aspect. In *The Birth of Tragedy* (1872) he contrasted the Dionysian and Apollonian spirit within humankind, the former bringing elation, intoxication and a stirring of the emotions, the latter bringing cool rationality. Art has the positive function of holding the two together.

For reflection

Plato was hostile to art and in favour of strict censorship. He saw art as subversive, replacing reality with fantasy, manipulating the emotions. Yet his dialogues are great works of literature; they are art!

(Contd)

- *How can you allow art to have its full effect on the person who sees, reads or hears it, and yet maintain some rational control on what art says?*
- *Should art be politically correct? Marx saw art as having a social and political function. Good art, from a Marxist perspective, is that which reflects the values of social revolution, and which stirs the emotions in line with certain political values and attitudes.*
- *Is a work of art its own justification? If so, does it make sense to speak of good or bad art?*

For those wanting to follow up on aesthetics, one could also look at Hume on matters of taste, and at Kant's *Critique of Aesthetic Judgement* (1790). In the twentieth century, philosophers of particular importance in this area include R. G. Collingwood, who published *Principles of Art* in 1925, written at a time when philosophy was much concerned with literal description (as in Logical Positivism), and, from the 1960s, E. H. Gombrich's *Art and Illusion* (1960) and N. Goodman's *Languages of Art* (1968).

Insight

Interestingly, much of this is an attempt to understand the place of art and creativity against a background of the obvious success of the literal use of language in science. One might explore the relationship between aesthetics and both the philosophy of science and the philosophy of language.

The range of problems associated with aesthetics may be illustrated by the practical dilemma of whether or not you are able to call something a work of art.

An example

I visit the home of a wealthy friend who tells me that he has just invested in a new work of art. I glance out of the window, and see a pile of bricks and rubble in the middle of his lawn. My friend has noticed me looking towards the lawn, and the glow of pride on his face leaves me in no doubt that the load of bricks and rubble is indeed his new work of art!

▶ *He sees a work of art; I see a pile of rubble. Is there any objective way of deciding between these two views ('seeing as')?*

▶ *If I agree that it is a work of art, where is that 'art' located? Is it in the art object (analyzed as a pile of bricks and rubble)? Is it in the mind of the artist? Is its beauty, as the saying goes, in the eye of the beholder? Is art something that takes place in a triangular relationship: artist, art object, person appreciating it 'as' art?*

▶ *Is it pointing to something beyond itself, some feature of reality that I cannot describe literally, but which I sense by looking at the work of art? Or is it simply being itself, and inviting me to give it my attention? And is the act of giving attention itself an aesthetic experience?*

▶ *Would the pile of bricks remain art, even if nobody appreciated it as such?*

▶ *What emotions does it evoke in me? If only irritation and embarrassment, are these still valid as an aesthetic experience?*

▶ *The pile of bricks on the lawn is part of an artificial social construction: an artist making a living; an investor wanting a new 'piece'; a financial deal. Is art still art if it becomes an investment commodity?*

▶ *What is the nature of artistic imagination?*

▶ *Does the artist create an illusion, trying to make me see something more than that which is actually before my eyes?*

▶ *If the artist thought of it as one thing and I see it as something else, are there two works of art here, or only one?*

Different periods have explored different aspects of art. In the eighteenth century, for example, primacy was given to natural beauty, and a sense of balance between nature and the mind perceiving nature. Kant saw a 'formal purposiveness' in those things that produced an aesthetic experience: art objects creating a sense of harmonious pleasure in the mind. The twentieth century has been more concerned with the nature of artistic production, and the process of artistic creativity has often become its own subject matter.

Art reflects the particular self-understanding of each age: wander through any art gallery and it becomes clear that the concerns and values of each period are clearly reflected in its visual art. It is not just a matter of style, but of the changing sense of what it is appropriate to depict in art. There is also great variety in the self-consciousness of creativity; in one period, the aim appears to be to render such an accurate depiction of external reality that the artist disappears from immediate view, in another period, perceived image is distorted in order to reflect the self-conscious intentions of the artist.

Thus, although aesthetics and the philosophy of art may be studied as a separate branch of philosophy, their real fascination comes from interlocking them with questions about the nature of perception, the self and its creativity, the self-transcending quality of religious experience, the ethics of what is expressed or depicted.

Insight

It could be argued that philosophy and art are two sides of the creative human coin, the one focusing on reflective thought, the other on creative expression.

The philosophy of history

What is history? We might be tempted to say that history is the account of what has happened in the past. But that will not do, for a theoretically infinite number of events have already taken place and, even if they could all be remembered and recorded, it would take an infinite amount of time to construct history out of them. In other words, history would unfold faster than it could be recounted.

History is therefore *selective*; most things are ignored. Without such selection, the sheer number of events in the past would smother any attempt to get an overall view of what happened. And this is a crucial point: history involves an interpretation of events, and that interpretation depends on the ideas and assumptions of the historian. *History cannot be an objective account of facts*. It is an interpretation of the significance of particular things that have taken place in the past.

More than one layer of interpretation may be involved; a modern historian examining ancient texts brings his own views to that study but, equally, the original authors of those texts were also interpreting the events they recorded. Much of the study of history is historiography, the study of historical writing.

This has led some postmodernist thinkers to argue that texts are simply based on other texts (the process called 'intertextuality') rather than on external 'facts'. The truth of a document is therefore related to the authority of those who wrote it, rather than to events it claims to describe. The American philosopher, Hayden White, in his book *Metahistory* (1973) put forward the view that the historian is actually producing a creative literary invention, rather than dealing in facts. *Some of the information which the historian uses may be factual, but it only becomes 'history' once it is part of a story.*

The postmodernist approach raises important issues for historians. If history does not present 'facts' about events that took place in the past, then any interpretation of the past would seem to be as good as any other. While no historian would claim that his or her account of an event is totally objective, there is a professional interest in gathering evidence in order to illustrate past events as clearly as possible.

THE MECHANISMS OF CHANGE

Part of the fascination of history is trying to understand the process by which change comes about. The German idealist philosopher Hegel (1770–1831) thought that it was possible to discern a particular 'spirit', or *Geist*, unfolding in the historical process. The process through which this unfolding took place is described as a 'dialectic': each age has its particular feature (its 'thesis') which then produces a reaction ('antithesis') which is then resolved (in a 'synthesis'). This process then repeats itself, always aiming towards a rational ideal and absolute.

Karl Marx was influenced by Hegel's theory of historical change. But he argued that the basis of society was economic and material. He therefore saw the economic conditions under which people lived, and the conflicts between classes, as the mechanism by which historical change came about. In Marx you therefore have a political philosophy which is also a philosophy of history, and you have a philosopher whose expressed intention is to change things rather than simply understand them.

Note

For further information on Marx, see Chapter 7, pp. 226–8.

One key feature of the philosophy of history is the recognition that as soon as events are described, they are interpreted, and as soon as they are interpreted, they are set within an overall pattern of understanding. The philosophy of history seeks to reveal that process of interpretation, and to relate it, as closely as it may, to the events which it seeks to present.

The philosophy of education

The philosophy of education is concerned both with the nature and purpose of education, and with the content of what is taught. As such it relates to many other areas of philosophy – to the theory of knowledge, to language, to ethics, religious and political philosophy. As a specialist area of philosophy, however, it is generally taught within departments of education rather than those of philosophy.

There are a number of key questions with which the philosophy of education is concerned:

- ▶ *What is education* for?
- ▶ *By what* process *do we learn?*
- ▶ *What should determine the* content *of education?*

In *The Republic*, Plato considers the nature of the state and the qualities of those who are to rule it, but he couches his argument in terms of the sort of education that will be necessary in order to produce leaders fit to rule. For Plato, therefore, education does not appear to be an end in itself, but a tool of social engineering – turning out the sort of people the state is going to need. However, that is not the whole truth, for Plato wants his rulers to be philosophers capable of seeing reality itself, rather than the passing shadows of sense experience. Hence it can equally be argued that Plato's scheme of education is aimed at an appreciation of the 'form of the good' (see p. 10).

His approach raises issues which continue within the world of education today:

- ▶ *To what extent should education be dependent on selection by ability?*
- ▶ *To what extent should education be aimed to equip students for particular tasks within society? Should society therefore set the curriculum?*
- ▶ *Should people of different classes and backgrounds be given different types of education?*
- ▶ *Should education be judged by its ability to turn out those who will maintain the social status quo?*

Insight

Should education be seen as having value in itself, or is it justified in terms of the need to train people for their roles in society? Your answer to that question will influence your views about funding for university departments, for example, or the giving of grants for research.

The process by which people learn is influenced by the general philosophical approach to knowledge of the world. Thus a philosopher such as John Locke, who sees all knowledge as based on sense experience, wants education to encourage experimentation and a rejection of the uncritical acceptance of tradition. A key feature of Locke's theory of knowledge is that people start with minds like blank sheets of paper (*tabula rasa*) and acquire knowledge though experience. (This contrasts with Plato, who held that we have innate knowledge of the 'forms', which we appear to have forgotten, but which enables us to recognize them as soon as we encounter them.)

John Dewey (1859–1952) was an influential American thinker who contributed widely in philosophy, but who is particularly known for his contribution to the theory of 'pragmatism'. This is the view that knowledge is achieved through practical problem-solving engagement with the world. The meaning of a statement can best be seen in terms of its practical application – the difference that it makes. Based on the scientific method of testing hypotheses, he suggested that education was primarily a process of problem solving, an approach which is generally termed 'instrumentalism'. This view has been enormously influential in terms of both educational theory and practice. Today, it is generally recognized that learning is most effective when it is based on practical, problem-solving methods, and the process of checking and testing out gives a clearer knowledge of the subject than the simple learning of facts.

With the pragmatists' contribution to education we have an interesting example of philosophy recognizing the significance of one sphere of life (the success of the scientific method), developing from it a general theory of meaning (that the truth of a statement is shown by the practical implications that follow from it – i.e. whether or not it works), and then applying it to another sphere of life (education) with overwhelming success. Throughout the world, primary school children learn through doing, examining and testing out, and this is largely due to the influence of pragmatism.

There are many other areas of education with which philosophy is concerned. For example, when it comes to the content of what is taught, there is debate about the appropriateness of religious or political education, about the point at which education descends into indoctrination. Equally, there is concern (often expressed by parents) about the methods and content of education in matters of sex and drugs. Does the teaching of contraception, for example, encourage promiscuity?

Central to many of these issues is the matter of personal autonomy. The essential difference between education and indoctrination is that the former seeks to empower and give autonomy to the individual learner, whereas the latter imposes on him or her an already formulated set of ideas. But how do you transmit culture from one generation to the next without at least some element of indoctrination?

The philosophy of education, therefore, arises naturally from the range of practical issues faced by those engaged in education. Both the process, the content and the purpose of education require to be linked to a broader understanding of life.

10 THINGS TO REMEMBER

1 *Aesthetics addresses the question 'What is art?'.*

2 *Art may be defined as what people accept as art.*

3 *Art often reflects the philosophy of the period in which it is produced.*

4 *Kant saw art as that which produced harmonious pleasure in the mind.*

5 *Art may deliberately reflect the self-consciousness of a artist.*

6 *Plato thought art subversive and in need of strict censorship.*

7 *History is always selective in terms of the facts upon which it is based.*

8 *History is always a matter of interpretation, never simply a factual account of the past.*

9 *There is a fundamental difference between education for itself alone, and purposeful training.*

10 *Pragmatism has been influential in terms of the practice of classroom education.*

10

The scope of philosophy today

In this chapter you will learn:
- *something of the range of issues considered by philosophy today.*

During the twentieth century there were a number of movements that attempted to reduce philosophy to some other discipline. The positivists wanted philosophy to follow science, throwing out all that did not conform to empirical criteria of meaning. Then the linguistic analysts insisted that the whole task of philosophy was the unpacking of statements to clarify their meaning. Marxists wanted everything reduced to its social and political matrix and postmodernists saw everything in terms of cultural and literary metaphors or signs, strung together. One might imagine that philosophy would be shaken radically by such drastic criticisms and re-interpretations of its task, but this has not been the case.

For anyone coming to philosophy at the end of the 1950s, however, at least in university departments concentrating on the Anglo-American analytic tradition, the task and scope of philosophy was precise but narrow. Still dominated by linguistic analysis, it aimed to examine problematic sentences and, through their elucidation, clarify meaning. It did not aspire to offer any new information on any subject. It saw itself as a necessary aid to all other subjects, rather than having a subject content of its own.

Over the last 50 years, however, philosophy has seen remarkable growth, both in its popularity as a subject and in the range and relevance of the topics it covers. One impetus for change came initially within the area of applied ethics. In the days of linguistic analysis, everything was focused on the meaning or otherwise of ethical propositions, and it was quite reasonable for a philosopher to claim to have nothing to say about moral issues themselves. But it was increasingly recognized that ethical guidance was needed by professionals, particularly in medicine and nursing, in order to develop and implement standards for dealing with the many difficult moral questions raised in their everyday work. Questions about abortion and euthanasia, the use of drugs and the conduct of medical research, all needed to be answered by sound moral arguments based on accepted professional standards.

At the same time, the rise of the cognitive sciences, information technology and artificial intelligence has raised questions about the nature of mind. International politics grapples with concepts – democracy, human rights, self-determination, national sovereignty – to direct and justify its action or inaction in various crises. Political philosophy is therefore utterly relevant to the human agenda. Issues concerning the philosophy of art – censorship, copyright, what distinguishes valid erotic art from pornography, what constitutes 'taste' or blasphemy, the nature of artistic expression – may be relevant when a Turner or other prize is judged, or when artists produce images that some find inspiring and others want banned. Relevant here also are legal debates about the ownership of intellectual property, about who should be paid royalties or claim copyright on ideas and words. Social awareness brings with it issues of feminism and of race, of inequality and the dynamics of free markets.

With the internet comes a whole raft of issues about self-expression, privacy, international controls, exploitation and the nature of communication. In a complex world, something more is needed of philosophy than the mere clarification of meaning. *Even beyond the obvious area of ethics, philosophy is increasingly becoming 'applied'*. And it is therefore also becoming more obviously relevant to everyday life – it is *the* subject for dealing with big questions.

Without doubt, philosophy as an academic discipline is alive and well, but the first decade of the twenty-first century has seen another phenomenon – the explosion of interest in 'popular' philosophy. Books by philosophers on a whole range of subjects, but particularly those related to human self-understanding and self-development, are increasingly produced for the general reader, rather than the academic specialist. The nature of status, or of love, of justice or of commitment, of work or of all the elements that go to make up the art of living, all require thoughtful reflection, and philosophy provides the discipline for doing just that.

Perhaps the last word should come from a traditional metaphysical philosopher, writing early in the twentieth century. In *Modes of Thought* (1938), A. N. Whitehead set down very clearly the value of the whole philosophical enterprise:

> **The sort of ideas we attend to, and the sort of ideas we push into the negligible background, govern our hopes, our fears, our control of behaviour. As we think, we live. This is why the assemblage of philosophical ideas is more than a specialist study. It moulds our type of civilization.**

If that is so, there is nothing more important than developing and maintaining an interest in philosophy.

Taking it further

Suggestions for further reading

The books listed here form a very limited, personal selection of those which should prove useful as a follow-up to issues touched on in this book. They are in addition to the classic texts and other books referred to in the text.

For those wanting to deepen their appreciation of the whole tradition of western philosophy, there are a good number of general histories, for example Bryan Magee's *The Story of Philosophy* (Dorling Kindersley, 1998, paperback, 2001) which offers an illustrated history of Western philosophy – lucid and very readable.

Of the older histories, my personal preference would be Bertrand Russell's *History of Western Philosophy* (1946, available in Routledge Classics, 2004). It is incisive, witty and readable, giving a vast panorama of philosophy, with particular reference to the social and political circumstances of philosophers, from the pre-socratics to the early years of the twentieth century. Don't expect Russell to suffer philosophical fools gladly; but he is always intelligently wicked in his criticism.

For general reference, there is *The Oxford Companion to Philosophy* edited by Ted Honderich (second edition, OUP, 2005), and the *Concise Routledge Encyclopedia of Philosophy* (Routledge, 2000), both of which give detailed information on the whole range of concepts, philosophies and philosophers. For quick reference, and for checking on the meaning of philosophical terms and which thinkers are associated with them, there are many valuable dictionaries of philosophy. See, for example, *The Oxford Dictionary of Philosophy*, by Simon Blackburn (Oxford Paperback Reference, 2008).

For clear expositions of key themes in philosophy, suitable for students and the general reader, there are a number of useful titles from Nigel Warburton, particularly his *Philosophy: the Basics* (Routledge, 2004), with useful extracts from the great texts in *Philosophy: Basic Readings*) (Routledge, 2004).

Some books deal with a particular issue, and yet touch on a whole range of philosophical questions and historical periods. Thus, for example, although Karen Armstrong's *The Case for God* (Bodley Head, 2009) is primarily about God, in the course of giving a historical overview of the way that word has been used, Armstrong draws in a wide range of philosophers.

Older books can also be useful. Iris Murdoch's *Metaphysics as a Guide to Morals* (Chatto & Windus, 1992), is much wider in its scope than the title might at first glance suggest. There are particularly valuable sections here on consciousness, on the traditional arguments for the existence of God, on will and on duty – a solid but stimulating book on a whole range of philosophical and religious issues, but those new to philosophy may find it quite difficult going in places. Two other older books that are well worth reading are transcripts of television interviews with distinguished philosophers – Bryan Magee's *Men of Ideas* (BBC Books, 1978), and *The Great Philosophers* (BBC Books, 1987). Magee's introductions and summaries are a model of clarity. The earlier book gives a good overview of twentieth-century philosophy up to the mid-1970s and is a superb example of lucid philosophical discussion.

This present book has outlined only Western philosophy; for those interested in getting a world perspective there is Ninian Smart's *World Philosophies* (Routledge, 1999), and *World Philosophy: an exploration in words and images* (Vega, 2005), a large-format illustrated book, edited by David Appelbaum and Mel Thompson.

For examples of philosophy applied to issues of everyday life, see recent publications by Alain De Botton or Anthony Grayling, and also *The Art of Living* series, published by Acumen, which takes a philosophical look at aspects of life from *Sex*, *Sport*, *Wellbeing* and *Fashion*, to *Middle Age*, *Hunger*, *Work* and *Death*. The present author's contribution to this series is about personal identity, entitled simply *Me* (Acumen, 2009).

Within the *Teach Yourself* series, the following titles cover particular areas of Western philosophy:

Thompson, Mel, *Understand Ethics* (Hodder Education, 2010)
Thompson, Mel, *Understand Philosophy of Religion* (Hodder Education, 2010)
Thompson, Mel, *Understand Political Philosophy* (Hodder Education, 2010)
Rodgers, Nigel and Thompson, Mel, *Understand Existentialism* (Hodder Education, 2010)
Ward, Glen, *Understand Postmodernism*, (Hodder Education, 2010)

The author will also be republishing titles on *The Philosophy of Science*, *The Philosophy of Mind* and *Eastern Philosophy* in late 2010 see www.philosophyandethics.com for more details.

And finally, for those who assume that philosophers live dull, thoughtful, untroubled lives, there is:

Rodgers, Nigel and Thompson, Mel, *Philosophers Behaving Badly* (Peter Owen, 2004).

MAGAZINES

Unlike academic journals, which tend to be specialist and sometimes quite hard-going for the uninitiated, the following magazines are likely to appeal to the general reader wanting to go further into philosophy:

Think, the journal of the Royal Institute of Philosophy, aims to bridge the gap between academic philosophy and the wider public by offering a jargon-free style. See its website for further information: www.royalinstituteofphilosophy.org/think/index.html

The Philosophers' Magazine offers a wide range of interesting and readable articles. See: www.philosophersnet.com

Philosophy Now is an attractively produced and readable general magazine on philosophy, showing just how broad and relevant the subject can be. Like the other magazines, it has useful book reviews. See: www.philosophynow.org

---

Websites

Today there are a large number of websites for those wanting to know more about philosophy, some hosted by philosophy magazines, but a majority by university websites. For further information on relevant sites, see the Websites page of www.philosophyandethics.com

For information on books, blogs and websites on Philosophy, for additional material of interest to students and teachers, or to contact the author with your views, suggestions or questions, log on to: www.philosophyandethics.com

Glossary

The following is a selection of terms used in this book, gathered here for quick reference. For more information on each of them, please refer to the relevant index entry.

agnosticism The view that we do not have sufficient evidence or other means of knowing whether a god exists or not.

atheism The view that there is no god. This may be taken in the narrower sense of the rejection of the theistic concept of God, or as a broad rejection of all religious ideas. It should be noted that some forms of Buddhism and Hinduism are atheistic, in that they promote a religious and spiritual path without requiring belief in God.

behaviourism The view that the mind can be understood in terms of observed physical activity.

blik A particular way of seeing something, used especially of religious language.

casuistry The process of applying general rules to specific cases; often used in a pejorative sense of an insensitive rejection of particular circumstances in favour of strictly applied rules.

categorical imperative A sense of unconditional moral obligation; used particularly in Kant's ethics for his general principles of morality.

category mistake (as used by Ryle in *The Concept of Mind*) The attempt to treat a collective term as though it were one of the particulars of which it is made up (e.g. right-hand glove/pair of gloves; university/colleges).

cosmological (arguments) Arguments for the existence of God, based on observation of the world.

deconstruction The process of examining a text in the context of the linguistic and social structures within which it was put together (see also **structuralism**).

deductive argument An argument based on logical principles, rather than on the assessment of evidence.

deism The view that God created the world and exists external to it, but is not (or no longer) involved or active within the world itself.

dualism The view that mind and matter are distinct and separate (of importance for the mind/body problem, but also for epistemology).

empiricism A theory of knowledge based on sense experience.

epiphenomenalism The theory that the mind is a product of complex physical processes.

epistemology The theory of knowledge.

existentialism The branch of philosophy concerned with the experience of meaning or purpose (or lack of it) in human existence; part of the 'Continental' tradition of philosophy.

foundationalism The attempt to find an indubitable fact as the basis, or foundation, for a theory of knowledge.

functionalism (as used in Cognitive Science) The view that the mind has a functional role in examining the input it receives from the senses and giving an appropriate response. Hence, the mind is not so much 'over and above' the brain, but is a way of describing the functions that are being performed by it.

fundamentalism Used in a religious context for the attempt to eliminate the superficial and return to the fundamental features of religious belief. Frequently associated with a radical and literal interpretation of doctrine and scriptures.

hedonism The view that pleasure, or human welfare and happiness, is the goal of life.

hermeneutics The study of the way in which texts are interpreted, used particularly for the examination of religious scriptures.

idealism The claim that the world, as we experience it, is fundamentally mental.

inductive method The process of coming to a conclusion based on the assessment of evidence.

interactionism The general term for theories of the mind in which mind and body are distinct (dualism) but interact.

intuitionism The view that 'good' is a fundamental term that is known intuitively, but cannot be defined in terms of anything else.

intuitive knowledge Direct knowledge which is not the result of conscious reasoning or experience.

materialism Reality is material (for example the 'self' is a way of describing the body and its actions).

metaphysics The study of theories concerning the nature, structure and general characteristics of reality.

modernism A general term for the self-conscious approach to philosophy and the arts, developed particularly in the first half of the twentieth century.

Natural Law The rational interpretation of meaning and purpose in nature, used as a basis for ethics.

natural selection Darwin's theory of evolution, by which only the strongest examples of a species survive to breed.

noumena Used by Kant for 'things in themselves' as opposed to things as we experience them.

numinous The 'holy', beyond rational definition (term used by Rudolph Otto).

ontological (argument) Argument for the existence of God, based simply on a proposed definition of God and independent of evidence.

panentheism Belief that everything exists within God (implied by theism, but not the same as pantheism).

pantheism The idea that God is identical with the material universe.

phenomenology The study of what people actually experience (a theory developed by Husserl).

postmodernism A modern, 'Continental' approach to philosophy and the arts, rejecting the modernist concept of a self-conscious, authentic, creative self in favour of a direct appreciation of symbols and texts in their cultural context (see also **structuralism**).

postulates Those beliefs that are implied by the experience of unconditional moral obligation (as used by Kant).

pragmatism The idea that a theory should be assessed according to its practical use, its implications for other areas of knowledge and its coherence with other beliefs.

rationalism The theory that all knowledge is based on, and shaped by, the process of thinking.

realism The view that scientific theories are capable of giving a direct description of reality.

reductionism The tendency to reduce everything to its component parts; the 'nothing but' view of complex things.

scepticism The view that all beliefs are equally open to critical examination and challenge and that none can claim absolute or permanent truth.

schema A cluster of rational terms by which the 'holy' is understood and described (the process is called 'schematization').

situation ethics The ethical view, as expounded by Joseph Fletcher's *Situation Ethics*, 1966, that the right thing to do is that which is the most loving, and therefore that general moral principles may sometimes be set aside in favour of the needs of particular situations.

solipsism The view that we cannot know other minds directly, but have to infer them from our experience of people's physical bodies, words and actions.

structuralism An approach to philosophy, developed within the 'Continental' school in the second half of the twentieth century, which interprets the meaning of a text, a word or an idea in the context of the structures of thought within which it is found.

syllogism A logical sequence of statements, leading from two premises which have a common term to a conclusion which does not have that term.

teleological Describes a theory or view based on the end or purpose of something, used particularly for the argument for the existence of God based on the idea that the world shows signs of purposeful design.

theism Belief in the existence of God.

utilitarianism The ethical theory that evaluates actions in terms of their predicted results ('the greatest good to the greatest number').

verification Checking the validity of a statement, used especially of logical positivist and other empirical approaches to language.

Index